# The Bodhisattva Question

*Krishnamurti, Steiner, Tomberg, and the
Mystery of the Twentieth-Century Master*

T. H. Meyer

with two lectures by Elisabeth Vreede

TEMPLE LODGE

Temple Lodge Publishing
Hillside House, The Square
Forest Row, E. Sussex RH18 5ES

www.templelodge.com

Published by Temple Lodge 1993
Second edition 2010

Originally published in German under the title *Die Bodhisattvafrage* by Pegasus
Verlagsbuchhandlung, Basel in 1989

© T.H. Meyer 2010

Vreede lectures © Els Drogleever-Fortuyn

Translation © 2010 Temple Lodge Publishing

Translated by John M. Wood
Translation of Vreede lectures revised by John M. Wood
Translation of material for second edition by Carla Vlad

All rights reserved. No part of this publication may be reproduced in any manner
whatsoever without the prior permission of Temple Lodge Publishing

T.H. Meyer asserts the moral right to be identified as the author of this work

A catalogue record for this book is available from the British Library

ISBN 978 1 906999 19 3

Cover by Andrew Morgan
Cover illustration shows the Bodhisattva Avalokiteśvara, China (probably twelfth
century)

Typeset by DP Photosetting, Aylesbury, Bucks
Printed and bound in Malta by Gutenberg Press

**Mixed Sources**
Product group from well-managed
forests, and other controlled sources
www.fsc.org  Cert no. TT-CoC-002424
© 1996 Forest Stewardship Council

The paper used for this book is FSC-certified and
totally chlorine-free. FSC (the Forest Stewardship
Council) is an international network to promote
responsible management of the world's forests.

FSC

# CONTENTS

# PREFACE TO THE NEW EDITION

The previous edition of this book sold out long ago. Between the first publication (in German in 1989) and the turn of the millennium, there have elapsed just as many years as from the beginning of the new millennium up to now. The author has been wondering whether a new edition is justified. Has the subject not long paled into insignificance, or yielded to more important matters? Who still takes an interest in such remote issues as the Bodhisattva in general terms, let alone the question of a Bodhisattva of the twentieth century? Who still cares whether Valentin Tomberg, formerly an anthroposophist who converted to Roman Catholicism, was regarded, after Krishnamurti and Rudolf Steiner, as the Bodhisattva of the twentieth century? Have these subjects not become irrelevant?

One look at certain tendencies within the present-day anthroposophical movement may enlighten us on these questions. The view that Steiner or Tomberg was the Bodhisattva of the twentieth century is still extant today, despite Steiner's direct statement (see Postscript and note 155), published for the first time in 1989, which expressed the exact opposite, and despite Tomberg's absolute estrangement from anthroposophy, which become known in the meantime. Moreover, a new candidate for the office of the Bodhisattva has been meanwhile nominated: the Danish seer Martinus. Further, there has recently been mention anew of a 'Master', who played a part in the initiation-phantasmagoria of Krishnamurti: the Master Serapis. Today, certain people who deem themselves to belong to the anthroposophical movement even link him to the individuality of Steiner.

To me all this indicates that the spiritual confusion which attended the Bodhisattva question at the beginning of the twentieth century has not only not been completely removed or eliminated, but rather seems to have 'blossomed' into new forms.

In the context of the theosophical-anthroposophical movement, all these confusions are rooted in the events of the year 1910, when they reached their peak for the first time. At the core of it all lay the erroneous theosophical conception of Christ, a conception which went hand-in-hand with an erroneous understanding of the Bodhisattva. The initiation of the 14-year-old Krishnamurti, who had been proclaimed to be both the reincarnated Christ and the Maitreya-Buddha, prompted Steiner to pronounce the truth of the reappearance

1

of Christ in the etheric realm. In his first mystery drama *The Portal of Initiation*, he sought to ensure that the tangled circumstances were further elucidated. Likewise, the Berne lecture cycle on St Matthew's Gospel served the same purpose of illuminating and juxtaposing the truth to the corresponding theosophical misconceptions.

Within the theosophical movement there arose a division of the spirits, which began to surface as early as 1909. Such a division of the spirits is currently unfolding again *within the anthroposophical movement*, both inside and outside the Society that bears the same name. Thus, 100 years after 1910, and 21 years after the first publication of this book, we have, objectively, good reason to publish it in a new edition.

It is not least Elisabeth Vreede's exposition, inspired by that of Adolf Arenson, which still deserves our attention. Without knowing about Steiner's verbal statement, Vreede brings out the ego and intuitive character—which differs fundamentally from the inspirational character of the work of the Bodhisattva—of Steiner's spiritual-scientific research. Her two lectures are prime examples of a careful conceptual approach, as well as a most dignified and deferential approach to a dissident.

There have been added an essay on the first scene of the mystery drama *The Portal of Initiation*, which premièred 100 years ago, as well as a Postscript in which the author seeks to render an overview of related publications since 1989. He considers two things to be of foremost importance from a present-day perspective:

1. Some of the personalities portrayed in the present volume have in later life undergone a development of a kind that should not allow of our simply identifying them with their former stage of development. This holds mainly for Krishnamurti, and, to a certain extent, also for Annie Besant.

2. Of crucial importance is not the depiction of spiritual misconceptions or of their temporary bearers but the potential, intense insight that we may gain out of having perpetrated errors, be they our own or somebody else's. In a lecture given on 6 December 1918, Rudolf Steiner made a remark which may serve as a motto for this new edition: 'He who really is capable of thinking knows something which is of no little importance: everything he has true knowledge of, he was once mistaken about. In fact, we can only gain true knowledge of something once we have learned what was created in our soul when we were in error about it.'

Thomas Meyer, Basel, 11 July 2010

2

# INTRODUCTION

Many confusing legends have grown up around the individuality of
Rudolf Steiner during the course of this century. One such legend,
which is still extant today, says that he is identical with one of those
exalted beings known to oriental tradition as 'Bodhisattvas'. Especially
since the early Thirties of this century the question has been mooted
again and again in anthroposophical circles as to whether Rudolf
Steiner himself is to be regarded as the Bodhisattva of the twentieth
century, one of whose missions, according to the inaugurator of
spiritual science, is to proclaim the 'reappearance of Christ in the
etheric spiritual realm'. Who, apart from Rudolf Steiner, has attempted
to do that?

This controversy over the Bodhisattva question was preceded by a
long drawn out dispute which had taken place within the Theosophical Society. The expulsion of the German Section of the Theosophical
Society in 1913 (Rudolf Steiner had been its General Secretary since
1902) stands in direct relationship to this question. We must remind
ourselves of the young Krishnamurti who had been presented to the
world in a rather indiscriminate way as both the supposed Christ and
also as the Bodhisattva of the twentieth century by C.W. Leadbeater
and Annie Besant. A special Order was created with the task of
preparing the way for the coming 'World Teacher'. But the Order
was suddenly and unexpectedly dissolved by Krishnamurti, its Head, in
the summer of 1929. No sooner had the young World Teacher
disclaimed all connection with the throne which had been assigned
to him than other claimants began to appear to fill the vacant seat. And
this was a phenomenon that occurred increasingly in anthroposophical
circles.

In order to spare the anthroposophical movement the travails of the
false idolization into which the theosophists had largely fallen, Adolf
Arenson, one of Rudolf Steiner's most long-standing pupils, decided in
1930 to bring the important matter before the members of the
Anthroposophical Society. In treating the delicate subject, which
required careful discrimination, he related it to Steiner himself.
Arenson's lecture was immediately copied and was quickly and widely
disseminated among the anthroposophists of that time. It was quite
different in the case of the two lectures that were given soon afterwards
by Elisabeth Vreede and which only now appear in print for the first
time (in German in 1989).

The work of Arenson, as that of Vreede on this subject, should arouse much more than mere historical interest in people. For, as became evident during recent years, through what could be called 'the Tomberg case', the Bodhisattva question has acquired renewed, though hotly contested, topicality. Due to Tomberg this question has meanwhile gained entrance into certain Catholic circles. This indicates that within the most varied spiritual streams there are strivings for enlightenment on subjects of the greatest human importance, in which at least the *names* of the highest human or spiritual leaders have a part to play. The Tombergian-Catholic 'solution' to the Bodhisattva question is remarkable through the fact that the Bodhisattva of the twentieth century is brought into juxtaposition with the figure of Ignatius Loyola.

★

Rudolf Steiner describes the Bodhisattvas as the greatest teachers of humanity, who are destined in the course of the millennia to prepare human beings to receive into their souls the ever-growing influence of Christ's deed on Golgotha. This deed is destined to become the most significant factor in human and earthly history and, in fact, has already become so. The Bodhisattvas are the great inspiring teachers of the Christ Impulse and from this point of view alone should arouse in us the most painstaking and profound interest.

One after another, each of the 12 Bodhisattvas descends in turn into earthly incarnation during the course of vast epochs of time, until in their final Earth life they duly fulfil their earthly mission. At this point they then rise to Buddhahood and are no longer obliged to return into an earthly body, as in the case of the last of the Bodhisattvas who, according to oriental as well as anthroposophical investigation, became the great teacher of compassion and love and was known thenceforward as Gautama Buddha.

Before a Bodhisattva becomes a Buddha he announces the name of his successor. The one whom Gautama named was said by Rudolf Steiner to have incarnated during the present century. He is known to oriental occultism as the future Maitreya Buddha, the 'Bringer of Good', as Rudolf Steiner portrays him.

What is the connection between this sublime group of the 12 leaders of mankind and the spirituality and mission of Rudolf Steiner? This was the starting point for Arenson's as well as Vreede's investigation, which led them to such diverse conclusions. It is just this difference of results which can make us aware of the enormous complexity of the whole Bodhisattva question. And so the combined views brought forward in this volume can in no wise presume to deal exhaustively with every side of the individualities of the Bodhisattvas. This is already expressed in the book's title.

Those who are already acquainted with the history of the Theosophical-Anthroposophical movement will be able to delve immediately into the account given by Dr Vreede. What precedes Vreede's lectures in the present volume is written for those lacking such knowledge, or those wishing to follow up the subsequent destiny of this question and that of the people mainly concerned in the events described. Over and above this the comments in Part One of the book are intended to show what are the basic requirements of someone earnestly seeking to come to grips with this particular question to enable him to make a clear anthroposophical assessment of the situation.

Whoever wishes to form his judgement directly from what Dr Vreede has to say will feel himself immediately cast adrift on the high seas, and will need to be equipped with some substantial spiritual provender in order to survive the rapid journey through the surging waves of opinion to that sheltered island which is the goal of the present work. For this reason the island will be circumnavigated several times and approached from various angles in the commentary. Of necessity this will somewhat prolong the journey.

Whoever hopes to obtain specific indications about the karmic relationships and former lives of Rudolf Steiner through reading this book may be disappointed, and he is referred to already existing works on this subject.* This publication is intended to provide a kind of basis for such studies. It seeks to elaborate on the intuitive nature of Rudolf Steiner's spiritual investigation and set it over against the revelatory character of all previous spiritual streams and of modern popular but unscientific methods of gaining spiritual enlightenment, for it is not so much the content of Rudolf Steiner's revelations which are so radically different from earlier pronouncements but the method by which he arrives at such knowledge. To put it in the words of Elisabeth Vreede:

Rudolf Steiner was really the first *Anthroposophist* and he pursued his investigations as a *human being*: he was not a theosophist in the sense that up to that time everything had been *revealed*, actually from out of the

---

* See Margarete and Erich Kirchner-Bockholt, *Rudolf Steiner's Mission and Ita Wegman* (privately printed, London 1977).

spiritual world. Dr Steiner was the first person of the modern age to research these things by means of his own clairvoyance ... and who thereby made it possible for us also to go that way—so that we ourselves, even if only in small measure, could become researchers of the spirit.

This individual clairvoyance does not need to start in the higher grades of advanced occult training. In the everyday processes of thought, in so far as these contain sense-free concepts, there vibrates what Rudolf Steiner once referred to as 'the inestimable pearl of clairvoyant vision',* which is at the same time both a rudiment of bygone faculties and also the basis of a future kind of clairvoyance. To discover this 'pearl' and to apply one's thinking unstintingly to such complex facts as are dealt with here—that can be considered the modest but perfectly legitimate *beginning* of spiritual research appropriate to the present day, as envisaged by Dr Vreede. It is true that progress in individual research also depends upon the development of the necessary organs of super-sensible *perception*. Nevertheless, the development of these organs can be promoted in no better way than through the independent activity of the organ of thinking which produces the clairvoyant vision of ideas and their interconnection.

*

The reader will discover that some of the many personalities involved in the theosophical-anthroposophical Bodhisattva question are illuminated from many different sides. This applies especially to Annie Besant and Krishnamurti. For the understanding of some of these connections much will depend upon a carefully built up approach. For what is of importance for the development of judgement and acquisition of knowledge in general—and in particular for the special subject here dealt with—is that 'all wholesale judgement must be shed',† even from the periphery of a question such as this, as surely as the proverbial water off a duck's back.

T.H. Meyer

---

* See lecture 29 May 1913 (GA 146).
† See lecture 1 December 1913 (GA 186).

# PART ONE

*The more people there are
who can discriminate correctly in occult matters,
the harder it will be for certain Brotherhoods
to 'fish in muddied waters'.*

*Rudolf Steiner
22 January 1917*

# 1. CONCERNING THE LIGHT OF FREE INSIGHT

> *'Our task today consists of grasping occult truths . . . through the purest element of thought.'*
>
> Rudolf Steiner, 7 March 1907[1]

Nothing today has a more beneficial influence upon the development of a spiritual movement than the cultivation of a capacity for clear individual discernment. Many people, no doubt, would like to give pride of place to the mystical feeling-element, or to the good will of persons supporting such a movement. But of what good are the most refined feelings and the most laudable intentions if they are accompanied by unclear thinking? Do the feelings know why or if they are refined, or does the will know why or if it is good? Feelings and the will can never have direct knowledge of themselves. Only through intelligent discrimination and a reasoned line of *thought* can their true essence come to light. In this sense there is nothing we can take for granted, either in the sphere of the feelings or will, let alone in the world of outer appearance. There is only one single reality which we can accept without question and that is pure, sense-free thinking, for this is the only thing which can comprehend itself. Every other thing which one seeks to understand clearly must be illuminated by something which is not itself. If the light of thought is not maintained in its pristine clarity the essence of all things will sink down into the uncertainty of shadowy speculation and subjective opinion.

It is not necessary for this light to be imposed upon a person by someone else claiming quite special faculties of knowledge on account of his office in some spiritual movement. It can be ignited in every single human being quite independently of other people.

And when this light has once been ignited it is able not only to illuminate the facts and occurrences of the sense world, but also those of the supersensible. If this happens then the intellectual element will also become spiritualized. And it is this spiritualization of thinking which Rudolf Steiner saw as the primary task confronting mankind today, if man is to gain a *true* relationship to the supersensible world: 'It is now necessary for higher truths to be grasped by human thinking ... Human thinking must now become spiritualized'. In essence this statement of Rudolf Steiner, recorded by Friedrich Rittelmeyer (*Rudolf Steiner Enters my Life*),[2] expresses a truth which can be applied to the whole of Steiner's life's work. Especially at the beginning of this century, when he was still active within the theosophical movement, his whole work was placed under the sign of this leading thought. This is shown in a letter written by Rudolf Steiner to Wilhelm Hübbe-Schleiden (the inaugurator of the theosophical movement in Germany) 16 August 1902: 'I would do all in my power to lead Theosophy today in the direction indicated by *your* words: "This path into the spiritual world leads by way of the intellect at the present day."'[3]

*

In ancient times no one was allowed to hold spiritual office or carry out certain spiritual functions without first having been appointed thereto by higher powers. In earlier phases of the Egypto-Chaldean epoch the saying still held good: 'Whoever holds office is at the same time endowed with the spirit which enables him to carry out that office, for it is the spirit which maintains him in it'. The Pharaoh of ancient Egypt was led to the throne by the spirit of the Horus-falcon which worked from behind and above him and it was not his own will which he carried out there. He was merely the mouthpiece for the divine spirit working from above.

During the course of human history this spirit, which formerly worked on the individual from outside, gradually drew into him. One could also say that it *died* into him, for this universal spirit became ever more abstract and 'intellectual' the further it penetrated human consciousness. That the spirit became increasingly abstract, i.e. powerless, as it began to be revealed in its intellectual form *as ideas*, was the necessary preparation to enable the individual human being to become a *free* spirit. Only now, since the spirit had entered in a dead, powerless form into man's consciousness and had come to a standstill there, could it be used by him consciously to perform free deeds, whereas formerly it had worked not only in

10

outer nature but also in man's inner being with power and out of a higher necessity.

Just as the spirit had once worked from without to illumine and inspire the soul of, say, an Egyptian or Babylonian priest engaged in his ritual observances, so nowadays it depends in the main upon personally attained spirituality which the individual must infuse into the one or other office he performs. The Horus-falcon of old has to express itself nowadays through the spiritual activity within man himself.

It is due to the radical change which inevitably had to come about in the relationship between 'office' and 'spirit' that man has been able to develop his *free* spirituality. But despite this fact, different pronouncements about the 'truth' are still made from various sides *in an authoritative and official manner*, and even though this 'truth' may turn out to be an undisguised call for murder, it still finds wide acceptance among people in high positions, as has recently been demonstrated in macabre fashion in the Salman Rushdie case.

The grotesque and fatal results of blind adherence to authority and irrational hopes attached to people holding particular offices are nowhere so clearly marked today as in the great religious and spiritual movements of the present century. It is no excuse to say that National Socialism has far exceeded everything else in this respect; for even that was in essence a thoroughly spiritual movement, although indeed an exceedingly anachronistic caricature of once-sacred ritual spirituality of the Egyptian epoch.

If one wishes to find the cause of just such a perverting tendency as this, one will always discover that a lack of discrimination is one of its chief factors. This lack of discrimination is usually met in the company of the much-prized indolence of thought, and it might even be the latter's offspring. When it is a question of truth we can only characterize this double deficiency by referring to the motto 'Whoever holds this or that office in an ecclesiastical, religious or other kind of spiritual community will speak the truth by virtue of his position alone'. And so the question of truth may be reduced to a matter of the office one holds and ultimately become a question of power.

Rudolf Steiner took such a serious view of this lack of discrimination, to which members of spiritual movements seem particularly prone, that he occasionally felt obliged to make very pointed remarks to rouse his pupils to an awareness of the grave consequences the lack of this faculty would have. Thus on 21 September 1923, in speaking about the question of opponents, he introduced to his audience the chief *inner* opponent to the anthroposophical movement as 'Right-living Baron Lack of Discriminatory Ability', and what we learn about this gentleman is that 'he attends all our meetings, even though he always turns up without his membership card. As an unseen confuser of thoughts he prevents a clear distinction being made between what is of inner significance in an anthroposophical sense and what is mere anthroposophical twaddle.'[4]

★

An effective measure to insure that this Baron gets his membership card annulled, to 'cock a snook' at him, as Rudolf Steiner puts it, is to make a study of the densest fog that he has produced in the theosophical-anthroposophical spiritual movement this century. When we speak of the theosophical-anthroposophical movement we do not do so, in the sense of the above mentioned Baron, to obscure the difference between the two; we merely wish to point out the historical fact of their original unity in as far as Rudolf Steiner, the inaugurator of spiritual science, made known the results of his spiritual investigation first of all within the Theosophical Society founded by H.P. Blavatsky and Colonel Olcott in 1875. The fact that he attributed his knowledge from the start, even among theosophists, to his own spiritual investigation (which he afterwards called Anthroposophy) and not to any theosophical tradition or the work of any other person, was stated quite clearly by him on very many occasions and does not need any further comment here.

## 2. A CHILDHOOD IN INDIA

The densest fog that hung over the theosophical movement at the beginning of this century concerned the question of the identity of the so-called Bodhisattvas and their relationship to Christ. As this double-sided question originally referred almost exclusively to the young Indian boy Jiddu Krishnamurti, discovered by C.W. Leadbeater at a time when this fog had reached its greatest density, we would like to approach it indirectly and focus our attention on the strange course of this Hindu boy's development.

Jiddu Krishnamurti, the eighth child of Brahminic parents, was born on 11 May 1895 at a place about 200 kilometres north of Madras. His father worked as a tax collector under the British Administration and thus the family was fairly well off according to Indian standards.

Krishnamurti was regarded as a dreamy child, with a definite aversion to book-learning. We learn from his biographer, Mary Lutyens, that he was often sunk in contemplation of trees or clouds for long periods at a time, as though in a dream. Thus the belief grew up in those around him that he might perhaps be retarded in his mind. Nevertheless, the youngster was able to sit for hours on the ground examining flowers and insects at very close quarters. He even approached the world of mechanical appliances with a kind of analytical interest. And so, one day, he took his father's watch to pieces after the latter had left the house, and refused to go to school, or even to eat his meals, until he had put it together again.

A very intimate bond existed between the boy and his mother, a person endowed with certain psychic-clairvoyant faculties. When he was 8 years old Krishnamurti's eldest sister died. His mother then often took the rather apprehensive boy to a certain place in the garden, where at first to her, and later to him too, the spirit of the deceased appeared. The other members of the family accepted these visionary occurrences, which were not granted to them, with reverent and trusting respect. From his autobiographical sketch, written when he was 18 years old, we learn that not only his mother but, at times, he too was able to perceive the aura of other people.[5]

The death of his mother in 1905 (her health had always been

delicate) brought about a great change in the family life, as was only to be expected. To her favourite child, however, her presence was still perceptible during the following years. She often appeared to him in clairvoyant visions and almost until the end of his schooldays he would regularly 'hear her footsteps following him on his way to school.'[6]

When Krishnamurti's father, Narianiah, retired, two years after his wife's death, he offered his services as assistant secretary to the Theosophical Society at its headquarters in Adyar, Madras, having studied theosophical doctrines for many years with great devotion.

But Annie Besant,[7] who had just succeeded to the post of President of the Theosophical Society on the death of Colonel Olcott[8] in the spring of 1907, rejected his offer on the grounds that there was no school for his children in the vicinity of Adyar. It was only after she had met Narianiah personally about two years later at a theosophical convention, in December 1908, that she agreed to his suggestion. And so the family with the four sons was finally able to move to Adyar in January 1909. It is a strange turn of fortune that the eighth child in the family of Narianiah, the future 'World Teacher', should be denied entry into the social environment of the Theosophical Society for two years, owing to the lack of a school.

But during these two years of waiting much was going on, both behind the scenes and partly on stage in theosophical circles. The final preparations were being made for the curtain to rise on the tragedy of the once so spiritual Society's decline, a performance acted out over the next four years on the world stage.

# 3. THE ORIGIN AND AIM OF THE THEOSOPHICAL MOVEMENT

Let us now take a brief glance at the theosophical movement. The important spiritual current embodied in this movement was brought into existence and nurtured by H.P. Blavatsky[9] and watched over by certain enigmatic individuals, who may at first sight appear hard to understand. However, to conduct any historical research that aims at giving more than a mere factual or convenient account of events, it is necessary to rise to a true insight into their essential nature.

Rudolf Steiner referred to these individuals as the 'Masters of Wisdom and of the Harmonization of Feelings',[10] and with the term 'Master' he denoted a human being 'who had absorbed into himself the whole of earthly experience, so that he was able to evaluate all objects and thereby work creatively'.[11] Rudolf Steiner further characterized them thus: 'A Master is one who has passed through all stages of human development, but at a quicker pace than others and raises himself up to be a leader of humanity.'[12] From this we can infer that, however exalted a Master may be, he is nevertheless of *human* kind. For 'the souls have developed at different speeds ... There are also such souls ... which have progressed very rapidly, who ... have used their incarnation more fully than others and therefore stand at such an exalted spiritual level that it will only be attained by the rest of mankind in a very distant future. But when we consider them as souls, we can say ... they have passed through a similar course of development to that of other people'.[13]

Such highly advanced human souls must be distinguished from certain other individualities who, according to Rudolf Steiner, have never needed to incarnate in human bodies for their own sakes, but have nevertheless entered the stream of human evolution through a free deed of sacrifice, either by inspiration or by incorporation. Rudolf Steiner called *these* beings 'Avatars', in reference to eastern terminology, and speaks of Christ as being the greatest of all the Avatars.[14]

The Masters stand in a quite special relationship to Christ, as the 'Master of all Masters'. They are the ones 'who know that the progress of humanity is dependent on the living comprehension of the great event of Golgotha' and they, 'as the "Masters of Wisdom and of the Harmonization of Feelings" are united in the great guiding Lodge of Humanity'.[15]

This Lodge is built up from a collegium of 12 such Masters; its task is to teach mankind, during the course of the cultural epochs, to *understand* the *deed* that Christ performed at the turning-point of time. It is the goal of all their striving. The light of understanding is received by these 12 from the Spirit who is called the 'Giver of Spiritual Courage' and by the writer of St John's Gospel as the 'Spirit of Truth and Knowledge'. He is known both to Christian tradition and to modern spiritual science as the Holy Ghost: 'As once fiery tongues hovered over the company of the Apostles like a living Word-Symbol, so does the Holy Spirit, announced by Christ Himself, reign *as the Light over the Lodge of the Twelve*. The Holy Spirit is the mighty teacher of those whom we call the Masters of Wisdom and of the Harmonization of Feelings.' At the same time Rudolf Steiner affirms with great emphasis that 'this Holy Spirit is none other than the Spirit through whom one can apprehend what Christ has wrought. For Christ desired not merely to work, but also to be apprehended, to be understood'.[16]

★

This 'personified universal wisdom of our world'[17] was sent out by the Christ Spirit into the 12 directions of space and is therefore to be considered under 12 different aspects. Each of these personified part-elements is known as a 'Bodhisattva' in oriental terminology and only the twelvefold Pleroma represents what in western occultism is called the 'Holy Ghost'. Rudolf Steiner often refers to the word Bodhisattva, not as 'a part of that being which is itself the personified wisdom of our world', but to indicate the human individuality which is illumined by this Being and is used again and again in the course of history as the vessel into which it incarnates at well regulated intervals. This point is essential for an understanding of the following and for that which is put forward in the two lectures of Elisabeth Vreede. Wherever Rudolf Steiner speaks of the earthly mission of a Bodhisattva in the *latter* sense it is the exact equivalent of the term 'Master of Wisdom and of the Harmonization of Feelings'.[18]

16

All these Masters, i.e. Bodhisattva individualities (among whom, according to Rudolf Steiner, are to be reckoned the Master Jesus and Christian Rosenkreutz), were long protected by the strictest anonymity as they went about their daily tasks, and could only be recognized by a small handful of specially prepared pupils. This fact is understandable if we consider carefully their exalted mission, which would be hindered and imperilled on every hand in the present world situation were they to work openly.

Such individualities as these, working behind the scenes of historical happenings and known to us through chronicles and documents, are the true inaugurators of the theosophical movement. It was they who, at that time, selected H.P. Blavatsky as the most suitable instrument to convey a large body of spiritual wisdom to the western world, which was in danger of sinking into scientific materialism.

★

According to an important indication by Rudolf Steiner, 'the whole vocation, the whole mission of the theosophical world-wide movement is the putting into practice of that inspiration, that force which Christ calls the Spirit'.[19] And through this indication by Rudolf Steiner concerning the real source of inspiration behind the movement, and through all that has been stated above, we gain a true picture of the movement's original aim: to understand what Christ has *wrought*. This is confirmed by the following statement of Rudolf Steiner: 'The treasures of wisdom gathered together by the theosophical movement in order to understand the universe and the spirits therein, flow through the "Holy Spirit" into the Lodge of the Twelve; and that is what will ultimately lead mankind step by step to free, self-conscious understanding of Christ and of the Event of Golgotha. Thus to "cultivate" Theosophy means to understand that the Spirit has been sent into the world by Christ; the pursuit of Theosophy is implicit in true Christianity.'[20]

By looking at Rudolf Steiner's early pre-theosophical writings one could easily prove that he had cultivated Theosophy in this sense long before he became involved in the theosophical movement in an official capacity.

## 4. THE FUNDAMENTAL CHRISTOLOGICAL ERROR OF THE THEOSOPHISTS

To however great an extent H.P. Blavatsky's soul had been specially prepared to 'let the Spirit's wisdom flow into it',[21] this in no way enabled her to lead the souls, thirsting for the Spirit, through the realm of intellect into the actual spirit world—in other words, to lead them by way of the freely ignitable *spirit-light of thought* into the realm where the Spirit itself rules.

The Spirit, which stands behind the initiators of the theosophical movement, which, as we have seen, is the real inspirer of this movement, has to be met by the light of *free creative thought* in this epoch of the consciousness soul. Whoever is to be freed by the truth must first offer up that grain of truth he has acquired and begin to *think* truth in freedom. If, however, one prefers to let the actual existence of the supersensible world work upon one or manifest by means of all kinds of physical or psychic phenomena, then it will be very difficult for such an endeavour as this to receive enlightenment from the Spirit of Truth and Knowledge; it will be much more likely that quite different spirits will work into it, quite irrespective of what grand names one likes to apply to them, or as to whether their pupils call themselves 'Master' or allow such names as this to be applied to them.

If Blavatsky herself, through her chaotic attitude of soul, had an overriding aversion to any thoughtful, scientific point of view, this became even more pronounced in her immediate followers. Thus the store of inspired wisdom of the theosophical movement became more and more distorted in a one-sided and dilettantish fashion through her and her pupils. Therein is to be seen the main cause why 'the initiators ... withdrew their influence to an ever greater extent from the official Theosophical Society and ... it thus became an arena for the activity of all sorts of occult powers which distorted the high aims of the movement'.[22]

We have plenty of evidence from the history of the theosophical movement of a change of course having taken place among its original occult inspirers. But this change of course did not take place all in a moment; it is much more likely to have occurred bit by bit in

18

imperceptible degrees, so that to well-meaning members of the Society it was hardly, or not at all, noticeable. Among the symptoms of this change of course belongs the growing habit of basing one's authoritative statements upon the supposed or real communications of the 'Masters'. This does not mean to say that in one or two cases and by one means or other the real Masters might not have revealed themselves. It does demonstrate, however, that instead of taking their revelations as a basis for free judgements and decisions they were taken as authoritative utterances to determine the thoughts and actions of thousands—an attitude of mind which would have been more appropriate to a Pharaonic decree during the Egyptian cultural epoch. But there is no doubt that we are confronted here not only with false assumptions concerning the statements of the Masters but with false Masters too, in cases where the claim to authority rests with the latter. We shall have to look more closely at this imperceptible change of course behind the scenes of the theosophical movement; it has to be mentioned here because of its bearing on the coming into being and setting up of the 'fundamental Christological error' of the theosophists.

★

Immediately after the death of Henry Steel Olcott,[23] the Founder-President of the Theosophical Society, in February 1907, the orphaned members began to turn for leadership to two of the 'Masters', who are supposed to have appeared at his death-bed in order to inform him that the post of President should pass to Annie Besant on his demise.

'The absurd business at Olcott's death' was for Rudolf Steiner 'the beginning of the final decline of the Theosophical Society'.[24] And yet, in that same year, Annie Besant, the successor to Olcott, conceded to Rudolf Steiner the fullest freedom to assert the validity of the Christian element within the theosophical movement—an element with which it was inseparably connected from the start. At the Munich Conference at Whitsuntide 1907, she declared to Rudolf Steiner and his helper Marie von Sivers that she herself was incompetent in matters pertaining to Christianity and that she relinquished this whole sphere to the General Secretary of the German Section.[25] This can be the only reason for Rudolf Steiner's note to Eduard Schuré in September 1907, after the 'beginning of the decline', that 'in spite of its shortcomings the Theosophical Society can still *for the moment* be regarded as an instrument of the spiritual life of today'.[26] At the same time, however, he strongly emphasized that 'its successful progress in the West depends entirely upon whether it can adopt among its tenets the principle of western initiation. For eastern initiation must of necessity leave the central cosmic factor of the *Christ Principle* out of consideration'.[27]

Apart from Rudolf Steiner most of the leading personalities in the Society had either very little or only a very hazy and muddled idea of what was meant by the Christ principle. Emil Bock coined the phrase 'the fundamental Christological error of the theosophists'.[28] It is true that this error was a threat to the Society *through its representative personalities* right from the start. Nevertheless, it was only from the beginning of our century onwards that it began to take firm root in the movement as harbinger of a quite different spirit to that which originally prevailed, and running in exact synchronization with the change of course already described.

Of what does this fundamental error consist? To reduce it to its basic elements: the confusing of Jesus of Nazareth with Jeshu ben Pandira, the leading personality of the Essene Order, born as early as the second century BC.

As can best be deduced from the Talmudic literature, Jeshu ben Pandira lived between the years 105 and 70 BC. After a long sojourn in Egypt he was active as the inspirer of the Therapeutae and the Essene order, and after his return to Palestine he prepared his pupils for the coming of Christ. Through that he came into ever greater conflict with the ruling class of the Pharisees and, about the year 70 BC, after having been cruelly stoned to death, he was subjected to the further indignity of being hung upon a tree.[29]

The confusion arising in respect of these two Jesus figures—quite apart from their similarity of name—came about as a result of their likeness of character. As early as the second century AD, the Greek philosopher Celsus fell a prey to this confusion. After his day it continued to grow over the next two millennia and appears again in, among other writings, such a widely dispersed text as the *Welträtseln* (The Riddle of the Universe) of Ernst Haeckel in 1899.[30] Wherever this most dire confusion has a leading part to play, it not only hides the true nature and importance of Jeshu ben

Pandira but it also necessarily veils the Christ-aspect of Jesus' life as well.

Blavatsky's first important work, *Isis Unveiled*, refers throughout to Jesus the Son of Panthera or Pandira, and her followers also perpetuate this mistake. Thus Annie Besant, in her *Esoteric Christianity*, puts the birth of Jesus 'in the year 105 BC, during the consulship of Publius Rutilius Rufus and Gnaeus Mallius Maximus'.[31]

★

According to Rudolf Steiner's spiritual investigation,[32] the Bodhisattva who is to rise to Buddhahood some 2,500 years from now worked through this much misunderstood individuality, whose task it was to teach about the descent of Christ through the 42 generations. For, as already explained in the Introduction to this book, every Bodhisattva finally arrives, after many 'incarnations', in the specially selected body of a 'Master' or 'bearer-individuality', at the most important of his lives on Earth, in which he is fully incorporated for the first time and which will also be his final incarnation. During this last life on Earth he will rise to become the new Buddha and from then onwards will only work down into human history out of the spiritual realms. In the moment of becoming Buddha the individuality concerned hands on the flame of his task on Earth to the Bodhisattva who is destined, five thousand years later, to become the next Buddha. Thus we are now looking towards the time, about 2,500 years hence, when the new Bodhisattva will become Buddha, named as his successor by the historically famous Gautama Buddha, who received enlightenment in his twenty-ninth year under the Bodhi-tree in the sixth century BC. This successor, who was the guardian and protector of Jeshu ben Pandira, is called by oriental occultism the Maitreya Buddha.[33]

It was previously pointed out that the Bodhisattvas, and those who act as their inspired bearers, work primarily as teachers and interpreters of the Christ event. Only by recognizing that fact can we in any way appreciate the very special task of Jeshu ben Pandira: the announcing of the coming physical incarnation of Christ to the members of the Essene order.

## 5. THE BEGINNING OF THE END OF THE THEOSOPHICAL SOCIETY

Because leading theosophists identified Jesus of Nazareth with Jeshu ben Pandira and, after a time, also with Christ, there was bound to be confusion about what was meant by the concept 'Bodhisattva' or 'Master' in connection with these different beings, particularly in respect of their renewed or continued activity in the twentieth century.

During the year 1889,[34] H.P. Blavatsky announced to a group of theosophists that the true purpose of the Theosophical Society was to prepare mankind for the appearance of the 'World Teacher'. Five years after Blavatsky's death, in May 1891, Annie Besant started to take up this theme herself.[35]

C.W. Leadbeater, who had made the acquaintance of Annie Besant in 1890 and was to become her mentor in the following years, took upon himself the very special task of keeping watch for this World Teacher.

Charles Webster Leadbeater was born in England on 16 February 1854[36] and in the year 1879 had been consecrated a priest of the Anglican Church. In 1883, a year after his mother's death, he became a member of the then recently formed Theosophical Society. On the strength of two 'Master letters', he gave up his priestly calling in order to travel to India with H.P. Blavatsky. In 1889, after his return to England, he became the tutor of some boys, among whom was the son of A.P. Sinnett, the well known author of *Esoteric Buddhism*.

While on a lecture tour in America about the year 1904, Leadbeater discovered the earthly receptacle for the World Teacher in the 13-year-old Hubert van Hook, son of the then General Secretary of the Theosophical Society of America. Leadbeater took care that his protégé received an appropriate European education during the following years to equip him for his future world task. The preparation of this 'vessel' received a setback however when, in the spring of 1906, pressure was put on his discoverer, C.W. Leadbeater, forcing him to resign from the Theosophical Society. Certain accusations had been made against him with regard to his influence upon boys under his care, which circulated even in non-theosophical circles. However the accusations might be judged, of which enough detailed information exists,[37] they have had a lasting detrimental effect upon the reputation of the theosophists. Even Annie Besant's relationship towards her esteemed friend and colleague received a considerable shock, for she began seriously to doubt if she had ever really stood with him in front of the 'Masters'.

Let us now look more closely at 'the absurd story at Olcott's death', for with the Masters who are supposed to have appeared at Olcott's deathbed we are dealing, at least in name, with the same individualities whom Annie Besant had till then invoked and whom she would invoke again later.

Henry Steel Olcott, the intimate and faithful colleague of H.P.B. and Founder President of the Theosophical Society since its inauguration, was taken ill at the turn of 1906/7 with a lung complaint. Doctors informed the 74-year-old that his illness was of a very serious nature and that an early approach of death was to be expected. Olcott was not able personally to open the Theosophical Convention that took place in Adyar in December, and so his prepared speech for the occasion had to be read by Annie Besant. A few days later he was carried into the lecture hall and gave his last public address there. He then read to the assembled theosophists the first speech he had ever made, which he had given at the founding of the Society in New York on 17 November 1875. Olcott seemed to feel that his life, which had been dedicated to Theosophy with such loyal devotion and organizational talent, was now coming full circle.

The main concern of the ailing President was the question of his successor. The one whom he regarded as most suitable for this office was Annie Besant, with whom he had worked for so many years. But as she had been appointed by H.P.B. to look after the affairs of the Esoteric School, which the latter had founded, she at first declined to accept Olcott's suggestion and put forward another name, albeit one which she did not divulge. Perhaps she was thinking of A.P. Sinnett, who was the Vice President at that time. Nevertheless, in spite of Besant's remonstrances, Olcott stuck to his opinion that someone else should be appointed for the work in the Esoteric School so that Annie Besant would be left free for the post of President. As all further persuasion was of no avail he noted in his diary for 4 January 1907: 'The Masters will have to decide the matter.'[38] And after having taken up contact that evening with Masters Morya and Kuthumi in far-off Tibet, the latter appeared next day at his bedside in astral form in the presence of Marie Russak, the Hon. President of the Society, and a second person, who also shared the vision and heard the conversation between the Masters and Olcott. A record of this conversation made by Marie Russak is still preserved in Adyar to this day. It runs as follows:

> Question (by Olcott): 'What is your divine will regarding my successor—whom shall I name?'
> Answer (Master M.): 'Annie Besant.'
> Question: 'She is so occupied with the esoteric work—won't this hinder her in her responsibilities as President?'
> Answer: 'We shall watch over her ...'
> Question: 'Shall I appoint her with or without the conditions which occurred to me this afternoon?'
> Answer: 'Conditions not advisable—do not fix anything.'[39]

The Masters appeared again on 11 January in order this time to give instructions about the Leadbeater case. Marie Russak reports the following exchange between the mortally ill Olcott and the two Masters Kuthumi and Morya:

> Colonel Olcott asks: 'Who is there?'
> Answer: 'Cashmere.'
> Olcott: 'Oh! That is the name I always give to K.H.'
> Answer: 'Certainly, it is I—wait a moment, the elements are rebellious.'

After some moments the Master Morya appeared with K.H. in clear outline and began to speak distinctly in a natural tone of voice.

Olcott asked the Masters if Annie Besant had actually been deceived with regard to the character of her occult work with C.W.L. (C.W. Leadbeater) as she feared.

The answer was given with the greatest emphasis: 'There had been no kind of deception in what had occurred; both she and Mr Leadbeater had worked together on a higher plane under the guidance of the Masters.'

And how should Leadbeater's views on sexuality be judged? The Masters explained that they did not agree with such views, but that esoteric knowledge would never be able to come into the world if it had to wait until perfect human instruments were found.

Olcott: 'Has injustice been done to him [C.W.L.]?'
Master M: 'Yes, but only in so far as the matter has been leaked to the general public.'
Olcott: 'I am extremely sorry, Master. What can I do about it now?'
Master M: 'Write to him and tell him that you regret the pain it has caused him by it being made public ... He has been a light to the Society.'[40]

The Masters asked Olcott to write a similar note of explanation to the Society members. It appeared in the February number of *The Theosophist* under the title 'A recent Conversation with the Mahatmas'. And in a personal letter to C.W.L., Olcott indicated that his reinstatement in the work was to be expected soon.

As for Annie Besant, who had been present during at least one of the several different visitations of the Masters in Olcott's death chamber, her wavering trust in Leadbeater, as well as her self-confidence in her own occult faculties, began to rally again under the influence of these events. And one of her first deeds after her election as President, in June 1907, was the official rehabilitation of C.W. Leadbeater, which, however, she was only able finally to put into effect after a good year or so had lapsed.

*

As Rudolf Steiner looked upon 'the so-called nomination by the Masters' as 'the absurd story at Olcott's death—the beginning of the end of the Theosophical Society',[41] one might regard further elaboration of this part of the story as superfluous. For has not Rudolf Steiner made sufficiently clear what the pronouncements of the Masters as a whole signify? Those who may never have heard of Steiner's comments about the 'nomination' may feel inclined to look at the alternatives: we are dealing here either with sheer fraud or with the duping of an innocent victim, or else with a real astral or physical manifestation of the Masters, and in the latter case we

25

should have to take the matter much more seriously. But that the affair cannot be judged thus in an 'either-or' fashion was another aspect pointed out by Rudolf Steiner on that occasion. Wherein then lies the 'absurdity'?

The fullest and most elaborated account by Rudolf Steiner concerning the appearance of the Masters in Adyar and its possible effect on the nomination of the President was expressed in a circular letter to the members of the *Vorstand* (Council) of the German Section of the Theosophical Society on 28 April 1907.[42] After alluding to the fact that Mrs Besant wished to conduct all her business in the sense of the Masters and that 'she only believed in the Society in as far as this was an expression of *their* work, whose present revelations were absolutely crucial to her', Rudolf Steiner adds a decisive pointer towards a reasonable view of the matter: 'I now wish to say something which may be of use to some people. One may have the wish to serve the Masters, one may wish to hold fast to the idea that the Society only has a meaning when it is carrying out the work of the Masters, and yet one still does not need to take the revelations now proceeding from Adyar as one's rule of conduct.' With that nothing is expressed which might indicate that these revelations are in themselves mere 'humbug', as one might presume if one reads them superficially.

'It is not correct, namely, as many seem to think, that these revelations either come from the Masters whom one is obliged to follow, or that they are illusions. There is, namely, as every occultist ought to know, a third possibility.'[43] But whoever hopes to learn more of this matter will be disappointed, for Steiner leaves it at that and says that what he knows about the appearances at Adyar (whereby he can only be referring to his occult *perception*) he is not able to divulge at the present time. And 'so it has to remain at that for now'.[44] Though Steiner was not able or did not wish to characterize this question more fully, he nevertheless apparently wished to stimulate the readers of the letter to think about it for themselves. And that is what will be attempted in what follows.

To this end let us draw upon some further statements of Steiner on this subject. 'To discuss the reality or otherwise of these statements is a matter for esotericism,' he explained on 12 March 1907, in a letter to all members.[45] From that we can unmistakably infer that the 'absurdity' does not in any way rest on the alternative 'genuine/spurious'.

'None of those individualities whom we recognize through supersensible vision would ever interfere in such a matter as that of the presidential election,' he goes on to explain in the same letter. 'To do so would be to fetter our wills, but these individualities are intent just on freeing our wills through the relationship which they bear to us, so that each single one can come to what is right. Therefore the spiritual life-currents which we receive from the Masters never come to us in a way which inhibits our freedom of choice.' For 'if we take the proper esoteric view that our *teachings* spring from supersensible sources, then we must be very careful not to let a purely functional matter of the Society such as the nomination of the President come into any kind of connection with supersensible powers'.[46] Because one had not guarded against *that* mistake but had wished to include the voice of the Masters among the votes of ordinary mortals—therein lies the actual absurdity of this 'absurd story'.

And finally we read in a circular letter sent to all esoteric pupils on 4 May of the same year:[47] 'Even though I said, "My experiences of the Adyar visitations are different from those of Mrs Besant," I must also say, "Esoterically Mrs Besant was quite correct in her appeal to the Masters."'

What answer can we draw from all the statements of Rudolf Steiner on this subject? His last statement can point the way for us. When Rudolf Steiner speaks about his different experiences with regard to the Adyar visitations from those of Mrs Besant, this does not refer directly to the appearances themselves, but only to the *medium* through which they were manifesting, in other words, to the individual consciousness of a particular human being. In *this* consciousness such appearances—as indeed all phenomena of the normal waking consciousness of the sense world—gain their *interpretation* or meaning through the faculty of individual thinking.

For our 'third possibility', therefore, the following is quite conceivable: 1) The appearances mentioned are actually produced by the real Masters; they are, however, 2) experienced or interpreted differently according to the consciousness in which they appear. So that 3) it is obviously of decisive importance as to how far these appearances are modified by subjective wishes, prejudices,

27

etc., or if a kind of thinking is brought to bear upon them which is free from these elements.

As a result of introducing *purely personal* elements into the assessment of the Adyar visitations, they might have been felt to be something absolutely *binding* to the free will of the one who experienced them supersensibly. Perhaps, therefore, something was introduced into them which of itself need not have been there. If water is poured into an unwashed glass and becomes tinged thereby with colour from the glass, nobody would dream of taking this coloration of the water to be an objective constituent of the water itself. Or, to use another comparison, if the surface of a mirror is not quite smooth and a distorted reflection is produced of someone stepping in front of it, nobody would take this distorted picture to be a true likeness of the person in question.

In like manner some of the above-cited utterances of the Masters could have been coloured or, more precisely, could have been formulated in part by the inner soul-attitude of the chief receiver of the messages, namely Olcott himself. The results of this would have been the production of such statements with the seemingly objective character of giving authoritatively binding directions. That, however, would be nothing less than that certain attributes attached to the subject would become so closely connected with it that they could be taken for such an objective appearance. In connection with such experiences *one thing* is of foremost importance—to be clear about the condition of the 'glass' before and while any kind of liquid is being poured into it.

# 6. THE TWO SOURCES OF ALL ILLUSION

It is possible, then, that in this 'third possibility' we may be dealing with an actual appearance of a Master with an *unnoticed* subjective coloration, that is to say, with a partial or complete lack of recognition of its true nature.

To a quite special degree we should have to reckon with such a third possibility in the case of all supersensible experiences, in so far and for so long as their character *is mainly imaginative or inspired*. The visitations at Olcott's deathbed, which brought about such decisive consequences were, at least in part, of just such a character as this. So were the later, no less decisive events connected with Krishnamurti's first 'initiation', which will be described in the next chapter. At these first two stages of supersensible knowledge there can never be complete certainty that one is free from all illusion, as will be demonstrated presently. This is only possible for *intuitive* knowledge which has become free from all shadowy elements, so that it no longer depends upon *revelations* of some actually existing being in the form of pictures or audible communications but is *in actual direct communication with the beings concerned*.

★

As Rudolf Steiner describes in the chapter 'Knowledge of Higher Worlds' in his *Occult Science*, there are two main sources of all illusion in the realm of knowledge, but especially that of supersensible knowledge. One of these sources of illusion belongs more to the soul, the other is of a more spiritual nature. The former bubbles up in our awareness when 'the reality receives a colouring from the nature and disposition of the pupil himself'.[48] The colouring matter is formed out of our own subjective wishes and interests and is apparently produced to a far greater extent in connection with the supersensible world than in respect of the sense world. That a zebra appears to our eyes in two contrasting and intersecting colours will not be difficult for our souls to accept. But that, for instance, these same souls are composed of a mortal and an immortal part is not always accepted with an equally open mind. Who is there

29

who has never been tempted to re-tint the one part of his soul with the other part, according to his interests and sympathies?

Even on entering the lowest sphere of the spiritual world (Rudolf Steiner calls it the 'imaginative world') *the pictures change under the influence of these desires and interests and the pupil then has before him, giving every appearance of reality, what are in effect merely his own creations, or forms, that he has at least helped to create.*[49]

The second, more spiritual, source of illusion flows through the life of the sense world in great profusion. It is the cause of wrong judgement of perceptions and *'shows itself when we interpret incorrectly some sense impression we receive.'*[50] An example of an illusion of *this* kind, taken from the sense world, could be the experience of a rail passenger who, perhaps having fallen asleep and then awaking and looking out of the carriage window, sees what he *thinks* are the trees moving towards the stationary train, whereas in fact it is the train which has started to move without the passenger having become aware of it. It is not the impression itself which is illusory, and the reasoning element too may be perfectly sound when considered on its own merit (that is, its connection may be quite logical); the error here lies *in the wrong combination of percept and concept.* But even this source of error is easier to block in the sense world than it is in the sphere of supersensible knowledge. For 'in the world of the senses the facts are not altered by our misconception of them; thus the way is open for unprejudiced observation to correct the delusion by reference to the facts. *In the supersensible world this cannot so easily be done. Suppose we are wanting to observe some supersensible fact, and as we approach it we come to a wrong conclusion about its nature. The incorrect conception we have formed we now carry into the fact itself, and it becomes so closely interwoven with the latter that the one cannot readily be distinguished from the other.* What we then have is not that the mistake is within ourselves, and the true fact is in the object observed; *the mistake has become incorporated in the outer fact—has become part of it.'*[51]

For the countering of both these sources of illusion there is really only the one remedy: the energetic cultivation and intensification of the powers of judgement, as well as the earnest determination 'to acquire sufficient knowledge about all that illusion and self-deception can bring about'.[52]

Whoever would understand with full consciousness the true nature of these sources of illusion which play such a big part in supersensible judgement must be willing to renounce all that he has acquired on both the imaginative and inspirational levels on his path of knowledge. And he will have to discern clearly which aspects of these achievements still have shadowy elements attached to them which could lead to illusion.

Imaginative knowledge of the supersensible still contains within it 'mental pictures of outer observation'—in the Adyar example, mental pictures of human figures as they can only be perceived in the sense world. And in the case of *such* mental pictures formed by man, Steiner writes: 'He is not the sole creator of the picture; something besides himself has shared in the creation of its content. This means that he may still be under an illusion as to how the content of the picture has come about: he may ascribe it to a mistaken source.'[53] A pupil, therefore, wishing to acquire a conscious faculty for supersensible knowledge free from illusion, 'must learn to banish this content from his consciousness when he embarks on exercises to acquire *Inspiration*'[54]—which, in addition, also provide him with an audible awareness. The exercises for attaining to the level of Inspiration are freer from sensuality and illusion than the previous attainments, because in the latter the pupil 'gives himself up entirely to the contemplation of his own activity of soul, which formed the [imaginative] picture'. Through that the possible illusions concerning the origin of the *picture* content are banished. Yet, 'here again error may creep in. For the particular character of his soul's activity he is indebted to his education—in the widest sense of the word. It is impossible for him to be fully informed of its origin. But now there comes the time when even the pupil's own activity of soul has to be expelled from consciousness. If there is still anything left, this remaining content is fully exposed to view. *Nothing* can intrude here that cannot be perceived and appraised in all its parts and aspects.'[55]

This third step in supersensible knowledge is called by Steiner '*Intuition*' and 'in this Intuition the pupil has something that reveals to him the essential character of pure reality in the world of soul and spirit'.[56] From this we can plainly infer that only through *intuitive* knowledge are all the sources of illusion banished and therefore it is quite rightly acknowledged as the highest and most important kind of knowledge.

It must not be overlooked, however, that this intuitive knowledge already has a certain role to play in everyday consciousness and it is brought to realization or becomes activated every time a human being has a sense-free thought. For, in contrast to a sense-filled *mental picture*, a pure thought has no sensual content and is therefore free from the illusory element which can attach itself to anything of an imaginative nature. But, to consider the matter further, it does not develop out of a 'soul activity' (leading to inspiration), about the origin of which one cannot be quite certain. The only criterion for judging the thought-building process is the activity of the thinking activity itself, and here, as every unbiased observation can show, the exact opposite applies: it is completely exposed to view, for this activity is not derived from any unconscious element but by its own nature has to come to fulfilment through man's conscious individual intention. Thus, for the sense-free thinking of ordinary conscious-ness the following holds good: we see 'how a perfectly straightfor-ward fact of the soul-spirit world'—the reality of a lucid and clearly comprehended thought—'is constituted'. In the same way that these thought-contents are comprehended, all other 'realities' of the soul-spirit world must be grasped. In this sense the intuitive knowl-edge of all particular 'thought-contents' is the prototype for intuitive knowledge in general. Already in intuitive thinking as a whole the spiritual reality is revealed directly and immediately in its *essential being* whereas in imaginative and inspirational knowledge only *the outer husk* of what is seen and heard is revealed, and that only indirectly. It is true that the spiritual essence is revealed in an abstract way in the thinking or, which is the same, in the form of *thoughts* (however, in this form actual self-contained spiritual reality is present which is, to begin with, nowhere else the case), and this self-contained reality is unaffected by any wishes or interests on the part of the subject.

So the everyday thinking consciousness of the present day—let us call it the intellectual consciousness—holds in its hand the key to the highest form of knowledge, a knowledge that is free from decep-tion. And it is important for us to take hold of this key where it at first presents itself, otherwise it may happen that, although two steps are taken on the path to higher knowledge, the degree of certainty attained at these levels might be less than that which we would have arrived at through intuitive thinking!

Further to our Adyar example, the following can be indirectly deduced from what has been presented up to now. We must not only take into account the subjective source of deception, which is connected more with the soul and from which to a great extent personal wishes flow, but also the second source of deception, which can affect the stages of objective, imaginative and inspirational *knowledge*, and so must be carefully closed as well. This can only be carried out at the stage of intuitive knowledge. For only he who is in a position to recognize and distinguish from one another spiritual individualities or beings in a purely intuitive fashion will be able to have infallible certainty about *what* is appearing to inspirational or imaginative vision. This intuitive faculty is, of course, not negotiable in respect of incontestable judgement concerning *physical* appearances of spiritual entities. For at different times quite different entities might use the same garment in which to manifest!

With that, in contrast to what we said at the beginning of this chapter, we do not wish to assert that real Masters could not *possibly* have made their appearance in Adyar; we merely wish to point out what *conditions* are necessary for an incontestable judgement to be made about that sort of appearance.

★

The following passages are quoted from the work of a former theosophist familiar with the conditions necessary for all illusion-free knowledge in general and all true knowledge of the Masters in particular: 'The path leading to the Master involves a distinct knowledge of noëtic action in a high grade of substance. The "Presence" cannot be described in terms of the senses ... The true Master is felt; he is not seen. When he who was unseen is seen, he disappears.' 'Before man can find the true Master, he must lose him.'[57] 'There is only one thing that reaches the ear of the Master, and that is *thought*; it is what you think he notices and sees and realizes, nothing else.'[58]

# 7. AN 'INITIATION' AT A YOUTHFUL AGE AND RUDOLF STEINER'S COMPENSATORY DEED

There were two events that took place in the Theosophical Society at the end of 1908 which do not outwardly seem to have anything to do with one another, but which can, nevertheless, appear to historical insight to have a secret inner connection. The first was when the new President, Annie Besant, readmitted C.W. Leadbeater into the Society, and the second was when, after two years of hesitation, she finally accepted the offer of Krishnamurti's father to move with his sons to Adyar, the Headquarters of the Society. In January 1909 Krishnamurti's family settled in their new abode. Already, a bare three weeks later, Leadbeater also moves to Adyar—and with that the stage is set, the last and most significant actor in the coming drama treads the boards. The curtain is about to rise.

*

C.W. Leadbeater, along with a Dutch colleague, is now faced with the task of dealing with correspondence from all over the world, as well as publishing the periodical *The Theosophist*. However, soon after the departure of Annie Besant in April (she set out on a lecturing tour lasting seven months), the deeper meaning of his move to Adyar became apparent to him.

The young 'Krishna', as the eighth child of Narianiah was usually called, was in the habit of going every evening to bathe in the sea with his younger brother and other children, where C.W. Leadbeater was also wont to go with members of his staff to relax after the day's work. One evening, on returning to his bungalow, he revealed to his young English secretary, Wood, what he had just discovered. One of the youngsters at the beach had the most wonderful aura he had ever seen; it was the expression of the most perfect unselfishness. When his secretary learnt that he was referring to 'Krishna' he was somewhat taken aback. Wood had at various times helped the youngster with his homework and had gained the impression that the latter was extremely slow in comprehension. But Leadbeater was not to be put off and declared that the boy would one day be a spiritual leader and a great orator. And to Wood's question 'How great? As great as Mrs Besant?' Leadbeater simply replied: 'Much greater!'[59] In spite of his physical frailty and uncleanliness, and in spite of his feebleminded look which Wood detected, for Leadbeater it was certain: Krishna is preordained to become the vessel or 'vehicle', as the theosophists called it, of the Maitreya Buddha. Leadbeater's only hint of a little modesty in his opinion, or caution in his approach to what was, at least in name, such an important discovery, can be seen in the fact that he added to his prophecy the words: 'unless something goes wrong'.[60]

In June, Leadbeater declared to another member of his staff that the Master Kuthumi had told him that 'this family had come here for a very special reason and that both those boys' (with the second is meant Krishna's younger brother, Nitya) 'will undergo training which you will hear more about later.'[61]

A short while later Leadbeater, authorized by the Master, took the occult training of his protégé in hand. He arranged for him to come to his bungalow accompanied by his father, where the 14-year-old boy was obliged to take his place beside him on the sofa. Leadbeater laid his hand on the youngster's head and began to describe to him his former life. Krishna then regularly visited Leadbeater in his bungalow on Saturdays and Sundays, at first accompanied by his father and afterwards alone. Leadbeater confided further details of Krishna's former incarnations—it had soon arrived at a plurality—and bestowed upon him his 'eternal' name *Alcyone*; Nariniah, the father, made notes of the fact.

The shy youth, who often received a caning in school and, according to his own witness, 'was, like most Indian boys, afraid of Europeans,'[62] soon lost his shyness and gained confidence in his new teacher. Leadbeater taught the boy English and set about ensuring that the family, which lived in a poor dwelling with inadequate sanitary arrangements, should move into a building in the Theosophical Centre.

He wrote to Annie Besant in September that 'if we are to have the karma of assisting even indirectly in the bringing up of one whom the Master has used in the past and is waiting to use again, we may at least give him the chance to grow up decently!'[63]

While Leadbeater is engaged in his investigations into the former lives of his Alcyone, Besant goes to America where, in August and September, she visits 31 Lodges and among other things holds a lecture in Chicago, 'The Coming World Teacher', in which she asserts, 'We look for Him to come in the Western World this time.'[64] The 'vessel' for this western World Teacher had been discovered by Leadbeater some years previously in the person of the 13-year-old Hubert van Hook. During her stay in Chicago Besant has another look at the boy and asks his mother to bring him to Europe and India for his further education. The President apparently knew nothing definite at this time about Leadbeater's Indian discovery! It was only on 6 October that he informed her of the identity of the vehicle he had discovered. Two days later Besant writes back to him: 'Krishnamurti is evidently brought to Adyar to be helped, and we must do our best for him and the Master will tell you what he wishes done.'[65]

★

In the meantime, Mrs van Hook had already set off for India with her son. Besant apparently was planning a combined education for the two 'candidates', whose karmic connections Leadbeater had already wanted to investigate. She held the opinion that the ultimate decision must rest with the Master: 'Whatever he wishes must obviously be done,' she writes in mid-October in the same letter to Leadbeater, 'and we cannot let other opinion interfere.'[66]

There were still some obstacles in the way of a fully responsible education for the two candidates to be faced by C.W.L., to which his name had now been shortened in theosophical circles. He was obliged to steer a slow and cautious course in view of the comparatively recent scandals: 'I must not take too prominent an interest in boys of 13. When you are here I shall be able to act more boldly.'[67] Step by step Leadbeater was able to win the approval of the at first hesitant father to allow him to take over the whole of the education of his son. One of his arguments was that the many blows which his son received in the school would damage his astral body; furthermore Mrs Besant would certainly see to it that a good education would later be provided for him in England.

Krishna engaged in sport under the supervision of Leadbeater, the point of which in the teacher's mind was that the youngster should become fearless in every respect. Yet the still dreamy character of the boy could not be entirely altered by this means. The boy still often stood with gaping mouth and eyes gazing into space. And when this happened again one day, in spite of every warning, Leadbeater shut his mouth for him with his own hands. According to Krishnamurti's later account this immediately put an end to their former relationship.

As far as Krishnamurti's spiritual education was concerned, he and his brother were guided in their sleep by Leadbeater in his astral body to the 'House' of the Master who promised to make them his pupils after a period of probation. Subsequently C.W.L. brought Krishna for a quarter of an hour every night before the face of the Master and the youngster was obliged next morning to try and recall what he had learned during the night in order to write it down.

His matutinal notes, edited by C.W.L., were published a year later under the title *At the Feet of the Master*.

★

In mid-November, the two van Hooks, accompanied by Olcott's confidante, Marie Russak, mentioned in Chapter 5, arrived in Adyar; the arrival of Mrs Besant was expected on 27 November. It would be her first meeting with the Indian 'vessel', discovered by C.W.L.

Krishna and his brother threw themselves respectfully to the ground, as is the fashion in India when one greets a person one reveres. But 'she lifted us up and embraced us' Krishnamurti later recollects. 'I do not remember what she said to us, as I was still very nervous, although full of a great happiness.'[68]

Three weeks later, in December, even before Besant continued her journey to Benares, she admitted the two brothers Krishna and Nitya into the Esoteric Section of the Theosophical Society. It was also arranged, among other considerations, as a result of new advice from the Masters, that the boys should sleep apart from their father, in the President's bedroom during her absence.

At the end of December, C.W.L. received a message from the Master K., according to which he was to accept Krishna as his pupil. That made it clear on which of the two candidates the choice had fallen. The further occult training of Hubert van Hook as well as his presence in India could now be dispensed with.

After further talks with the Masters, the start of the initiation was now fixed for 10 January 1910. Leadbeater sent a telegram to the President asking her to be astrally present, and the young neophyte also wrote to her whom he so greatly revered: 'Please be there, dear Mother.'[69] The ceremony, in which, according to Leadbeater, the Lord Maitreya himself officiated, was carried out with the exclusion of all but Leadbeater and Krishna. The neophyte and his teacher locked themselves into Mrs Besant's bedroom at the prearranged time and further saw to it that the room was well guarded from the outside, in order to prevent any unexpected visitors from intruding. Except for short intervals for the taking of a little food, mainly consisting of warm milk—both were brought to the room by specially selected people—the discoverer and his pupil remained motionless most of the time, with C.W.L. on the floor and Krishna lying on Mrs Besant's bed.

In order to give the reader as broad a basis as possible to judge the memorable 'initiation' which now took place, the following passages will be quoted from Krishnamurti's account, which he prepared for Mrs Besant about his initiation experiences.[70]

> When I left my body the first night, I went at once to the Master's house and found Him there with the Master Morya and the Master Djwal Kul. The Master talked to me very kindly for a long time and told me all about the Initiation, and what I should have to do. Then we all went together to the house of the Lord Maitreya ... and there we found many of the Masters—the Venetian Master, the Master Jesus, the Master the Count St Germain, the Master Serapis, the Master Hilarion and the two Masters, Morya and K.H. [Kuthumi].

As with certain appearances during Olcott's last weeks, we are also dealing here with experiences which, at the most, bear a certain imaginative or inspirational character. As was demonstrated in the last chapter, this kind of supersensible awareness is in itself prone to illusion. In our case there is the added factor that the young Krishnamurti had been 'transplanted', as it were, in a most intimate fashion, into the atmosphere of the thoughts and opinions of his Guru C.W.L. for a whole year. Through that we are dealing here not merely with the potential effect of the already mentioned two sources of error in the *one* person, but with the multiplied effect within *two* people, who are in a condition of a deep interpenetration of soul. But let us follow the report further. Krishnamurti describes how he is thereupon led by his Master before the Lord Maitreya and how the latter is at first anxious to learn from the Master if the candidate has proved worthy of initiation, which the former conceded. Then the Maitreya addressed the neophyte directly, to test how well he was versed in the rules of the Great Brotherhood. The candidate was questioned thus:

> 'Do you know the object of this Brotherhood?'
> I replied: 'To do the work of the Logos by helping the world.'
> Then he replied:—'Will you pledge yourself to devote all your life and all your strength henceforth to this work, forgetting yourself absolutely for the good of the world, making your life all love, even as He is all love?'
> And I answered:—'I will, with the Master's help ... '
> Then He showed me many astral objects and I had to tell Him what they were. I had to distinguish between the astral bodies of a living man and a dead man, between a real person and a thought-image of a person, and between an imitation Master and a real one ...'[71]

Interesting, for its own sake, as is such a motive of discrimination at the youth's initiation, it can, of course, in no wise confirm that such a discrimination on the part of Krishnamurti or his guru could actually be exercised in concrete cases in truly incontestable fashion! In consideration of Krishnamurti's dreamy nature one might conversely arrive at the conclusion that a motive of appeasement of the young neophyte had been woven into the proceedings. Did perhaps the orchestrators of this initiation, of whom we shall speak later, wish thereby to remove from Krishnamurti doubts as to whether the 'Masters' were real or only imaginary or imitation?

> Then He showed me an image of my worst enemy ... and He said:—'Will you help even this creature, if he needs your help?' But there can be no hatred in the Master's presence, so I replied:—
> 'Surely I will.' At the end He smiled and said that the answers were very satisfactory and then He asked all the other Masters:—

'Do all present agree to the reception of this candidate into our company?' And all said that they did.

Then the Lord turned away from me and called towards Shambhala:— 'Do I this, O Lord of Life and Light, in Thy Name and for Thee?' And at once the great Silver Star flashed out over His head ... And the Lord Maitreya turned and called me by the true name of the Ego and laid His hand upon my head and said:—

'In the name of the One Initiator, whose Star shines above us, I receive you into the Brotherhood of Eternal Life; see to it that you are a worthy and useful member of it. You are now safe for ever, for you have entered upon the stream; may you soon attain the further shore!'[72]

One can gain an idea of what conceptions and feelings of the neophyte were being played upon as on a keyboard: upon his fear of his former Indian schoolmaster (here the Great Teacher is satisfied with his answers); upon his boundless trust in all equally revered personalities around him (here it seems to him that he is surrounded by the quintessence of everything that is worthy of respect); upon his need for assurance of soul (let us not forget that when he was 9 his beloved mother was snatched away from him, and here a lasting security was promised him), etc.

All too obvious are the references to things seen and heard by the 14-year-old—to which, of course, belongs all that his teacher Leadbeater had told him about the Masters, about initiation, and so on—for this to be understood merely in a naive, realistic fashion.

Towards the end of the account, we are told how the 'keys of knowledge' are handed to the young initiate. And as the latter, after having been blessed by the Maitreya, starts towards 'home', his way leads him, among other things, 'past enormous ruins' such as he had never seen before.

Thus far goes the report of Krishnamurti, written on the last day, 12 January 1910. On the same day the President of the Theosophical Society writes to C.W.L. her impressions of the initiation, which she had followed in spirit from afar:

'I went over ... at five and stayed till 6.15 [11 January].' And now there follows a sentence of which the full import can only be appreciated after due consideration. It is, so to speak, a time-bomb that, after a mighty explosion, would wreck the old Theosophical Society.

'So it is definitely fixed that the Lord Maitreya takes this dear child's body.'[73] And a concluding sentence which at the same time would 'guarantee' that the catastrophe would come about: 'The dear boy looked so beautiful, *like a picture of the child Christ* with his large solemn eyes, full of love and trust.' Let us take into account that Besant was unable to see in the Maitreya Bodhisattva, respectively the Buddha, any other individuality than the 'Christ', so that thereby is expressed: in this child the Christ is to reincarnate. And it was exactly in this form that the result of this 'initiation' was proclaimed through the theosophical world press very soon afterwards.

★

At the same historical moment that this 'truth' was finally 'confirmed' by the President Besant, and was conveyed in writing by her to her chief aide, Leadbeater, Rudolf Steiner, the General Secretary of the German Section of the Society, performed the compensatory deed. On *the same day*, 12 January 1910, in far off Stockholm, he speaks *for the first time* to members of the Theosophical Society about the reappearance of Christ *in the etheric spiritual realm*, as an event which was to take place in the course of the twentieth century.[74]

The contemporaneity of these two events must be regarded as one of the factors which makes this first announcement of the Etheric Christ so significant! That it was not 'by accident' or, more irrelevantly, for the want of a more 'appropriate' theme, that Steiner spoke thus to his theosophical audience is attested to by the following fact: the German General Secretary 'insisted that this lecture was to take place at what was, for the custom in Stockholm at that particular time, a quite unusual hour, namely, at 5.30 p.m.'[75] Steiner must have chosen this theme quite deliberately and for a special reason. Its cause must be looked for in the details of this parallel spiritual event taking place on the Indian sub-continent.

For years Rudolf Steiner had carefully studied the various tendencies within the Theosophical Society with regard to the question of Christ, and we can see from what he said to Schuré how much he thought the well-being of the Society depended on its capacity to accept the knowledge of the Christ-principle. Now such a fatal turn of events had been inaugurated by Annie Besant on 12

January 1910 and *published on the physical plane*, that Rudolf Steiner was obliged to *speak out* on the very same physical plane about the reappearance of the *Etheric* Christ, which fact was certainly not something which had only just occurred to him but must have been spiritually investigated by him for a considerable time.

This temporal coincidence of deed and counter-deed goes to show what a polar spiritual antithesis existed in reality within the leadership of the Theosophical Society, and lets us surmise what radically different sources of inspiration were involved in this struggle for supremacy. This struggle had not yet been settled; it had only entered its final stage when, on 12 January 1910—the year when Halley's Comet made its first appearance this century—it began its offensive on the *physical plane*.

★

There is certainly no intention to condemn Annie Besant, C.W. Leadbeater or even Krishnamurti for having been swayed by their experiences, which have been shown more and more by the preceding account to have, at least in part, been illusory. It is much more important to bring both the Adyar-visitations of 1907, and also the 'initiation' proceedings of 1910, into connection with the change of course behind the scenes of the theosophical movement. That the *original* inspiring Masters or Bodhisattvas standing behind the movement could confuse the Christ-perception with the Buddha-perception cannot be accepted. The General Secretary of the German Society knew this as an absolute fact. The question is not so much to what degree Besant and Leadbeater had fallen prey to an imaginary-inspirational phantasmagoria, but rather: which 'Master'-beings made use of these personalities in order to mix anti-Christian substance into the theosophical movement? For that is assuredly the deeper intention of both the Adyar events, as was to become ever plainer during the following years. In the first place the observation of such events is concerned with the question of truth and illusion, or respectively with a mixture of both, and *this* is what we have been considering up to now.

Now, however, in the case of a deception that may have been deliberately engineered from a particular direction, it is not only a question of whether a lie has been placed into the world. Much more important is the fact that this lie is enabled to work with such force that it becomes *a real fact of life*.

The events of the following years within the Theosophical Society, which will be described in later chapters, will show that in the Adyar current the Bodhisattva question becomes less and less a question of truth and illusion and ever more one of power against opposing power.

It would be naive to suppose that the increasingly powerful spiritual errors within the Theosophical Society were solely and unconditionally due to the subjective proneness of its generally well-meaning and assiduous members to succumb to illusion. This proneness to illusion certainly provides the necessary subjective occasion for the origin and spread of certain errors; yet the actual causative forces must in some cases be sought in quite a different direction. Why then should there not be quite 'objective' reasons for certain powers or beings which are able to make use of this proneness to illusion of countless members of a spiritual community to carry on a struggle unto death against particular spiritual views precisely because they are able, at least partially, to recognize their truth?

Among such 'objective' reasons belongs, for instance, what Rudolf Steiner described once to a Russian audience as 'a strong karmic debt' which the European West felt towards the East, especially towards India. At a time when the theosophical current, which was predisposed to become a worldwide movement rising above all specialized interests, was just new, India, which had been physically enslaved by the English, 'took this first opportunity of revenge on encountering an occult movement of the West to merge its own nationalistic egoistic occultism into it'. Through that, 'the spiritual forces which sought to bestow upon mankind a new impulse without distinction of race, creed or any other merely human attributes were dammed back ... Through the very way in which England and India are karmically connected with one another in world affairs lies the possibility of a falsification of those supreme powers which presided at the inauguration of the Theosophical Society.' And about the *method* employed in this damming back and falsifying Steiner gives a very definite and important indication: 'For it occurs quite frequently in occultism that powers, wishing to follow their own special interests, *take on the appearance of those who had originally inspired the impulse.'*[76] In other words: behind the appearance of a 'Master', experienced through Imagination or Inspiration alone, there might lurk quite a different being in reality.

This provides a key to the understanding of a significant technique employed in the change of course we have already mentioned. It can throw a bright light on the forces of deception working in the subjective illusions of the Adyar events of 1907 and 1910. It can also explain with greater clarity why there is always a third possibility beyond the mere alternative of 'true' or 'false', in all occult experiences which *do not stretch beyond the region of Imagination and Inspiration*—a third possibility in which the 'false' has already become established within the objective sphere by means of a chameleon-like factor of deception. It is true this *objective* illusory factor can only become effective in cases where the sources of error from Imagination and Inspiration have not been stopped. Yet, nevertheless, regarding life in general, the deceptions belonging to the 'third possibility' seem to be in a quite different relationship to objectivity than the ones which arise from our own incapacity alone. Even in ordinary life there is a certain difference between a misconception about another person in which only one's own feelings and judgements are involved and one in which somebody else has the 'positive' intention of actually deceiving one. In the second case one's own proneness to falling under an illusion could only be a partial explanation of the whole case and would leave the objective fact of the other's intention to deceive out of consideration. With the 'third possibility' the illusions can have an actual objective existence besides the subjective one, and just from this point of view certain things that went on in the Theosophical Society arouse a great deal of interest. Only through such 'third possibilities' as these are we able to understand how for Rudolf Steiner 'from a certain moment in the theosophical movement onwards there was no further possibility to accept without question all that went on there'.[77]

# 8. THE ONE SOURCE OF ALL INFALLIBILITY

Let us turn once again to the urgent question of the vulnerability to illusion of certain leading theosophical personalities. They could not have fallen prey to objective powers of deception working in the sense of the 'third possibility' had not their subjective proneness to illusion been involved. The reason for this was mainly the lack, or at any rate insufficient development, of the intuitive cognitive element. Let us look more closely at this deficiency with regard to what was mentioned in the last chapter about the catastrophic results it brought to the leading theosophists.

Why does Rudolf Steiner attach such tremendous importance to pure thinking? In the first place, it is because sense-free thought, e.g. the thought 'circle' in general, as opposed to an 'imagined' or 'particularized' circle with a fixed radius, colour, etc. (that is, with elements that are of *no importance* for the sense-free concept), must be grasped intuitively by a purely spiritual act of perception.[78] And secondly, it is because 'the way in which the thought content meets us ... is a guarantee to us that we here *have the essential nature of the thing before us*'.[79] There is, therefore, in the case of a thought (e.g. the thought 'circle'), no sense in asking what the 'essence' of the thought is, for the 'essence' of the thought is the thought content itself. All other contents of the world appear before us in such a way that their 'essence' is not included within the object itself. It is only in the case of thinking itself that this can be said. Rudolf Steiner has expressed it thus in his *A Theory of Knowledge Implicit in Goethe's World Conception*: 'Thought is the essential nature of the world, and individual human thinking is the phenomenal form of this essential nature.'[80] With that, however, all intuitive cognition is characterized—this is direct essential cognition. And that is the reason why unsureness of knowledge and proneness to illusion *must of necessity* occur when one wants to approach the 'essence' of a thing while avoiding looking for its essential thought-core, for it is in thinking, to begin with, that we are able to put into effect the most accessible form of all intuitive cognition of things.[81]

★

In 1906 Rudolf Steiner warned Annie Besant in respect of the Leadbeater affair that what concerned him most was not the moral aspect or how one judged his actions, or what took place, but that through Leadbeater's inadequate method of acquiring knowledge the same or similar situations *were bound* to occur as a side-effect. Then Steiner explained what this inadequacy was:

'A western person may only advance in his psychic development to the stage which Leadbeater had attained if that part of his training that cannot be guided by a Guru is replaced by a *mental* training up to a sufficiently high level. And this mental training was lacking in Leadbeater. I do not refer here to a merely intellectual-philosophical training, but to the development of that kind of consciousness which consists of *thoughtful inner vision*.' And as the deeper reason for this demand he told Besant: 'The explanation for all this is that *thought is the same for all levels of consciousness*. Wherever thought is produced . . . *it will prove a sure guide as long as it remains sense-free*.'[82]

Steiner's indication of the supreme importance of sense-free intuitive thinking for *all* realms of knowledge constituted perhaps his most fundamental 'compensatory deed' of cognition that he introduced into the Theosophical Society right from the start and of which his intuitively acquired knowledge of Christ was, from this point of view, 'only'—though most significantly—a 'special case'.

Had the 'President-to-be' taken the German General Secretary's hints seriously at that time, then perhaps the inundation that swamped the original theosophical spiritual substance so violently with an ever-increasing pseudo-esoteric (because illusory) phantasmagoria might have been prevented.

## 9. DIVISION OF THE SPIRITS

The 'recognition' by the President of the Theosophical Society that the Maitreya Bodhisattva (respectively Christ) would incarnate in the young Krishnamurti was bound to polarize the whole Society into two opposing camps. The various stages in this polarization process are documented in the events of the following years and reach their climax in the forming of the independent 'Anthroposophical Society' which was led by Rudolf Steiner, though not actually founded by him. The following is not intended as a complete chronological account of these happenings but a description of particularly symptomatic events.

From April 1910 onwards, the results of Leadbeater's occult Alcyone investigations began to be published in *The Theosophist*, a periodical appearing in Adyar. They were printed under the heading 'The Lives of Alcyone' and claimed to reveal his *30* (!) past lives. As one would expect, many of the theosophical personalities of the time appear in the one or other guise woven into these many different lives, first and foremost among them being Annie Besant as 'Heracles' and C.W.L. as 'Sirius'.

From that time on, according to Krishnamurti's biographer, among theosophical circles a very common question was: 'Are you in the Lives?' Whoever answered in the affirmative was further questioned: 'How closely related have you been to Alcyone?'[83]

Parallel with this in time we can observe how Rudolf Steiner discloses his knowledge of the reappearance of Christ in the etheric realm, first of all on 12 January 1910 in Stockholm, then in different German towns, and in Rome and in Palermo at the southern tip of Europe in April.[84] So while the Adyar version of the Christ-event of Besant and Leadbeater was spreading from its centre in the East, from India towards the English-speaking West, Rudolf Steiner's compensatory words were travelling simultaneously from Scandinavia in the North to the Sicilian South of Europe. In other words, during these few months a kind of 'crossing' or 'crucifixion' of the earthly life of Theosophy was taking place. 'Without the testimony of books or documents this great event of Christ's reappearance stands there for all who prepare themselves for it in a worthy manner,' asserts Rudolf Steiner in Hanover on 10 May 1910. And not only since becoming an anthroposophist, but very decidedly while still a theosophist, the General Secretary of the German Section declared in this hour of increasing polarization or 'crucifixion' that: 'It is the duty of Theosophy to proclaim this ... There are people today who believe that we have been victorious over the dark period and are moving towards a more enlightened age. Theosophists will have to tread this path consciously.'[85]

★

Instead of this 'worthy manner of preparation' for the coming of the Etheric Christ, those belonging to the Theosophical Society along the East-West axis were preparing for the presumed *physical* reappearance of Christ in a most unworthy manner. On the anniversary of Krishnamurti's 'initiation', on 11 January 1911, George Arundale created the 'Order of the Rising Sun'. The 32-year-old former pupil of Leadbeater, who figured in the *Lives* as 'Fides', had got to know Krishnamurti only in September 1910, after studying ethics at Cambridge and having become the headmaster of the Central Hindu College, founded by Besant in Benares. Arundale's Order was formed to spread an 'atmosphere of welcome and reverence' around the coming World Teacher.[86] Besant and Leadbeater took up Arundale's initiative with enthusiasm and re-christened it the 'Order of the Star in the East'. The Order acquired an international structure with a social representative in every member state. Its first principle ran thus: 'Expectation of the Coming of a Great Teacher'![87] Besant and Leadbeater were proclaimed patrons, Arundale its Private Secretary and Krishnamurti its true and proper Head. Further to this a special publication was produced called *Herald of the Star*.

In addition to the membership cards—and probably at the instigation of C.W.L.—medals of the Order were prepared. They consisted of a silver five-pointed star, an unmistakable allusion to the great silver star which suddenly appeared above Krishnamurti towards the end of his initiation ceremony. A very clever idea! For in a way a more or less unconscious, and therefore more effective, connection was established between the outward symbol of membership and certain occult realities. A similar use of outward

48

symbols with hidden or unmentioned reference to occult realities has been seen in other places during this century working with fatal consequences.

In June, Annie Besant travelled to Paris with the young Head of the Order and his brother. There, on 12 June, she held a lecture to a full audience in the Sorbonne entitled 'Giordano Bruno, the Apostle of Theosophy in the Sixteenth Century'. Following that she spoke in the Queen's Hall in London on 'The Coming World Teacher', whose 'vessel' she had beside her.

The next Congress of the Federation of the European Sections was on the programme for autumn and was to take place in Genoa. Annie Besant was intending to take with her the 16-year-old Head of the new Order, the supposed 'vehicle' of the Maitreya Bodhisattva. There would therefore have undoubtedly been a notable confrontation between Besant and the German General Secretary who, to put it mildly, saw no necessity for the formation of such an Order. However, the Congress was cancelled at the last minute and Steiner had no opportunity of coming to an understanding with Besant and of making her aware of his point of view.

Annie Besant considered it more important to train Krishnamurti to become a 'star' lecturer than to prepare him to take part in the Genoese Congress. Just one day before the planned start of the Congress, Besant announced in London with great satisfaction that the otherwise mainly reticent Krishna 'had grown very "manly" and had spoken "to over two hundred people at a meeting of the Star of the East, and had really spoken very well. It seemed wise to grasp this opportunity, although it was quite an ordeal for him." '[88] This announcement clearly shows where the chief interest of the President lay at that time.

Besant maintained later that it was not the Congress as a whole that she had cancelled, but only her participation in it. The fact remains, however, that it did not take place. Rudolf Steiner, who regarded this manoeuvre as a piece of impossible behaviour, did not for a moment consider abandoning his travel arrangements on account of the President's mood. At the arranged time he set off with Marie Steiner for the Tessin and Italy, and gave altogether four lectures during the time in which the Congress was to have been held. These were in Lugano, Locarno and Milan, and are of the greatest importance for the subject we are dealing with. Once again, by means of these lectures, a kind of spiritual compensatory deed was performed by Rudolf Steiner in an unassuming way, for with this *he revealed for the first time a special law connected with the incarnation of a Bodhisattva, namely, that he could not be recognized as such before he had attained his twenty-ninth or thirtieth year.* 'The Maitreya Buddha especially [Rudolf Steiner here refers to the Bodhisattva who will one day rise to become the Maitreya Buddha] will live with a certain individuality until his thirtieth year, and then an exchange will occur in him, as we find with Jesus of Nazareth during the baptism in the Jordan.'[89] And without any doubt it was to these intentions and opinions of the President he was referring when he said: 'Any true occultist would find it ridiculous for a Buddha to appear in the twentieth century ... It is part of an occultist's basic knowledge *that the Maitreya Buddha will be unknown in his youth.*'[90]

To revere this unknown youth of 18 and found a special order in his honour can be seen, from this point of view, not only as ridiculous, but as quite absurd.

'All those individuals who live as Bodhisattvas and will later become Buddhas have the particular destiny on Earth, as every serious occultist can see, of being in a certain respect unknown in their youth,'[91] said Rudolf Steiner two days later in Locarno on 19 September. And he expresses the same rule in the succeeding lecture in Milan. It is evident, then, that the primary announcements of this Bodhisattva rule, at these places and at this particular time, is Rudolf Steiner's concrete answer to the endeavours of the President. It is the essence of that with which he would have confronted her had she appeared in Genoa with her 'Maitreya candidate'. But she, full of misgiving, preferred to avoid hearing it with her physical ears.

★

The Annual Convention of the Theosophical Society took place in Benares at the end of December; in a very remarkable way it also served as the first Congress of the Star of the East, for when the young World Teacher made his appearance on 28 December, towards the end of the Convention, his mere presence was enough to create an atmosphere of 'such tremendous force that a member standing beside him fell down at his feet completely overcome by the wonderful radiating force … One was involuntarily reminded of the mighty rushing wind which was poured out by the Holy Spirit over the Company of those assembled at the first Whitsuntide'.[92] That was how it was described by an eyewitness whose lack of judgement confused a psychic experience of power with an experience of the spirit and even called this spirit 'holy'. 'Everyone present in the hall was noticeably affected by this force. We experienced something in the manner described in old writings which we always think of as being an exaggeration; but it took place here in the twentieth century in front of our very eyes. *Afterwards everyone threw himself to the ground before him in turn.*'[93] At a sign from Mrs Besant, Krishnamurti closed the Convention with the significant sentence: 'May the blessing of the great Lord [Maitreya] rest upon you for ever'.[94] Apart from his sheer presence this was Krishna's only spoken contribution to the Conference. It had sufficed to make this into a 'holy day' of the new Order for all who were present at the Convention, as well as for all Star members from afar. Mrs Besant herself was so overwhelmed by this unexpected 'Whitsuntide event' that, as she explained to a gathering of members of the Esoteric School next day, 'from this time onwards it will not even be possible to hide the fact that Krishna's body has been chosen by the Bodhisattva who is now engaged in slowly adapting himself to it'.[95] From thenceforth the President was able to lay her cards on the table.

★

But it was not just in distant India that the grotesque Star drama was moving solemnly on from one act to the next. In Theosophy's own 'home' of the German Section strange developments were taking place. We shall not try to judge such things here in a moralizing way inasmuch as they concern definite personalities— they merely go to show how at every step, with regard to the things of the spirit, there is no more untrue saying than the one suggested to the young Krishnamurti at the high point of his initiation in which he was guaranteed 'eternal safety'.

The following is an example. During the course of the year 1911, Dr Hübbe-Schleiden had allowed himself to be nominated to represent the Star of the East in Germany. And this same man

51

who had once spoken to Rudolf Steiner about the necessity for guiding mankind into the spirit realms only by way of the intellect now, nine years later, suggests to him in all seriousness that he should 'avoid using the word *Christ* in his lectures'.[96] In justification of this, Hübbe-Schleiden pointed out that 'Mrs Besant used this word in referring to the *Bodhisattva, because people in Europe would not understand the word Bodhisattva*'.[97] Whoever holds office should not only be endowed with 'spirit' but, as Hübbe-Schleiden saw it at that time, should have the inalienable right of determining which *words* were to be used. Those who stand at a lower hierarchical level must be content to use the words available to them! Hübbe-Schleiden had evidently penetrated into spirit worlds during the past years by completely avoiding the realm of the intellect—which is the realm of sound human reason—not to speak of the obvious question as to *which* spiritual realm he had entered.

But in spite of this presumption on the part of an old comrade-in-arms, and in spite of the fact that the new Order spread very quickly and was propagated also within the circle of the already established Society, the Secretary of the German Society did not say anything in a general way regarding these occur-rences. The following words spoken by him were still applicable: 'It is the opinion of those individualities who are the leaders of our theosophical movement that we should preserve the Society for as long as it is at all possible.'[98] And with these individualities is meant 'the Masters of Wisdom and of the Harmonization of Feelings' who were mentioned above and among whom can undoubtedly be reckoned that 'Master' who, at the beginning of the century, was able to convince Rudolf Steiner that 'in spite of everything', that is, in spite of the difficulties at that time, 'Theosophy is necessary for our Age'.[99]

But for how long would it still be possible to continue? This was the question that confronted the destiny of the Theosophical Society at the turn of the year 1911.

In the following year, too, the process of polarization continued apparently irresistibly. C.W.L. considered that the time was ripe for his exalted pupil to be gradually prepared for his second 'initiation'. In order to make things ready for this he went abroad in January; in view of the renewed mistrust of Krishnamurti's father in the moral integrity of his chief male instructor, it seemed wise to arrange for the coming initiation to take place far away from the Asiatic sub-continent. While Krishna's father in India was actually preparing to take legal action against Besant and C.W.L., the latter was travelling through Europe looking for 'a place with the right magnetism and the right atmosphere'[100] for the forthcoming initiation ceremony. His choice finally fell on Sicily where, according to a biography of Besant, he is supposed to have worked as a magician in a former life.[101] Rudolf Steiner had visited Sicily two years previously, to make known the knowledge of the Etheric Christ.

Sicily is a very special part of the Earth. People of the most divers races have left traces of their great and significant cultural achievements here. In addition, the island was known to medieval occultists as one of the mightiest strongholds of black magical forces. According to a statement by Rudolf Steiner, this is still perceptible in the atmosphere of the countryside. It was here, strangely enough, that Henry Lord Stanhope, the later opponent and corrupter of Caspar Hauser, suffered a peculiar loss of consciousness, which took hold of him like some extraneous influence, a hundred years before Leadbeater arrived on the scene.[102] Just as appropriate to the occasion might appear the fact that one of the shadiest pseudo-occultists of the twentieth century, who called himself the 'Great Beast' of the Apocalypse, stayed here for a while until the Italian authorities ordered him to leave the country.[103]

Here Wolfram von Eschenbach's Klingsor worked with his hordes from the Sicilian Mystery centre at Caltabellotta. Must it be regarded as mere coincidence that Leadbeater, too, in search of a 'place with the right magnetism', was attracted to this many-tiered island (a fact upon which Elisabeth Vreede lays particular stress)?

The second 'initiation' took place in the upper suite of a hotel in Taormina, to which Krishna with his younger brother and George Arundale among others had gone on ahead. The exact timing of this 'second step' is also notable: it was the night of the full Moon between 30 April and 1 May, the same night as that in which Mephisto and Faust set out towards the Brocken in the Walpurgis scene of *Faust*.

We learn from a lecture by Steiner, given in the year 1916, that when Faust and Mephisto make their way to the 'Brocken' it means that they 'come together with others who are disembodied on a similar journey, for obviously the physical bodies of those who undertake such a journey are lying in bed'.[104] In other words, the 'wanderers' to the Brocken are in a condition similar to that of sleep, in which the ego and astral body are dynamically released from the living physical body. If now certain quite specific spiritual experiences are to be induced, this normal loosening of the astral body and ego must undergo an additional modification. Steiner describes this modification in the following way:

> During the times when such things were particularly intensively practised, those who wished to take part in the Brocken journey— the day, or rather the night, lay between 30 April and 1 May—anointed themselves with an ointment which caused a more complete separation of the *astral body and ego* than is otherwise the case during normal sleep. With this they could participate in spirit in the Brocken journey. That is an experience—naturally of a very low kind—but it is an experience which can be made.[105]

On the very day that could be called the traditional international 'Ascension Day of the semi-occultists who fish in muddied waters', C.W.L., who had led his pupil into the 'witches kitchen' two years previously, now staged a journey together to the 'Brocken'. And of far greater efficacy than any ointment in this second 'initiation' were certain elements of the Sicilian ether-aura. Whatever the content of these 'initiation experiences' may have been (Krishnamurti himself only referred to them very briefly), the place and timing of the ceremony speaks in a very clear language, quite apart from the already characterized 'Star-goals' of C.W.L.

★

Meanwhile, Wilhelm Hübbe-Schleiden, the chief representative and votary of the Indian Order of the Star in Germany, more and more persistently was closing in on Rudolf Steiner with his ideas and endeavours.[106] He had apparently expected at the outset that the latter would fully endorse and integrate the new Star religion into the German Section. On realizing that Steiner had no use for the Anglo-Indian humbug, he started to circulate the dictum that 'there is not a single member of our German Section who does not quite literally imitate Dr Rudolf Steiner'.[107] In October 1912,

Hübbe-Schleiden wanted to found a 'Freedom Branch' in the sense of the Star of the East, and the German General Secretary had to refuse the issuing of the corresponding Lodge diplomas. For similar reasons Steiner had to refuse permission for the founding of a Leipzig Lodge, as it was 'based on hostile intentions from the outset'.[108] Steps had to be taken by the German Council (*Vorstand*), not in order to oppose the adherents of the Star of the East but to enable them to continue their work with Rudolf Steiner undisturbed. It was thanks to the initiative of Mathilde Scholl that an extraordinary meeting of the *Vorstand* was called on 8 December 1912 for this purpose. The following resolution was passed: 'The *Vorstand* of the German Section of the Theosophical Society regards membership of the Star of the East ... as incompatible with membership of the Theosophical Society ... and requests the members of the Star of the East to resign their membership of the Theosophical Society. The *Vorstand* of the German Section will be obliged to exclude members from the German Section who do not comply with this request.'[109] No members belonging to the Star of the East were thereby excluded altogether from the Theosophical Society—for that step the German Section of itself had no authorization—but only from this Section. Furthermore it was decided at the meeting—again not on the initiative of Rudolf Steiner, though he assented to it—that Annie Besant should be asked to step down. This was confirmed three days later by telegram.

With that Dr Steiner took the unavoidable risk of himself and his Section being excluded from the Theosophical Society. And so the 'Anthroposophical Society' was formed on 28 December 1912 in a quite informal way in the presence of about three hundred people out of a prophetic foreboding of this eventuality.[110] Is it to be regarded as mere chance that this first Anthroposophical Congress should have taken place on the 'holy day' of the Order of the Star of the East, which had received its baptism, so to speak, exactly one year before?

★

At the General Meeting of the Theosophical Society which also took place simultaneously during the last week of December in Adyar, these two resolutions of the German *Vorstand* were vehemently discussed. And the President did not refrain from fabricating an absurd, but none the less effective, lie to explain what was happening in Germany:[111] 'The German General Secretary, brought up by the Jesuits, has not been able to free himself from their fatal influence, and this does not allow him to preserve freedom within the German Section.'[112]

That is the gist of Annie Besant's reaction to the two *Vorstand* resolutions.

This mean slander of premeditated calculated effect was followed in the middle of January by a written reply in which Annie Besant, while apparently offering the German Section a chance for further co-operation, in actual fact recommended to them that they should comply with her intentions without question if the threatened exclusion of this section were to be avoided. 'If not,' her letter concluded, 'we must wish them all the best ... and trust that their future as a separate Society will bring its reward.'[113] This reward came to the former General Secretary of this Section as early as 3 February with the opening of the first Constitutional General Meeting of the Anthroposophical Society. Outwardly free of the Adyar tendencies, a phase of undisturbed activity could now ensue for the former General Secretary.

Rudolf Steiner and his faithful followers were not standing at the start of a completely new undertaking on this occasion but, in his own words, 'at the starting point of a significant endeavour to consolidate and increase the scope of the earlier work'.[114] On the same evening he commenced his important lecture cycle *The Mysteries of the East and of Christianity*.[115] It would be possible to read into these lectures—particularly the fourth—an explanation of certain happenings within the Theosophical Society, although Steiner himself does not make any direct references to this. Elisabeth Vreede had already tried to draw attention to it. When Rudolf Steiner spoke in the fourth lecture about the 'evil after-effects of Klingsor' still persisting in the Sicilian atmosphere, and also about the bad influence of Klingsor's union with 'Iblis',[116] this may have thrown into sharp relief the Sicilian ingredients of the 'Star' under-takings the previous year for many of those present.

On 7 March 1913, the anniversary of the death of Thomas Aquinas, the Scholastic philosopher and greatest Christian thinker of the Middle Ages, the deeds of the founding of the German

Section were officially pronounced invalid by the President of the Theosophical Society.[117]

★

'There is no religion higher than Truth'—H.P. Blavatsky had tried to stamp this motto onto the soul of the theosophical movement. For all who regard Blavatsky's saying as a more or less established truth, it will appear evident that a President who pays homage to the exact opposite to an ever-increasing extent, by founding a new 'religion' regardless of any truth, must of necessity cause a rift in the whole Society. This is a shattering self-testament made by a President, about whom Leadbeater had said that he had 'stood with her before the Director of the Globe'—a statement that Steiner brought to mind again a month after the exclusion. For 'perhaps the opinion might be allowed that a different way of dealing with the truth can be learned from the Director of the Globe.'[118]

Behind Steiner's irony there lies, in addition to a strict regard for truth, the bitterest disappointment that a lover of truth can ever experience in a fellow human being: the disappointment caused by human untruthfulness. This cannot simply be looked upon as a failing like other failings; in a certain respect it towers high above all other human weaknesses. Its mere approach is sufficient to immediately provide all other negative qualities unlimited scope for growth. Still more: when breathed upon by the breath of untruthfulness which blurs all outlines, these weaknesses, at least in a person's own eyes, begin to appear as 'strength'.

A servant of the Masters of Wisdom and of the Harmonization of Feelings may possess all kinds of weaknesses. Untruthfulness alone can ban him from their field of vision—until he has learned 'a different way of dealing with truth'.

## 10. A DREAM COMES TO AN END

*'Submerge him in a sea of madness.'*

*Mephistopheles*

Many well-known former theosophists joined the newly formed Society of their own accord.[119] One of these was Edouard Schuré, the author of *The Great Initiates*, whose mystery plays had been produced by Rudolf Steiner in Munich from 1907 on. Another, also a well-known writer of that time, was Mabel Collins, the author of *Light on the Path*. And among the many intimate, German-speaking pupils of Rudolf Steiner were Marie von Sivers, Ita Wegman, Carl Unger, Adolf Arenson and, of course, Elisabeth Vreede.

Thus the theosophical movement suffered a sudden loss of many of its noblest spirits. And the 'soul' of the movement, too, Helena Petrovna Blavatsky, might well have stood on the side of the spiritual guide of the new movement at this critical juncture. The former General Secretary of the German Section felt himself 'in full harmony with the individuality of H.P. Blavatsky' when he gave a candid appreciation of this great founder of the theosophical movement on the occasion of her annually celebrated death and memorial day on 8 May. For 'it was a characteristic of hers, when quite true to her own higher self, *to wish above all else to speak the truth*'.[120]

★

Unswervingly, after their fashion, Annie Besant and Leadbeater continued to promote their youthful World Saviour with new and unimpeded vigour during the following time.

Also the guardianship case being pursued by Krishnamurti's father for over a year did not for a moment prevent the President and her helpers from keeping their eyes firmly fixed on their goal. Before the case ended George Arundale took Krishna and his younger brother once more to Europe. During this journey—

amid all the contention of the guardianship question in respect of his and his brother's education—the young Krishnamurti was suddenly taken hold of by a strong breath of independence such as had never been evinced in him before. 'I think the time has now come when I should take a hand in my affairs myself,' the now 18-year-old writes to C.W. Leadbeater on 31 October from Genoa. 'I have never had a chance to look after my own concerns and have been carried around like a baby all the time.'[121] What a new and invigorating note is being struck! It seems as though the first real dawning of the entelechy was being announced, two months before the first Moon-node, that time in the life of every young person when, at the age of 18 years and seven months, the pre-natal aims of their *individuality* may begin to make themselves more strongly felt. It is true that Krishnamurti also writes in the same letter about the Masters, whose instructions he intends to follow now as heretofore, only he believes that he is better able to carry out what is required of him when he is not 'impelled to do so'.

For the first time Krishnamurti's own voice is perceptible! However much it may be drowned by the confusion of those other voices to which he has become so accustomed for years past, nothing in the world will ever force it to be silent again.

★

During January 1914, the Head of the Order of the Star and his small group of followers were once more in Taormina in Sicily, but this time without C.W.L. Full of expectation, the company waited about in the well-known magnetic surroundings for a 'third' revelation to take place. The *genius loci* apparently called forth the old pictures which had filled Krishnamurti's mind for the last years and he, with a voice that could not be described as his natural one, exclaimed at supper on 10 January, the anniversary of his 'initiation': 'I am sure something is going to happen tonight. I am so excited.'[122] But, to the great disappointment of the little party who had travelled there, nothing occurred. Could it have been that C.W.L., following every step his protégé made, even from the greatest distance, and well aware of the significance of the place and of this particular night, did not co-operate in the events? Was this his answer to the bold, independent statement of the young Head?

Was the small group to be made aware of the fact that without him and his psychic involvement nothing could happen?

★

Until 1921, Krishnamurti remained in Europe with Nitya, mostly in England. The brothers had been endowed with a considerable annual income by a rich American theosophist, and this enabled them to lead a carefree existence from a material point of view. Under the guidance of specially chosen tutors, Krishnamurti was introduced to Keats, Shelley, Shakespeare and others; parts of the Old Testament were also read to him. For the rest he loved the theatre, exciting films, watches and clocks, cameras and cars. He was an enthusiastic and skilled golfer. The two brothers, who were inseparable, developed the taste for a European style of clothing and acquired an aristocratic life-style. Could they not have continued thus for decades, unhampered by all the fine words and high aims with which they had been surrounded during their youth? Krishna had gradually ceased to believe any more in the 'Masters' and in the 'Maitreya' and the mere thought of the role that had been assigned to him must have filled him with terror at times. Krishna often turned to Emily Lutyens, the mother of one of his later biographers and a person with whom he felt as closely united as he did with his brother Nitya, and in these years of ambivalent light-heartedness he is said to have often addressed the question to her: 'Why should they have picked on me?'[123]

Annie Besant, who still considered herself to be the spiritual guide of the future World Teacher, began to tighten the reins of the two boys in 1920, because she was worried about their inner and outer development. Not only in her capacity as President of the Theosophical Society but also as the educator of the World-Teacher, she followed the very effective principle 'divide and rule'. Krishnamurti, who had failed his matriculation examination three times in England, was sent to Paris, whereas his brother Nitya was to remain in London to study law.

Krishna came under the care of a Russo-French theosophist in Paris who understood how to interest him in concerts and art galleries, and also attempted to win him again for the aims of the Order of the Star. At first she was hardly able to succeed, for again and again the primeval urge for independence broke forth in him, mixed with scruples and an altogether modest self-appraisal. So he once informed his trusted Emily Lutyens of the deification attempts of his Parisian guardian, who literally worshipped him, and he added: 'I begged her not to turn my head ... I am not worth it.'[124] Two books made the deepest impression on him during his time in Paris: Dostoyevsky's *The Idiot* and Nietzsche's *Zarathustra*. Just as great as the contrast between these two literary figures was the contrast in the soul condition of this young man, hovering between docile acceptance of the 'image' imposed on him and his urge towards spiritual revolt. Towards the end of his stay in Paris, however, the scales dipped down decidedly in favour of the Star goals. Was this to be attributed to the persistence of his guardian, Madame de Manziarly, who had read to him so impressively from a book about Buddha that he chose among other excerpts the passage 'Whom shall I call my teacher? I have found the way'?[125] Or was it perhaps the shadow of one who is possibly the most evil of the 'Walpurgis Night' occultists working publicly in this century, who was to settle in the same street where Madame de Manziarly tended her young charge, just after the latter left for India, in the rue du Colonel Renard.[126]

However that may be, Krishna seemed to have veered gradually but surely back to his foreordained course by the end of 1920. On 28 December, the 'holy' day of the Order of the Star, he gave a talk in Paris on his own initiative for the first time for some years. It is true it cost him an effort to do so and, according to his own account, he approached the rostrum 'trembling and in a fit of nerves'. But he soon regained control of himself and by the end of his talk he was showered with applause. His public appearance had inspired the 25-year-old with a renewed feeling for his 'mission'. He wrote to Annie Besant at the beginning of January to say that he would contribute the monthly leading article to the *Herald of the Star* in future and explained: 'I have only one wish in my life: to work for you and for Theosophy.'[127]

Krishnamurti's change of attitude seems to have sprung much more from his personal love of and gratitude to his benefactress than from an objective acceptance of Theosophy as such. In November 1921, Annie Besant called Krishnamurti and his brother Nitya to India. The latter had in the meantime been diagnosed as suffering

61

from tuberculosis. Besant considered that the moment had arrived for the Head of the Order of the Star to don his appropriate costume and to assume his appointed role. At the end of December Krishnamurti spoke four times during the Theosophical Convention in Benares and Mrs Besant decided to bring him into closer contact with C.W. Leadbeater once again. Leadbeater had been living in Sydney since 1917, where, since his conversion to the Old Catholic faith, he had been working as a bishop, which he combined with the aims of Theosophy. He had not seen either of the brothers for nine years and it may have occurred to him, as it had done once to Krishnamurti, that perhaps 'something had gone wrong'. This he had foreseen as a possibility in 1909.

A reunion between Leadbeater and his 'discovery', Krishnamurti, came about in 1922 at the next Theosophical Convention in Sydney.

Krishnamurti felt repelled by the ecclesiastical ceremonial with which he was confronted. Furthermore, on account of his visit, the 'Leadbeater case' flared up again on the spot when a leading Australian theosophist proposed a vote of no confidence in C.W.L. and Annie Besant. It was decided to send the controversial pair to Switzerland, where Nitya could recuperate from his tuberculosis and Krishna, according to his own wish, could study economics, theology and pedagogy. It is true that Besant and Leadbeater agreed to the plan, but this time they saw to it that their 'vehicle' would not be allowed to slip away again in spirit or threaten to get completely lost in following his distant educational goal. Precautions were taken from 'higher authority' to prevent this happening: Leadbeater arranged a 'message from the Master' which alluded to Krishna. 'We also have the highest hopes of you,' announced the Master. 'Become stronger in yourself, broaden your horizon and *strive to subordinate your spirit and your brain more and more strongly to your true inner self.*'[128] We are left in no doubt as to where this 'striving' was to lead: to the complete subordination to the aims of the Order of the Star. By means of what one might call blasphemous roundabout ways, and through the agency of a so-called Master, Bishop Leadbeater attempted to keep his 'vehicle' subject to his own will and to direct his 'true' aims from a distance. And Krishna? Was he to fall a prey to this complete parody of his higher self? Indeed, yes. Perhaps words written to Emily Lutyens when the brothers were meanwhile living in Ojai in California, where an interim stop had been arranged, indicated that the recent talk of a 'Master' had had its desired effect on his pliant disposition. 'I will take up my old connection to the Masters again, for that is after all the only thing that matters in life,'[129] Krishna wrote to his confidante at the beginning of August. The stop-over in America turned into a longer stay, for in an idyllic, secluded valley in California, where the brothers had a comfortable house at their disposal, what Mrs Besant and C.W.L. were later to describe as Krishnamurti's 'third initiation' was soon to take place. We get the impression from Nitya's account as well as from Krishna's own testimony of the strange event which began on 17 August[130] that certain spiritual powers lurking behind the appearances of the 'Masters', and other disguised figures, were intent upon paralysing once and for all the still hesitant vessel of the future World Teacher, so that from then onwards it would remain continually receptive without constantly wasting any of the precious spiritual substance.

At first, during the next days, cramp-like, feverish conditions set in, interrupted ever and again with phases of apathy. 'It was exactly the behaviour of a malarial patient, with the exception that Krishna complained of a terrible heat,' reports Nitya.[131] At times the consciousness became dulled and Krishna 'would talk of Adyar and the people there as if they were present; then again he would lie quiet for a little while until the ruffle of a curtain or the rattling of a window ... would rouse him again and he would moan for silence and quiet.'[132] Two days later his condition had worsened. More frequent lapses into unconsciousness occurred, and as soon as he appeared to regain awareness of his surroundings he started once more to hallucinate about Adyar, Annie Besant and the Order of the Star. 'I want to go back to India,' he feverishly announced. 'Why have I been brought here? I don't know where I am.' Suddenly the whole house seemed filled with a 'terrible power and Krishna was like one possessed'. Then everything appeared to him to be soiled and he experienced a strong wish to go into the woods. 'He was sobbing aloud, we dared not touch him and knew not what to do; he had left his bed and sat in a dark corner of the room on the floor, sobbing aloud that he wanted to go into the woods in India.'[133] In the meantime, evening had come and he wanted to go for a walk; luckily he could be dissuaded from doing so. Finally he sat down on the verandah some distance away from his friends, but his body soon appeared deserted by soul and spirit and produced disconnected sounds.

It will be the task of psychopathology based on spiritual understanding to elucidate these events one day in all concreteness. But a quite normal and healthy human understanding is able to conclude that all kinds of beings attempted, with varying degrees of success, to gain possession of Krishna's tortured soul—an incorporation of the 'Lord Maitreya' could hardly have come about in such a fashion as this!

The 'crisis' was finally reached when the General Secretary of the American Section of the Theosophical Society of that time, who lived locally, hit upon the idea of gently persuading Krishna to seat himself beneath the pepper tree that was growing in the garden. A miracle happened: Krishna suddenly intoned a mantric song which he had been taught in Adyar—and fell silent. His brother Nitya later described how he experienced these moments with him: 'Long ago in Taormina, as Krishna had looked with meditative eyes upon a beautiful painting of our Lord Gautama in mendicant garb, we had felt for a blissful moment the divine presence of the Great One, who had deigned to send a thought. And again this night, as Krishna, under the young pepper tree, finished his song of adoration, I thought of the Tathagata [the Buddha] under the Bo tree, and again I felt pervading the peaceful valley a wave of that splendour, as if again He had sent a blessing upon Krishna.' Then Nitya suddenly beheld 'a great Star shining above the tree' and knew 'that Krishna's body was being prepared for the Great One'.[134]

And how did Krishna experience the events that took place beneath the pepper tree? 'When I had sat thus for some time,' his report runs, 'I felt myself going out of my body ... I was facing the east. In front of me was my own body and over my head I saw the Star, bright and clear. Then I could feel the vibrations of the Lord Buddha; I beheld Lord Maitreya and Master K.H. I was so happy, calm and at peace ... The Presence of the mighty Beings was with me for some time and then They were gone. I was supremely happy, for I had seen. Nothing could ever be the same. I have drunk at the clear and pure waters at the source of the fountain of life and my thirst was appeased.'[135] How might not Besant and C.W.L. have rejoiced when they read this report! And still more at the words directed to Leadbeater two weeks later: 'I feel once again in touch with Lord Maitreya and the Master and there is nothing else for me to do but to serve Them. My whole life now is consciously on the physical plane, devoted to the work.' But, as if issuing from a deeper layer of his nature, he adds the words: 'And I am not likely to change.'[136] These are harmless sounding words, which though they seem to reinforce what he has just said suddenly envelop it with an aura of doubt.

It is in these final words, and also in certain details stretching over several days of ever-changing conditions of experience, that not only what has been impressed upon him but what springs from his deeper or higher self seems to have been at work.

The following experience came to Krishna while he was fully conscious, as a man happened to be repairing the roadway just opposite his house: 'The pickaxe he held was myself; the very stone which he was breaking up was a part of me; the tender blade of grass was my very being, and the tree beside the man was myself ... The birds, the dust, and the very noise were a part of me. Just then there was a car passing by at some distance; I was the driver, the engine, and the tyres; as the car went further away from me, I was going away from myself. I was in everything, or rather everything was in me.'[137] Fantastic and illusory as all previously described happenings may appear—at least in so far as concerns their interpretation—in the last mentioned episode one can at least detect the germ of a kind of mystical experience that lies deeper in Krishna's real inner being than the psychical manipulations of his gurus.

★

After this third 'initiation', one would think everything should have run smoothly. And thus it appeared at first during the next years, even though, as a kind of side effect of the 'initiation', a strange and very disconcerting phenomenon made its appearance. Every evening, between 6 and 7 o'clock, Krishnamurti was overcome by weakness that was accompanied by a terrible headache and pains in his throat and spine. Simultaneously he grew so sensitive during this time that the smallest noise occasioned him such agony that he could not bear anything to touch him. The pain began to ebb after a time but left its victim completely exhausted. This 'process', as his biographer called the strange event, continued for years in greater or lesser degree! No doctor, apart from a helpless theosophical lady doctor, was ever consulted, and Krishna, who regarded the whole thing as a necessary side effect of a still uncompleted change of consciousness, took no pain killers! Perhaps this unusual ability to bear pain was one of the noblest strands of this soul inclined towards true devotion—and perhaps the only side of his nature which could never be misused either at that time or at any future date.

★

In the following year, a Dutchman, Baron van Pallandt, gave Krishnamurti an eighteenth-century mansion with estates at Ommen. As the recipient did not want such personal possessions, a trust was formed and it was made into the headquarters of the Star Order. Shortly after Rudolf Steiner had held his three elaborately planned lectures in neighbouring Arnheim in July 1924,[138] in which for the first time he introduced the Michael theme into his karma lectures, the Order of the Star at Ommen held its first Summer Camp in a dissolute parody of Steiner's Archai announcement.

In February 1925, Krishna, who was greatly worried about the health of his seriously ill brother, received a consoling message in his dreams from the greatest of all 'Masters', the Master 'Mahachohan', containing the following words: 'He will recover!'[139] During the same summer, Annie Besant, as a precautionary measure, named the first of 12 'Apostles' in the absence of the promised 'World Teacher', Krishnamurti. Perhaps she hoped thereby to speed up the long overdue arrival of the 'World Teacher' into his earthly 'vessel'. When the far-off predestined one heard of this proposal it proved too much for him to accept quietly. He thought that the 78-year-old President had become senile, as he informed Lady Emily. The naivety and passivity of his devotional attitude seemed once again to have received a healthy shot of scepticism. And yet he later begged Emily Lutyens to destroy the letter containing these references to Besant, out of consideration for the aged President.

Stronger, more profound doubts about the sense of the whole undertaking beset Krishnamurti when he heard about the death of his brother while he was on his way to India, whither Besant had persuaded him to go. Krishna had a complete nervous breakdown and sobbed for nights on end. Had not the 'Masters' lately reassured him that Nitya would not die? When Krishna began to recover after some days, the great dream seemed to have finally ended. And so it is all the more incomprehensible how, only six weeks later, in Adyar, on the 'holy' 28 December, that moment for which the whole starry world and, first and foremost, Mrs Besant herself, had waited—the first 'spoken' manifestation of the 'Maitreya-Christ' in the body of the tested 'vehicle'—could come about. Only a few months previously, Rudolf Steiner, a *real* World Teacher, had left the physical plane, on 30 March 1925.

While Krishna was speaking at the opening of the Star Congress about the World Teacher, a dramatic change took place in him. His biographer reports, 'As he was speaking the following words: "He only comes to those who want, who desire, who long . . .", his face suddenly acquired a new, radiant expression, and in a completely different ringing tone he continued: "And I come for those who want sympathy, who want happiness, who are longing to be released, who are longing to find happiness in all things. I come to reform, not to tear down, I come to build, not to destroy." '[140] For all who noticed the sudden switch from the third to the first person, there was no doubt as to *who* it was that was speaking!

Certainly there are many components at work in this event. Alongside the mood of anticipation, acting like a force of suction in the masses of adherents of the Order of the Star, there was the susceptibility of the young Krishnamurti towards psychic influences and his very noticeable lack of spiritual discrimination. But one factor ought not to be overlooked, which might provide the key to the surprising change: the soul of Krishna's brother who, until he was taken ill, had hardly left his side! In a previous chapter we saw how very sensitive Krishnamurti had been as a child to the psychic influence of his deceased mother. And it was not just up to the end of his schooldays that she had accompanied him inwardly; during his enigmatic illness following his third 'initiation' she had played a decisive role in his soul-experiences. And for months he had taken a nurse, of whom he was especially fond, for his reincarnated mother, although she had been born before the latter's death! So why should it be any different in the case of his brother, who had accompanied him in close proximity of soul and body throughout all the stages leading to the 'throne' prepared for the 'World Teacher', particularly as he had himself to a certain extent received initiation (that is to say, he had become acquainted with the 'initiatory' part of the completely farcical proceedings)?

The President, absorbed in distant starry goals, would probably have disdained, as tasteless triviality, to have followed up such obvious thoughts as these about the very close connection of the fraternal pair. That is not to say that Nitya actually spoke through Krishna directly. But could he not have exerted a very strengthening influence on his brother-soul on this 'holy' occasion, as a result of which the latter, suddenly flooded with new confidence, was enabled to give utterance at last to illusions bred in him over many years? How could Krishna himself have suddenly brought to an end this great 'waiting for Godot' of many years after experiencing the great pain of the outward loss of his brother and the probably still greater pain over his own loss of faith in the Masters and their instructions?

Things were simpler for the aged President and her followers. She regarded what had happened as the 'definite consecration of the chosen vehicle'.[141] And the dreaming 'vessel' himself appeared in his own eyes as 'a crystal vase, a jar that has been cleaned and now anybody in the world can put a beautiful flower in it and that flower shall live in the vase and never die'.[142] He could not remain unaware for long of the inner hollowness to which he already basically points in these flowery words.

Such emptiness of soul eventually causes a sucking action, and if it is not *consciously* evoked and annulled again by a sovereign Ego-being it can attract all kinds of 'inspirations'. A participant at the Ommen Star Camp of the following year received the impression one day that a 'black magician' was actually speaking through Krishnamurti. This assertion might at least have sprung from the right feeling, the feeling that, on occasion, all kinds of things could speak through Krishna, only *not* that of which all Star-followers dreamed. This utterance struck Krishnamurti like lightning. Perhaps it contributed not a little to his imminent awakening.

'The World Teacher is here' was the message that Besant released in April 1927 to the Associated Press of America for world-wide distribution. And with great consistency it was decided to change the name of the publishing firm of the Order of the Star from *Herald of the Star*, as it had previously been called, to *Star Review*—the Star having finally been revealed in its Herald! But hardly had the laboriously prepared house, which had taken so many years to build, become ready to have the final touches added before opening its doors to the world at large than the 'World Teacher' began to search about for other possibilities for himself, quite regardless of his prearranged commitments. Thus he suddenly announced quite openly at the Ommen Camp in August of the same year: 'No one can give you liberation, you have to find it within.'[143] One had not expected to hear such statements, which seemed quite uninspired, coming from the 'World Teacher'. Was Krishna on the point of discovering that he was also able to speak with his *own* voice?

The consternation he caused his followers the next year was even greater when he explained to them that he would 'abolish the Order at once if it claimed to be a vehicle which held the Truth and the *only* Truth'.[144] And Jiddu Krishnamurti drew a conclusive line through all expectations of an easily attained peace of soul and blissful spirit-sleep when, on 3 August 1929, he announced in the presence of Annie Besant and more than three thousand members of the Order of the Star: 'We are going to discuss this morning the dissolution of the Order of the Star.' Thus he began the first, and also the last important address that he ever gave within the Order: 'Many will be delighted, and others will be rather sad. It is a question neither for rejoicing nor for sadness, because it is inevitable, as I am going to explain ... I maintain that Truth is a pathless land, and you cannot approach it by any path whatsoever, by any religion, by any sect ... It cannot be organized; nor should any organization be formed to lead or coerce people along any particular path. If you first understand that, then you will see how impossible it is to organize a belief. A belief is purely an individual matter, and you cannot and must not organize it ... I do not want to belong to any organization of a spiritual kind ... You are depending for your spirituality on someone else ... You have been accustomed to being told how far you have advanced, what is your spiritual status. How childish! Who but yourself can tell you if you are incorruptible? ... For two years I have been thinking about this, slowly, carefully, patiently, and I have now decided to disband the

Order, as I happen to be its Head. You can form other organizations and expect someone else. With that I am not concerned, nor with creating new cages, new decorations for those cages.'[145]

The first and last 'miracle' had taken place within the 18-year history of the Order: a single person had finally had the courage to express what *he himself* thought—and with one blow had silenced the Babylonian hubbub of countless voices issuing from all possible 'Masters'.

'*My only concern is to set men absolutely and unconditionally free.*' Thus ended the address of the now 34-year-old Krishna.

★

It is true that the founder of the Order had pointed out from the very start that the World Teacher might very well bring a doctrine which would be quite the opposite of what everyone expected. Nevertheless, hardly anyone could have been prepared for such a radical contrast as this, in spite of all their many presentiments! As Krishnamurti himself had now seen to it in no uncertain fashion that the reappearance should 'go wrong', he withdrew from the Theosophical Society himself at the end of the year. For it was quite clear to him: 'Personally I am out of their Society, their quarrels and their politics. There is something far more important.'[146] At one blow Krishna had rubbed the slightly less than two decades of sleep from his eyes. That he was serious about it is made evident by all his subsequent years of activity, *completely on his own account*, as lecturer and writer. And so energetic and profound was the gesture with which he opened his own eyes and the eyes of some of his followers that it almost extinguished the memory of his erstwhile glamorous existence. Never again in future talks, which were to take him all over the world, would he mention the 'Masters' or the ancient spiritual traditions of mankind stretching back for many thousands of years. With elementary force he turned his back not only on his own past but, as it were, *on the past as such*. From duration itself he sought to draw his inspiration for every subsequent moment of his life. As to how far he succeeded in this and to what extent his later evolved teaching corresponded to the condition of western mankind's consciousness at the present day is another question, and one which must be left to the reader to answer for himself.

'If I was writing my life,' said Krishnamurti in later years to his biographer, 'I would begin with the vacant mind.'[147] That he was able to make himself the watchman and guardian of this 'emptiness', into which the remarkable destiny of his youth had poured such a multitude and variety of things, only not his own spiritual substance, this, above all, lends to his biography an air of unusual purity and unpretentiousness. And though the world has not put its flowers in the 'cleansed vase', he himself became a rare pure soul of the twentieth century, both vase and flower in one.

★

Mrs Besant was a sorry sight when she bid farewell to Krishnamurti for the last time.[148] 'She recognized me,' he wrote to Lady Emily, 'she said how beautiful I was with my beard, that I must drink grape juice to get strong, that I must write to her . . . It is tragic to see her in this state. It's all so sad for them all.'

'Sad, yes, for all those who have got stuck in the treadmill of their traditions,' adds his biographer, 'but for K., who had shed the burden of the past, each day was to be a fresh discovery of joy as with the passionate energy of freedom he continued on his way as a teacher of the world.'[149]

# 11. RUDOLF STEINER AND THE BODHISATTVA QUESTION IN THE TWENTIETH CENTURY

While Jiddu Krishnamurti was distancing himself ever further from the throne which all the 'Barons of Discriminatory Ability' of East and West would like him to have occupied as Bodhisattva or as 'Christ', the whole Bodhisattva question had suddenly gained topical interest once more among that circle of people who, almost two decades previously, had left the Theosophical Society on account of that very same question. As far back as the spring of 1930, divers rumours were being circulated among anthroposophists concerning the various candidates for the throne Krishnamurti had vacated. The Bodhisattva 'mantle', which he had abandoned—in reality a very dilapidated, patched up straightjacket created out of illusory notions—seemed to be awaiting a new heir. We have to thank the initiative of Adolf Arenson for preventing a recurrence of the infectious madness which had previously been warded off with such great difficulty. On the fifth anniversary of Rudolf Steiner's death Arenson attempted to enlighten a surprised audience on the subject of an 'anthroposophical topic which still remains largely unsolved at the present day'. So he went into the question of the relationship of Rudolf Steiner to the Bodhisattva of the twentieth century.

It was not only the above-mentioned rumours but a quite definite statement made by Rudolf Steiner to Friedrich Rittelmeyer which played a prominent part in the argument. It was in Basel in 1911 that Rudolf Steiner mentioned, among other things, that the individuality who was to be the bearer of the Bodhisattva would never be recognized as such before his thirtieth year, as that was the age at which this being would enter the body.[150] In a further remark made to Rittelmeyer, in the summer of 1921, concerning Jeshu ben Pandira, the bearer-individuality, Steiner said: 'If we are still alive in 15 years' time, we may be able to experience something of that ... Jeshu ben Pandira was born at the beginning of this century.'[151] According to this remark, it would be just at the beginning of the Thirties that the Bodhisattva could be expected to incorporate.

It is therefore not surprising that in some circles a certain mood of expectation was beginning to be felt, which needed to be given direction! Through his carefully thought out reasoning Arenson not only brought a new point of view to the Bodhisattva question after Rudolf Steiner's death but was also able to put it on a broader and more worthy basis by bringing together the various remarks Steiner had made on the subject. His lecture, which he repeated at the General Meeting of the Anthroposophical Society in Dornach on 28 April of the same year, was immediately printed and then republished a few years later.

The gist of Arenson's reasoning was that the mission that Rudolf Steiner attributed to the Bodhisattva of the twentieth century—the announcement of the Etheric Christ—had been completely fulfilled by Rudolf Steiner himself. Nevertheless, Arenson hesitated to proclaim Rudolf Steiner as the reincarnated Jeshu ben Pandira, which would have been the logical conclusion. 'There remains, therefore, an obvious contradiction in Arenson's exposition,' states the most recent publisher of his lecture.[152] This contradiction had immediately attracted the attention of Elisabeth Vreede and incited her to counter Arenson's thesis in a factual and altogether worthy manner, or at least to make a correction to it. She spoke about the complexities of the case in the Hague on 26 April and continued her dissertation on 28 April—on the same day that Arenson repeated his lecture. On 14 May Vreede spoke on the subject once more, this time in Stuttgart, where two months later she delivered the two lectures printed in Part Two of this book. Arenson's Stuttgart lecture and its repetition in Dornach gave Vreede the incentive to lecture about the Bodhisattva question five times during the next three months. From this we can see how important it was for her to create an immediate balance to what Arenson had said, even though she did this in a quite free way. In her eyes, what Arenson had said, if uncorrected, could have led to quite wrong concepts being formed, not only about the Bodhisattva but also about the individuality of Rudolf Steiner, and these ideas could have sunk deeply into many people's minds. The details of Vreede's answer can be taken from her lectures printed in Part Two. Only a few of the points which appear especially important to the present author will be dealt with, shortly, in as far as they throw light on the question of Rudolf Steiner's individuality.

Whereas Arenson characterizes Rudolf Steiner's way of spiritual research as mainly *Inspiration* from the Bodhisattva, Vreede on the other hand emphasizes more its ego-character. She recognizes the special and important feature of his mission as the fact that he was 'the first truly modern man and that he investigated these things [to which the question of the identity and mission of the Bodhisattva also belongs] out of his *own* clairvoyance'. This kind of research based on the ego can, however, only be *intuitive*. Vreede therefore sees no reason to attribute Rudolf Steiner's method of research to 'Inspiration'. That of course does not mean that he was incapable of receiving Inspiration to the highest degree, and this, moreover, in a fully conscious way! Vreede even says that she sometimes had the impression that he provides us *par excellence* with the great example of what Inspiration should be.

This knowledge of the reappearance of Christ in the etheric realm Rudolf Steiner characterized as *being inspired by the Bodhisattva of the twentieth century*.[153] He would only be able to gain illusion-free certainty in such matters, however, if according to the methods of spiritual investigation he himself describes he could establish a direct intuitive relationship to such an inspiring *being*.

By attributing this deep knowledge given by Rudolf Steiner about the return of Christ in the etheric realm to an Inspiration coming from the Bodhisattva, we can infer that the individuality of Rudolf Steiner himself is to be distinguished from this other inspiring being. It could be contended that this also applies to the individual who is the bearer of the Bodhisattva. Rudolf Steiner could therefore be this Bodhisattva-bearer, as Arenson's contradictory assertions would lead one to suppose. In reply to this we might ask: is Rudolf Steiner then the only one who can be inspired in this way by the Bodhisattva? Does he not say himself that *everyone* who wishes to know anything about the Etheric Christ must gain his knowledge from the Inspirations of this being?[154] Inspiration by the Bodhisattva does not therefore prove that the one who is inspired is himself the bearer of this Being!

And how plausible is Arenson's argument about the supposed important turn in Rudolf Steiner's life that was to indicate the incorporation of the Bodhisattva into him as the bearer-individuality? If one can speak at all about an important turn in Rudolf Steiner's life, it would not be something that occurred between his thirtieth and thirty-third year but rather an event that took place in his thirty-fifth year as he described in his autobigraphy. The period between Rudolf Steiner's thirtieth and thirty-third year is just the time in which it is least possible to speak about a step-by-step penetration of his being by a continuing Inspiration through the Bodhisattva. Out of his own inherent ego-forces Rudolf Steiner soared up at this time to the heights of his *Philosophy of Spiritual Activity*. Among all his works there is no other piece that can be less attributed to the inspirational influence of another being than *this* one, in which every line is the result of pure intuitive activity!

This turning point in Rudolf Steiner's life, cited by Arenson as an indication that he is the 'Bodhisattva', is problematical, and so too is Arenson's interpretation of the fact that Rudolf Steiner spoke detachedly about himself in the third person in his autobiographical lecture of 3 February 1913, in response to the Besant lies.

From the foregoing it can be concluded that Rudolf Steiner cannot be regarded as the bearer of the Bodhisattva, i.e. the reincarnated Jeshu ben Pandira, though he might have had a connection to the Bodhisattva Spirit or his bearer-individuality.

However grateful we may be to Adolf Arenson for having raised the complex and elusive question of the reciprocal relationships of these individuals, just as grateful are we to Elisabeth Vreede for having been the first to give an explanation, albeit a negatively restricting one, to this same question. According to a little known report by Walter Vegelahn, Rudolf Steiner himself pointed to the necessity of distinguishing between his own individuality and that of the Bodhisattva. This was in a personal remark made on the occasion of his Berne lectures about the St Matthew's Gospel and seems to have been unknown to Elisabeth Vreede.[155]

★

It is not surprising that the illuminating explanations of Vreede and Arenson were not able to prevent further speculation about alleged other candidates for the role of bearer-individuality for the Bodhisattva. This received even more encouragement through the fact that the Vreede lectures left the space vacated by Krishnamurti still unclaimed. The candidate for this 'throne' most often mentioned even today and the one best known in this connection is Valentin Tomberg, who converted to Roman Catholicism at the beginning of the Forties. Whether Tomberg, who was the leader of a Group of the Anthroposophical Society in Estonia in his younger years, thought of himself as the Bodhisattva or was merely nominated thereto by his followers, to fulfil the double need of an anthroposophical and a Catholic substitute for Krishnamurti, need not be discussed here. It is, however, a well-known fact that Tomberg, who was born in St Petersburg in February 1900 and died in 1973, was, and still is, regarded in certain circles as the Bodhisattva of the twentieth century. They offer as evidence backing their point of view the remark of Dr Steiner to Friedrich Rittelmeyer, that Jeshu ben Pandira, the Bodhisattva-bearer, had been born at the beginning of the century.

Tomberg's absorption of the Christological side of Anthroposophy was remarkable, and his earlier essays and writings offer much food for thought. Through his way of expressing himself it is not always clear what he derived from Rudolf Steiner and what was the outcome of his own thoughts and knowledge. Nevertheless, he emphasizes in his *Anthroposophical Studies of the Old Testament*, which appeared from 1933 onwards and was still addressed to the members of the Anthroposophical Society, that he attributed all his knowledge to Rudolf Steiner. It was no less a person than Elisabeth Vreede who wrote the Foreword to the English translation of these studies, thereby providing an indication of the well-intentioned recognition that Tomberg's writings evoked among anthroposophists at that time. During a stay of some years in Holland, against a background of some differences of opinion with Willem Zeylmans van Emmichoven, the General Secretary of the Dutch Society, he became estranged from these circles. In 1945, Tomberg, the former pupil of Rudolf Steiner's Anthroposophy, brought up in the Protestant faith, joined the Catholic Church.

Tomberg's conduct of life and spiritual conversion present deep enigmas to the observer. Undoubtedly Tomberg was a universal and in some ways highly gifted spirit. Yet Rudolf Steiner's individual spirituality and the particular mission that arose out of it remained a sealed book to him in its essential nature. Steiner's endeavour was to investigate the facts and beings of the super-sensible world by means of his clairvoyance based on thinking, in order to be able to formulate his results in a way that was comprehensible to the healthy human consciousness. In a posthumously published work, Tomberg refers to this, stating: 'Rudolf Steiner elected to give his work a scientific form, so-called "spiritual science".'[156] But this scientific slant to Anthroposophy was taken by Tomberg as a sign of weakness. It appeared to him that in Steiner's work 'the third aspect of the indivisible threefoldness of the Way, the Truth, and the Life—namely Life—was not given enough attention. For the form which is proper to the scientific attitude leaves no room for pure mysticism or the magic of the spirit, that is, for Life itself'.[157] No one familiar with Steiner's monumental work *The Philosophy of Spiritual Activity* will find the slightest grain of truth in this assertion. One can even go back to an earlier phase of Rudolf Steiner's life and find in his very first publication dealing with Goethe's scientific writings the remarkable sentence: 'Becoming aware of the Idea within reality is the true communion of man.'[158] Has not the communion of the believer a mystical, as well as a ceremonial-cultic and, in this sense, a 'magical' side to it? Right at the beginning of his research work Steiner raised mystic-magical experience out of the realm of ignorant belief into the lucid region of thought experience, and sublimated therewith the *mystical* element (which tends to become nebulous when acting alone) into the sphere of *truth*, i.e. into thought-filled mysticism. Tomberg was unable to discover anything of this thought-mysticism in Steiner. Nevertheless, for Tomberg there still remained 'a magnificent achievement of thought and will in Anthroposophy',[159] in spite of the supposed lack of mysticism.

To everyone who possesses some insight into the basis of Anthroposophy, this characteristic might be of interest first and foremost as a piece of self-characterization of Tomberg himself. That could apply to a heightened degree to the following passage in which he attempts to explain Steiner's reference to the Bodhisattva of the twentieth century out of his 'deficiency-diagnosis' of Anthroposophy: 'Rudolf Steiner himself was conscious of this, therefore it was with a certain amount of hope that he indicated the necessary appearance of a successor (the Bodhisattva) who would remedy this lack and would bring the trinity of the Way, the Truth and the Life to full fruition.'[160]

Whether or not the Bodhisattva individuality would choose for his purpose a tool with *such* a conception of Rudolf Steiner's Anthroposophy (which after all is there to prepare for his activity)

remains, luckily—even though the ways of God are rightly pronounced inscrutable—a doubtful question . . .

Far-fetched as it would seem to take this particular view seriously,
it is just as remarkable to find elsewhere in the same book an
apparently positive assessment of Rudolf Steiner and a specially
important view of his spiritual research, which runs as follows:

> The teaching of the heavenly hierarchies was renewed in the first
> quarter of this century through the life-work of the great Austrian seer
> and thinker Rudolf Steiner. The depth and profundity of Rudolf
> Steiner's contribution to a new understanding of the spiritual hierar-
> chies is such that this theme cannot be seriously taken up today without
> taking into account his remarkable accomplishment. For his achieve-
> ment in the domain of the teaching concerning the angelic hierar-
> chies—as far as the wealth of stimulation, the depth and multiplicity of
> viewpoints, the inner lack of contradictions, the consistency and
> organic cohesiveness is concerned—cannot be compared with the
> accomplishment of any seer or thinker of the present, or from the
> Middle Ages or antiquity. It towers way above them.[161]

What is astonishing about such words is not just that they come
from a man who has sought refuge in the Catholic Church but that
they appear in a book whose German edition is published by one of
the most renowned and traditional printing houses of the Curia.[162]
Does this perhaps indicate that it has already been perceived, or that
the discovery is about to be made in ecclesiastical circles that Rudolf
Steiner's teachings about the hierarchies are 'a mighty confirmation
of the Church teachings about the Angels . . .' as Tomberg stresses?

A still greater amazement, however, might strike the hearts of
many of our anthroposophical friends when they learn from the
Epilogue to the same book that, although Tomberg may have
turned away from the Anthroposophical Society, '*he never willingly
forsook Rudolf Steiner, with whom he felt connected and whom he felt was
connected with him from the spiritual world.*'[163]

What an affirmation of *mutual* posthumous relationship between
a pupil of spiritual science and the inaugurator of Anthroposophy!
There can hardly be its equal in the relevant biographies of the
pioneers of Anthroposophy! Should the tireless contributions of the
anthroposophical friends for the things which they hold dear be
rewarded by divine decree at the end of the century by their

suddenly being joined in their battle by quite new comrades at arms? Or has this intimate confession escaped the censor and slipped into print in an unguarded moment of the book's production?

Or perhaps it was not by error after all, for this is not an isolated case. The same publishing house had started two years previously to accept works by Tomberg and had printed the German edition of his *Meditations on the Tarot* in 1983, whereby his desire for anonymity was strictly respected. In this work, too, very appreciative and in some places even enthusiastic words about Rudolf Steiner are to be found, quite apart from the many ideas it contains which are quite obviously derived from Anthroposophy. And in this same work Tomberg points in a truly remarkable way to Steiner's statements about the Bodhisattva of the twentieth century, and writes: 'Of all the things which have been published or publicly spoken about on this subject, the most pertinent is that which Rudolf Steiner said.'[164] And yet, Steiner's conception of the way in which the Bodhisattva would be revealed was not quite the same as what Tomberg had in mind, but 'he was at least on the right track,' says the latter. Following on along this 'right track', Tomberg develops the idea that the Bodhisattva event and its real aim is to unite spirituality with intellectuality, a subject about which Rudolf Steiner once spoke to Hübbe-Schleiden—though it was in quite a different sense!

According to Tomberg this union should take place in the following way: 'Since it is a question of the work of the fusion of revelation and knowledge, of spirituality and intellectuality, it is a matter throughout of the fusion of the Avatar principle with the Buddha principle. In other words, the Kalki-Avatar awaited by the Hindus and the Maitreya Buddha awaited by the Buddhists will manifest in a *single personality*. On the historical plane the Maitreya Buddha and the Kalki-Avatar will be one.'[165]

This union is inevitably interpreted as a union of *prayer* and *meditation*, and as the great historical forerunner of this 'unique personality' and his work of unification Tomberg names *St Ignatius of Loyola*, the founder of the Jesuit Order! The latter, we are told, was 'not only the Master of Prayer, but also the Master of Meditation'. And we learn, furthermore, that Ignatius 'had to a large extent set the example of fusing spirituality and intellectuality, prayer and meditation, which was the mission of the future Buddha

Avatar'.[166] Devious, if not to say unfathomable, as this stylization is, which sees in St Ignatius a fuser of intellect and spirituality (the former giving man freedom and the latter spirituality, which just in their fusion is something so alien to St Ignatius), as interesting is it on the other hand to find this Tombergian work prefaced by a former member of the Jesuit Order, one of the best known of their sect, the recently deceased Hans Urs von Balthasar. Balthasar's writings are among the most read in educated Catholic circles, and thus the Polish Pontiff himself, who is also Head of the Jesuit Order, who raised the deceased to the rank of Cardinal just before his death, cannot have been quite ignorant in all these matters.

It will not be easy to unravel the innermost reasons for Tomberg's conversion. But obvious, on the other hand, is the tolerant attention paid by members of certain Catholic circles to the remnants of Anthroposophy still retained by their convert.

It is true that Rudolf Steiner did not address the contents of Anthroposophy exclusively to members of the Society of that time, but to humanity in general. It is therefore a matter for rejoicing if more and more people start to take an interest in it, even those in ecclesiastical circles. Nevertheless, certain as it is that this can really happen among the laity and higher echelons of the Church, we must be aware of how the actual leading Church circles stand with regard to such an interest in Anthroposophy and its propagation, considering their allegiance to Jesuitism.

Cardinal Joseph Ratzinger, the present adviser on Church doctrine 'through whom the Holy See encourages the deepening of faith and oversees its orthodoxy',[167] felt himself obliged to make the following statement some years ago: 'Christians [he means Catholics] are again in the minority, more than they have been since the end of antiquity.'[168] According to him, this fact is associated with 'a crisis of belief in the dogma'.[169] Has the crisis arisen perhaps because the radius of Church dogma has become too narrow for more and more souls? Should this radius now be widened to include Anthroposophy, so that the spiritual needs which have transcended the former body of dogma can be met in future within the framework of the Church? Perhaps it is not a coincidence that this same adviser on Church doctrine is known to the Cologne editor of Tomberg's work. And in view of this precarious situation and the growing and successful spread of the anthroposophical movement, why should one not long ago have recognized the futility of the direct assault against Anthroposophy as it was practised at the beginning of the century, and have decided on a change of strategy and, more or less behind closed doors, have breathed a policy of 'the gentle approach of brotherly embrace'?

For there is *one* thing about which everyone who is at all familiar with the aims of Jesuitism can be certain: the Jesuits must under all circumstances adhere to the Ignatian rule of making converts—a maxim reiterated by Pedro Arupe, the late head of the Society of Jesus, in an interview held just before his death, wherein he spoke of the wholesale 'conversion of hearts'. To this end every means must be employed. Why not, then, the one recommended by Ignatius himself? This is characterized somewhat as follows in the thirteenth of his 'Rules' laid down for 'the attaining of the right attitude in the service of the battling Church': 'In order for us to be protected in every respect we must always remember "What to us seems white becomes black as soon as it is so decreed by the hierarchical Church."'[170]

Did the hierarchical Church—and that means, first and foremost, the actual Pontifex Maximus, whoever happened at the time to be head of the Society of Jesus, and the latter's adviser on Church doctrine—'decide' perhaps on the 'blackening' of Rudolf Steiner and his followers—that is to say, 'Catholicizing' them?

Such questions as these, it should be emphasized, do not infringe upon or set in doubt either the absolute inviolability of freedom in matters of faith or the genuine interest of *individual representatives* of the Catholic Church in Rudolf Steiner's Anthroposophy. All that is here intended is to try to relate the behaviour of the Church just described with its strategic centrepiece resting on the ultimate aims of St Ignatius. To what extent these aims are known in Catholic circles or are really taken seriously is, of course, a different question, which cannot be gone into here. Yet, just as little as it is decisive in the waging and outcome of a war what the ordinary footsoldiers or NCOs think about the general strategic situation, of equal indifference is it to the aims of the hierarchical heads of the Church what views and intentions, even of the most sincere kind, are held by individual believers. In other words, no reasonable person possessing a more or less clear understanding of the aims of the hierarchical Church can allow himself to believe that the more than four hundred year old sightline of Jesuitism could be lowered, or even abandoned, during the course of the twentieth century on account of the very 'dangerous' spread of the anthroposophical movement! One should not forget that the first principle of Jesuitism consists of complete and absolute inner submission through meditation to the figure of Jesus, and that the latter is regarded as the most powerful earthly-spiritual *conqueror*. The meditative pupil of the Jesuit Order must aim to identify himself more and more with this power. Then, in time, the one who submits himself thus in the sense of a world-wide conversion impulse can become a powerful ruler over the souls of others. It is self-evident that this 'submissive, but over-bearing' Janus spirit of Jesuitism *cannot* ever truly be drawn towards the anthroposophical principle of the freedom of the individual spirit as long as it remains faithful to its own 'eternal' principles. That, of course, does not prevent it from *appearing* to be drawn towards the spirit of Anthroposophy in varying degrees. (A modern illustration of this is provided in Bernhard Grom's publication *Anthroposophie und Christentum*.) Whoever thinks with dreamy, unclear thoughts, out of vague feelings of tolerance or communal desire, that it is possible to achieve a substantial amount of co-operation between the *essence* of these two spiritual currents, should study the exercises of Ignatius Loyola followed by the content of Rudolf Steiner's lecture given in Carlsruhe on 5 October 1911,[171] and then consider again the symptoms described here.

★

To the symptoms of a strategic change within the politics of certain ecclesiastical circles belongs, in the first place, the cautious way in which the reincarnation motive is placed, with an expec-tant experimental gesture, in the publications we have mentioned and in others. Thus von Balthasar, at the end of his introduction to Tomberg's *Tarot* book, delivers a gentle reprimand to the latter for upholding the idea of reincarnation, which appears to him 'to deviate a little too far to the left'. At the same time, however, any uneasiness which might have been caused by this idea is set to rest by the assertion: 'The author certainly tries his hardest to stick to the middle way of Christian knowledge.'[172] In other words: in spite of such rather risky deviation from the central path, Valentin

Tomberg can still be looked upon as a worthy son of the Church.

The same reincarnation thought meets us a few years later in the Introduction to the German edition of the book *Covenant of the Heart*, from the pen of a well-known public lawyer from Munich. 'Tomberg,' we learn, 'expressed himself very clearly on the subject of reincarnation. It is personal experience with him. As such . . . it is not to be refuted by theories, but from its side throws a light of deeper understanding on the life of individuals and on that of mankind as a whole.'[173]

One could imagine that one is reading an introductory handbook on the study of Anthroposophy. Not a bit of it: quite other illuminated and well trained sons of the 'hierarchical Church' have thought upon these lines during the twentieth century and so Tomberg's experience 'has unexpected points of contact with the work of Gabriel Marcel, who holds the teaching of reincarnation to be a reasonable hypothesis to explain empirical facts'.[174] And finally we learn that the New Testament 'has attested to the fact that at least *one* person returned to a new earthly incarnation—Lazarus!'[175]

It may appear very questionable to choose just Lazarus of all people to support *this* particular argument, but as it is actually alluded to briefly in this connection in the Bible, we can be in no doubt as to what lies behind it: reincarnation is an archetypally Christian phenomenon, which has always rested at the heart of Church doctrine. We do not need a Goethe or a Lessing, least of all a Rudolf Steiner, to disclose this truth to us. The mass of Roman Catholics may now start to *believe* in reincarnation, just as 120 years ago they were encouraged to believe in the infallibility of the Pope. And why should reincarnation not be raised to the level of a dogma in the not too distant future, if this would be of benefit in spreading the faith? (At any rate, the present Pope is considered to be a private adherent of the doctrine of reincarnation, according to a statement by Professor Robert Spaemann.)[176]

★

Over against all considerations discussed up till now the simple objection could be raised that they only serve to blacken the name of the Church and are furthermore unrealistic in that so many opposing writings issue from the Catholic camp today, such as the recent vitriolic attack against Waldorf pedagogy by the 'Working Community of Catholic Societies for Education and Schools', in which the tactics of 'brotherly embrace' do not come into the question. Nevertheless, one has to ask oneself if such attacks as this are a reflection of *every* aspect of present Church policy. Of course, the 'stalwart' Catholic who, uninitiated, cannot imagine how 'what to us seems white becomes black as soon as it is so decreed by the hierarchical Church', must be allowed to carry on his polemics against Anthroposophy for quite a while yet. Why should not the higher echelons take account of the law of inertia among the lower ranks and allow the infantry to proceed in its manifest opposition to Anthroposophy? Is it only by pure chance that this sort of Catholic publication does not usually have an introduction by high-ranking personalities or be published by such a renowned firm as that which brought out the writings of Tomberg, a publishing firm moreover that produced five works during the last six years, which to a greater or lesser degree appear to invite one to an ardent study of Anthroposophy,[177] and which during that time did not publish one book in opposition?

So perhaps, after all, it would not be too unrealistic to search for the real, present-day Church opposition in quite a different quarter from that in which it still clamours with the same insistence and crudity as it did 70 years ago.

Should the setting up of the dogma of reincarnation be successful, then the Church would be able to put its foot in the door to Steiner's spiritual science in accordance with Goethe's interpretation of the attitude of ecclesiastical policy (adapted, of course, to the present situation):

The Church has an excellent stomach,
whole *doctrines* has she swallowed,
but never yet had indigestion. (*Faust*: Promenade)

Of course, in the sense of Rudolf Steiner, neither reincarnation nor any other spiritual fact or being can ever become an object of belief through a doctrine without immediately losing its essential connection to the ability of every man to develop independent *knowledge* of the spiritual world. In other words, in every endeavour to make supersensible realities into a dogma we must recognize a kind of pasteurization attempt with respect to the contents of anthroposophical knowledge according to the motto 'Contents *yes*, independent comprehension of the contents by individual believers—*never!*'

The creator of Anthroposophy never wished for people to *believe* in him; he only hoped that his insights, acquired by means of his own supersensible experience, would be met by unbiased *thinking*, which is a necessary step towards acquiring one's own supersensible experience—a kind of thinking that cannot be restricted by any dogma. In the sense of Rudolf Steiner one must recognize that as soon as a spiritual fact becomes changed into a tenet of dogmatic belief it ceases to be true, for in modern times *truth has become inseparable from its discovery by the independent spiritual human individuality*.

The reason why the goodwill shown by certain ecclesiastical circles towards the idea of reincarnation, at any rate as far as its propagation in the lower Church ranks is concerned, must as a matter of policy be kept strictly *within the bounds of a belief* becomes immediately clear to us if we consider the disquieting effect which would be produced in the Church if this policy did *not* succeed. For what would the consequence be if more and more Catholics not only developed a general trusting belief in this idea, which allowed them to remain in ignorance of the immediacy and pertinence of Rudolf Steiner's spiritual science, but awakened to a serious study, say of his Karma lectures? And what if ever more and more Catholics should for instance occupy themselves with studying what Rudolf Steiner had to say about Ignatius Loyola, about his life after death and his subsequent incarnation? Strange and perhaps not easily guided stirrings towards truly independent forming of thoughts, possibly also about the sense and justification for a Universal Church led by Jesuits might be the outcome! For it would become evident through this study that the founder of Jesuitism was, in his succeeding incarnation, anything but a dogmatically restricted believer, and a man who had many more real spiritual experiences than Loyola, who, in fact, through his gift of spiritual insight, saw whole armies of spirits in all concreteness.[178] Just the possibility of this swing from a general feeling of goodwill towards reincarnation to a serious thinking acceptance could lead from a 'crisis in belief in dogma', as foreseen by Ratzinger, to a 'crisis in belief in Jesuitism'!

Great as this 'risk' might appear, it is not actually *that* big, for Rudolf Steiner has characterized the later manifestation of the individuality who formally worked in Loyola as an individual who can be described as the 'father' of all modern spiritualism.[179]

What we call 'spiritualistic' is any attempt to draw near to the spiritual world with the wish to see the spirit *in a material garb*. Thus if Jesuitism were to take seriously this concrete result from Steiner's reincarnation research, it might actually get a boost from it that would work out in two different ways: 1) by widening its field of vision into the manifoldness and richness of the spiritual world; 2) by strengthening its endeavour to materialize the spiritual in doctrine and cult.

In view of what was said above regarding the symptoms of a more open approach, one might now ask if—thanks, strangely enough, to Rudolf Steiner's own research—such a further development of Jesuitism is not already long since in full swing. *This would mean that in certain non-anthroposophical circles the realities of reincarnation and karma might be taken just as seriously as by the pupils of Steiner.* Might not the strange benevolence of certain ecclesiastical circles towards Anthroposophy and its creator in essence arise from an acceptance of certain facts and relationships with regard to reincarnation?

In the year 1879, Pope Leo XIII published the famous encyclical 'Aeterni Patris'. It raised the theology and philosophy of Thomas Aquinas by the highest authority of the Papal throne to be the dogmatic basis of all Catholic thought and research. The historian Karl Heyer once described this encyclical as the 'expression of a most important but "backwards-looking" world-historical will'.[180] Why should not the intention be present within the Church of one day publishing a similar encyclical with regard to Rudolf Steiner? It would only be a consequence of the benevolent attitude towards the idea of reincarnation within a further developed Jesuitism.

Should the so striking *entente cordiale* of certain ecclesiastical circles towards Valentin Tomberg's writings be only the public expression of the fact that the Church, at least in its higher echelons, is seeking to satisfy the ever-growing soul hunger with anthroposophical spiritual nourishment, so that in face of the changed spiritual needs of millions of our fellow human beings the Church does not have to remain in a cultural cul-de-sac, no genuine lover of Anthroposophy should be disturbed by that. For access to the spiritual inheritance of Anthroposophy cannot and must not be denied to anyone, even to him who may misuse it. However, it is very doubtful if the stage managers of these and other *ententes* belonging to the 'Church militant' would be willing to abstain completely from diluting the anthroposophical movement, wherever possible, with Roman infallibility doctrines and dogmatic thinking with truly Ignatian conscious intent. No lesser personage than Pedro Arupe, the last General of the Order of the Society of Jesus, during the above-mentioned interview, reminded his hearers of the brilliant epigram of St Ignatius of Loyola summarizing the tactics of spiritual conquest, 'In at their doors, out through mine'—a saying which, in view of the *glasnost* mood in certain ecclesiastical circles towards Anthroposophy,[181] should not be forgotten.

Among the self-evident 'duties' of tolerance, esteem and good will which every person owes his fellow men belongs also the maxim 'live and let live', of which not only the first part must be practised but also the second part. However, along with this greatest possible social tolerance and respect should go the greatest possible spiritual clarity and refusal to compromise, from which it should never deviate. If goodwill is an indispensable element in a social respect, so can it become a disintegrating force in spiritual concerns when it begins to dissolve the boundaries of facts and what they comprise. And one of these facts consists in the utter irreconcilability of the *inner kernel* of Catholicism with Anthroposophy.

Perhaps we might here remind our readers of those impressive words which Rudolf Steiner once spoke to the active members of the Threefold Commonwealth movement on this very subject:

> You see, there are always well-intentioned people among anthroposophists who, however, attach a certain value to going beyond the facts. It sometimes becomes a kind of addiction for them to want to go beyond the facts, and that expresses itself in the case with which we are at present dealing by them frequently emphasizing the fact that one would be doing a service to a particular confession or confessional community by aligning oneself with it as far as this is possible. In the case of the Catholic Church it would only antagonize it if you tried to draw near to its dogma. The more the Catholic Church finds a similarity of belief in some other community or discovers that it is

seeking the Christian truths, the more it will hate that community or that truth, for the Catholic Church aims at carefully avoiding Christian truth and increasing its own power as much as possible. That is the aim of the Catholic Church. You will never move it by becoming ever more and more 'Christian'. You can only be reconciled to it if you are a human being upon whom it can depend as upon someone who belongs to Rome. And in no other way can you be reconciled.

Now the Church feels itself in a position to increase its power very greatly under the present conditions of the time. It knows very well that to build upon dynasties will not be of any use to it, because it is generally better informed about such things than other people. It also knows that such dynasties as still retain the Crown are on the road to extinction. Therefore it does not wish to bind itself to what is foredoomed. On the other hand the Church will make use precisely of the upward striving of the broad masses of the people to increase its power. And the Catholic Church makes use of everything it can lay its hands on for this purpose. In its great world strategy which sometimes shows an ingenious streak—ingenious in the sense that humanity is thereby brought more and more under the domination of Rome—it makes use of a situation such as the nationalizing of the Polish clergy; *and Poland will become of importance in the game which the Catholic Church plays* ... These things are not radicalism when one describes them thus; it is simply an objective fact. The bad thing about it is that, through human prejudice, a large part of humanity does not yet see that it is actually impossible to speak the truth when one stands within one of the confessions. It is a fact, one can become a tragic figure within a confession; but one cannot hold office within a confession and still speak the truth. It is not possible nowadays. Therefore the attitude towards the Catholic Church can be thus described: *one should ignore the aspirations of the Church as long as possible and then proceed to reveal their mendacity in single cases.* Then, at least, one would be taking a way consistent with the facts.[182]


These words appear meanwhile to have become more pertinent, specially when one takes into account the probability of a further development of Jesuitism in the above sense which can be diagnosed from certain symptoms. They would be very suited to sweeping away any possible 'well-intentioned' but, in fact, adversely working attitude of 'door opening' in the anthroposophical movement. Or should one prefer to continue in this way of 'going beyond the facts'?

★

'There must be no Intuition of Evil,' we read in Tomberg's meditation to the fifteenth tarot card of the Great Arcana (The Devil).[183] 'For intuition becomes Identification and Identification Communion ... One can only intuitively grasp what one loves ... But one cannot love evil. *Evil is unknowable in its essential nature.*'[184] According to that its effects must also essentially remain unknowable ... 'Essentially unknowable': Mephistopheles must secretly rub his withered hands together in glee at such 'wise knowledge'! These words fit extremely well to those Goethe once put into his mouth:

> The Devil your good folk ne'er scent
> e'en though he has them by the collar.
>
> <div align="right">(<i>Faust</i>: Auerbach's cellar)</div>

In this respect one should compare this statement of Tomberg with the last utterance of Ahriman in Rudolf Steiner's fourth Mystery Drama:

> Now 'tis time for me to haste away
> From his environment, for whensoe'er
> His sight can *think* me as I really am,
> He will commence to fashion in his thought
> Part of the power which slowly killeth me.

★

Should that kind of Tombergian theory of the knowledge of the essence of evil be labelled as 'unfathomable meditative profundity' in anthroposophical circles too, then—to visualize the almost unimaginable—there would be quite good prospects for a still more gloomy sequel to the Star-of-the-East farce appearing on the world stage towards the end of the century.

Yet we can be very grateful for the Tomberg phenomenon. For the attentive observer of the spiritual currents of our time certain symptomatic tendencies towards entanglement or fusion are laid bare which allow us to see clearly through the veiled nature of the present struggle.

Many a reader of the foregoing may perhaps be of the opinion that we have allowed ourselves to stray too far from the main theme. It was however nothing but the Bodhisattva question which led us in its Tombergian-Catholic guise to the figure of St Ignatius Loyola and therewithal into the heart of the Roman Catholic concern. And perhaps after all it is a remarkable symptom for the Bodhisattva-being to have caused himself to be talked about in recent years, also among members of a confessional Church, through the mouth of a well-known convert, after theosophists had played with the idea for several decades. To the oriental version of the Bodhisattva caricature there seems thus to be added a more South-European variety, though in germinal form and having a Catholic flavour.

At the end of this chapter a third kind of caricature will be discussed, which attempts to spread itself and influence chiefly the Anglo-American West.

A book entitled *The Reappearance of Christ and the Masters of Wisdom*, was published in England in 1980.[185] Its author, Benjamin Creme, explains in it his view of the reappearance. The book contains notes of lectures that Creme held during the seventies, and includes replies to questions. We read on the back cover that according to him 'the One whom people call Christ appeared on Earth in a present-day well-known country' on 19 July 1977.

Then, in April 1982, there appeared in many of the leading newspapers of the world a proclamation-like announcement which manifestly had a connection with Creme. It informed readers that 'Christ' who had come into the world would announce Himself through loudspeakers and from cinema screens to all mankind within two months. How would He, however, make Himself known among the innumerable 'showmasters'? The answer was: 'Look out for a modern man who is engaged in modern political, economic and social problems.'[186] Who would not in this connection be reminded of Soloviev's *Antichrist*? Furthermore, the great World Teacher 'Christ' is identified in the same announcement with the Jewish Messiah, the Muslim Mahdi, the Hindu Krishna and the Buddhist Maitreya, the latter identification having been already put forward by the theosophical conception. More interesting for our consideration is perhaps the fact that Creme—who seems to confine himself to synonymizing the expressions 'World Teacher', 'Christ' and 'Maitreya'—pays heed to a question from a member of his audience respecting certain statements by Rudolf Steiner. 'Rudolf Steiner seems to indicate,' said the questioner, 'that Christ would not reincarnate in a physical body. Did changes occur later?' Creme's answer: 'Yes, of course. Rudolf Steiner died in 1925. The revelation of Christ's need to come back to the physical world occurred only in 1945. The decision to come back took place indeed earlier, but the *way* in which He was to appear was still undecided at that time. Actually there were certain initiates in the world . . . who had been prepared as possible vehicles for the Christ. Altogether there were four: one of them is known to all of us [Krishnamurti was meant]. Then, however, the plan to make use of a vehicle was abandoned.'[187]

The event announced by the medium seems until now not to have occurred, although in his latest *Newsletter* at time of writing (1992, No. 3) it is announced that 'Maitreya has made a series of appearances on Sundays before large gatherings in different parts of the world, on which we still await media comment and reaction. He speaks fluently in the local language outlining His plans and concerns and asking for help and co-operation. Benjamin Creme's Master has confirmed that, after each such appearance, between 70 and 80 per cent are convinced that they have indeed seen the Christ.'

Indeed the Creme version of a 'Bodhisattva-Christ' caricature could find wide acceptance among different groups of people. For it contains a perfectly justified grain of truth, which Rudolf Steiner has long ago indicated: the imminent initial physical incarnation of a spiritual being who will usurp the name of Christ, although he is of a quite different nature.

1. Rudolf Steiner and Annie
Besant, Munich, 1907

2. Helena Petrovna Blavatsky and Henry Steel Olcott

3. Henry Steel Olcott

4. Helena Petrovna Blavatsky, 1889

5. Valentin Tomberg

6. Krishnamurti at Brockwood Park, around 1984

7. Adolf Arenson

8. Elisabeth Vreede, 1924

9, Rudolf Steiner, 1907

10. Annie Besant, around 1925

11. Krishnamurti (right) and brother Nitya, after their first 'initiation', Adyar, 1910

12. Besant, Leadbeater and Krishnamurti (right), Benares, December 1911

## 12. CONCLUDING PERSPECTIVES

Let us return once more to the drama of the Bodhisattva question and to its solution to which Elisabeth Vreede contributed so much. Even though the fog which *then* surrounded it has lifted, riddles still exist, particularly that of the destiny of Jiddu Krishnamurti, who just at the stage of the thickest fog began to show his true worth. How did Krishnamurti himself later judge the happenings of that time? And to what extent has he not only freed himself from the hubbub of those events but also managed to penetrate to their well-concealed causes? Has he come into relationship with the mystical primordial fact of Christianity, or did it remain closed to him during his lifetime? Regarding these and similar questions let us cast a final glance at the former protagonists in the theosophical Bodhisattva drama.

★

On 17 February 1986, the erstwhile candidate for the throne of 'Christ' died at Ojai, California, in his ninety-first year. For the last five weeks of his life he lay suffering from cancer of the pancreas, in the same 'Pine Cottage' where he had undergone such strange experiences 66 years previously, as described in Chapter 10. During his last days he had beseeched the small circle of his closest friends not to allow anyone to make pilgrimages to 'salute the body; he did not want any of that business—sandalwood and all that put over the body'.[188] This urgent plea is the final expression of Krishnamurti's view of life which, since his deed of emancipation in the summer of 1929, left no further place for outer authorities, earthly hierarchies, or any kind of personality cult. Through many utterances during his last days there shines with a gentle light the fruit of spiritual independence which had begun to ripen during those years. 'I like to talk to lots of people, not that they influence me,' he confessed in looking back over his life. His biographer writes: 'Nobody, not even Mrs Besant, had ever told him what to say. When he dissolved the Order of the Star, *he* did it.'[189]

Krishnamurti called upon people all over the world to perform similar acts of inner emancipation. In innumerable talks he had persistently attempted with passionate energy to show people how they could free themselves from all conditions of their inner and outer lives. He had become a man of the world who was eager to hold long, serious conversations with ordinary people just as readily as with well-known artists, politicians or scientists. The former idolization with which he had been met had changed to an attitude of universal respect from people, even where his presence remained a deep enigma to them. Nobody who ever heard him speak in later years would deny that his passionate endeavour to lead people to inner independence—even from himself, the speaker—was sincere. He never gave the slightest impression of being a person who wished to influence his audience or his pupils in any way; rather he would appeal to their inner judgement, sometimes with a soul-stirring entreaty. The absolute respect which he showed towards every single person seemed to have become second nature to him. He had experienced all too keenly in his own 'body' what it feels like for the dignity of man to be violated by somebody wishing to impress his own nature on another person from without in a suggestive fashion. As a result of this painful experience, Krishna-murti had not only overcome the illusion of a fictitious conscious-ness of self but had also gone beyond the much more fundamental error of believing that he was an entity completely different from the rest of mankind and the world. Identification with a particular race, or nation, or family group, or with one's own body, etc., all these were only special cases for Krishnamurti of that fundamental deception of being an absolutely separate being. Therein he saw the deeper cause of all personal, national, or international crises and conflicts of our present age. For that reason he called incessantly upon people to seek for deeper unity amidst all that appeared separate. Krishnamurti wished to see people growing up with a thinking stretching over the whole world, feelings which strove to go beyond egoism and deeds which were of significance for the whole planet Earth.

One of his last talks was given in Los Alamos, USA, to a gathering of 700 scientists and technicians, on the same spot where the first atomic bomb, developed by Robert Oppenheimer, had been fired 40 years earlier. In the discussion which followed Krishnamurti was asked how he would have directed the National Laboratory if he had been in charge and had been given the task of defending the nation. In his answer he explained to his audience that, among other things, certain psychological facts had first to be considered before any questions about outer defence were dealt with.

We have divided the world. You are a Christian, I am black, you are white ... you have given your time for destruction. You are doing a great deal which is of benefit, and on the other hand you are destroying every human being on Earth, because you only recognize *my* country, *my* responsibilities, *my* defence. And the Russians are saying exactly the same thing on the other side. India, which has immense poverty, is saying the same thing ... If I have a group of people who say, let's forget all nationalism, all religions, let us, as human beings, solve this problem—try to live together without destruction—then perhaps there is something new that can take place ... Nobody has a global outlook—a global feeling for all humanity ... If you went around the world as the speaker does, you would cry for the rest of your life.[190]

Touching as such utterances of the 90-year-old are, it is doubtful whether they would be of use to bridge the gap to which they themselves point. Krishnamurti draws our attention, it is true, to certain underlying causes of the destructive forces inherent in natural science and technology—the restricted province of the ordinary 'me' and 'my' consciousness. And maybe a person here or there might be roused by what he says. Yet the 'soul' of modern science, in so far as it has strayed along the path towards exclusive materialism, will hardly find help in any other way than by being shown concretely how it can enter into a science of the invisible which is just as detailed and clear as the physical sciences.

*

Throughout his life Krishnamurti had a great love of music. During the war, which he spent in California, he had a great predilection for Beethoven's Ninth Symphony. Apart from his long-familiar Indian music, what he also treasured was the work of Mozart. He loved the poetry of Shelley and Keats, and, perhaps more than all other ancient and modern poems, he liked the Song of Solomon. According to his biographer, among all the buildings and sculptures which impressed him most—apart from a gigantic statue of Shiva in India and a head of Buddha in Boston—was the *Nike of Samothrace* in the Louvre, and Chartres Cathedral.

★

The years of his 'discovery' and 'initiation' in Adyar seem to have slipped from his memory more and more after his deed of emancipation. In one of the very few statements of an autobiographical character that he made in later years, he recollects in very general terms that he had once been discovered 'and all the fuss and sudden importance given to him was around him'.[191] And when in 1980, in response to a request made by a female attendant from the Indian Centre of the Theosophical Society, he revisited for the first time the room Annie Besant had prepared for him and his brother some decades previously; it awakened no decisive memories in him!

Nevertheless, the destiny of his early years must have accompanied him throughout life as a profound inner riddle. Just a year before his death this riddle met him again in a surprising way and from a quite unexpected quarter and caused him deep uneasiness as nothing else had done during the latter decades of his life. His biographer relates how, at a conference in England in January 1985, 'he began to speak in a very confused manner about a meeting he had recently had with a Brahminic scholar in Madras'. This Brahmin apparently had discovered some ancient Tibetan manuscripts—as far as Krishnamurti could remember they dated from the sixth or ninth century AD—which not only made reference to the future Maitreya Buddha but also referred by name to Krishnamurti as the human vessel that would be used by the Maitreya! Let us leave the question open as to whether such a manuscript exists and whether it is genuine or a fake—Krishnamurti was 'deeply moved and impressed' by this disclosure, even though 'at the same time he was sceptical about it' and did not in the least wish to admit that the theosophists might have been right after all. And yet he still treated the whole thing as a secret nine months later and spoke about it without ever mentioning the name of his informant. 'It seems,' said his biographer, 'as if he were becoming more and more interested in the riddle of his own destiny.'[192]

'He has never been hurt, though many things happened to him, flattery and insult, threat and security. It was not that he was insensitive, unaware: *he had no image of himself.*'[193]

In such a way as this, the almost 80-year-old Krishnamurti pointed to the two basic traits of his character in a quite impersonal manner. This short characterization of himself shows his immense openness of soul, malleability and unaffectedness which was almost the undoing of him in his youth. At the same time it provides at least *one* clue to the understanding of the tremendous power of regeneration of this human being who was always able to put behind him all the shocks and convulsions that his ordinary self was forced to undergo. Only the light shed on his former lives, however, would be able to answer satisfactorily the questions raised by this one.

★

Krishnamurti would have met Rudolf Steiner in Genoa in 1911 if Mrs Besant had not at the last minute cancelled the Theosophical Congress that had been planned there at that time. When the English writer Rom Landau questioned Krishnamurti about Rudolf Steiner during long conversations in the year 1935, the latter made reply: 'I have never studied Steiner and I wish you could tell me more about him. All I know about him comes from Dr Besant's occasional remarks. I think she had a great admiration for Steiner's unusual gifts.'[194] And then, far removed from any of the 'fuss' with which his life had been befogged for decades, he said on the same occasion, 'A man infinitely greater than any of us had to go his own way that led to Golgotha.'[195]

★

'Tonight I shall go for a long walk in the mountains. The mists are rising.' With these words Krishnamurti bade farewell to Pupul Jayakar, his Indian biographer, on the evening of 16 February 1986. 'During that night,' writes his biographer, in conclusion of her work, 'Krishna slept to start his long walk into the high mountains. The mists were rising, but he walked through the mists and he walked away.'[196]

Even though C.W. Leadbeater had been the actual 'discoverer' of Krishnamurti, without the trusting relationship that started to develop between him and Annie Besant the Hindu boy at that time could hardly have been brought up to become a World Teacher. For whereas he always showed a great respect for Leadbeater, the undivided veneration of his heart was towards Annie Besant. The Indian lady who wrote Krishnamurti's biography describes Besant as 'the only constant and reliable influence of his early youth'. 'To begin with, she was his mother, anxious to protect him from injury and distress, then his teacher and later, as the years passed, she sometimes took over the role of a disciple, sitting at his feet and listening to his words ... Krishna's love and respect for her lasted throughout his whole life undiminished. She did not influence him by shaping his thinking or his teachings, but by providing him with an absolutely sure foundation of love.'[197] One who observes this unique bond between Krishnamurti and Annie Besant 'existing beyond space and time' will not only wish to learn about the individual karma of these personalities, but will also want to know more about their common destiny.

★

One of the enigmas of Rudolf Steiner's life-story is the question as to why he felt obliged to serve in the Theosophical Society for a good decade with the best forces of his life, instead of merely turning a friendly glance towards it as he had done previously. In a letter from 9 January 1905 to Marie von Sivers after he had been appointed General Secretary of the German Section of the Society for more than two years, he wrote: 'I can only say that had the Master not convinced me that, in spite of all this, Theosophy is necessary for our age, I would only have written philosophical books and lectured on literature and philosophy even *after* 1901.'[198] With what arguments he had been persuaded to make his momentous decision we are not told.

Did this conviction rest in the emphasis on the general need for Theosophy, or had the Master, besides this, drawn the attention of his pupil to the presence of the one or other important individual within the Society, for whose sake risks could be taken? We do not know the answer. Nevertheless there are a number of unusual indications to show that when Rudolf Steiner officially started his work in the Theosophical Society in autumn 1902 he had full knowledge of certain karmic relationships and insight into past incarnations. A few days before the founding of the German Section Steiner gave a public lecture to the Giordano Bruno League about 'Monism and Theosophy', in the course of which, after saying a few words, he 'characterized Mrs Besant and her whole spiritual tendency'.[199] *With the lecture held in this circle Steiner had for the first time publicly shown his support for the idea of Theosophy which he had developed out of his wish to advance German cultural life.* He was taking a risk by showing support for the theosophical movement and for one of its leading members in a circle of scientifically minded people who were not very sympathetic towards such things. Yet the result was 'surprisingly favourable',[200] as Steiner reported to Hübbe-Schleiden. 'The dice has been thrown ... now it will all depend on whether we are able to work in such a way that we shall not find ourselves compromised by our union with the theosophical movement.'[201]

Rudolf Steiner first made personal acquaintance with Annie Besant at the Theosophical Congress in London at the beginning of July. At the Foundation Meeting of the German Section in Berlin on 20 October Steiner was nominated its General Secretary in the presence of Annie Besant, the Head of the Esoteric School.[202] He was accepted by her into this Esoteric School three days later.

On 29 February 1904, a Giordano Bruno Branch was founded in Cologne through the initiative of Mathilde Scholl, the translator, among other works, of Besant's *Esoteric Christianity* into German.[203] A few months later Rudolf Steiner's *Theosophy* appeared as a basic work for theosophists. Up to this time Annie Besant's book *Ancient Wisdom*, published in 1897, had been a standard work on theosophical knowledge of the world and of man. Steiner was, however, convinced that people in search of the truth 'could not gain a pure answer to their questions from this work' and through his *Theosophy* he sought to supply this need. Thus, instead of directly criticising Besant's work he placed the results of his own spiritual striving quite freely *alongside* it. This is how he expressed himself about it: 'To give a true answer I would say that, whereas *Ancient Wisdom* has provided people with a dogmatic book, I did not worry about *Ancient Wisdom* but have written my own book, *Theosophy*, in which I provide answers to questions which I know people ask. That was the positive answer. Further than that one does not need to go. One must allow people their absolute freedom to decide if they wish to take up *Ancient Wisdom*, or if they wish to take up *Theosophy*.'[204]

The first edition of Rudolf Steiner's *Theosophy* was dedicated to 'The Spirit of Giordano Bruno' and contains a passage referring to his concept of the 'Monad', which was left out in later editions. Why does Steiner dedicate his *Theosophy* to Bruno of all people? Whoever allows what Steiner says about Bruno in his *Mysticism and Modern Thought* to work upon him will not conclude that Steiner imagines Bruno to be that spirit which embodies modern Theosophy in its purest and clearest form. But the book is not dedicated to the Bruno of those days but '*to the Spirit* of Giordano Bruno'. 'The meaning of this dedication,' writes Christoph Lindenberg in his chronicle of Rudolf Steiner's life and work, 'and above all its absence from later editions is not in any way only a result of Rudolf Steiner's participation in the Giordano League, *but of the fact that in certain circles of the Theosophical Society Annie Besant was regarded as the reincarnated Giordano Bruno*.'[205] On the day of the founding of the Section, Rudolf Steiner had already attempted to introduce the assembled theosophists to a new concrete trend concerning karma and reincarnation by announcing lectures about 'Practical Studies in Karma'. How little success was achieved by this attempt was emphasized by Rudolf Steiner several times during his last great year of activity after the Christmas Foundation Meeting. *In the abstract* and in general most theosophists were 'convinced' of the reality of reincarnation and karma; *in the concrete*, however, and in individual cases they showed so much 'fear of spiritual creativity' and 'hate of spiritual revelation' that on 20 October 1902 Steiner was forced to discontinue this attempt. He was only able to take up the threads again 21 years later with a better prepared audience and in a grand style and to carry it forward for several months in this fashion.

In consideration of this so important and in part unfulfilled spiritual intention of Steiner on the first day of his official activity within the Theosophical Society, it appears very questionable if the aforesaid dedication in *Theosophy* is really to be attributed to the factors just mentioned. Can it seriously be believed that Rudolf Steiner merely wished to uphold a reincarnation *rumour* by his dedication? If not, then what was the dedication for?

A few days after the publication of *Theosophy,* Rudolf Steiner travelled to London with Marie von Sivers to talk to Mrs Besant. On 22 June he gave Besant a copy of the book with a personal dedication,[206] and invited her to take part in a lecturing tour of Germany which was to take place in the autumn. Shortly afterwards he announced Besant's autumn tour at a lecture given in Berlin and described her then as 'one of the most important spiritual forces of the present day'. During the following year a 'Besant Branch' was founded in Berlin on Rudolf Steiner's initiative.

Several other important facts could be mentioned to substantiate Steiner's high esteem for Mrs Besant at that time and to document his evident pains to support her as Head of the Esoteric School whenever possible. Should one not regard, at least provisionally, such words as these about Besant being 'one of the most important forces of the present day' as a quite concrete expression of a quite concrete piece of insight into a particular individual rather than just a conventional piece of polite rhetoric—or even something worse?

In reply to the question as to what *his* particular mission was, apart from the one inherited from Karl Julius Schröer of editing the works of Goethe, Rudolf Steiner once answered: 'Reincarnation and karma.'[207] Whoever would take this remark seriously and concretely might perhaps arrive at a different conclusion to that of 'pretty rules in the art of social behaviour' when one considers certain earlier and later remarks concerning Annie Besant and the motivation for his Giordano Bruno dedication.

★

Annie Besant 'had certain qualities that made her an interesting personality' for Rudolf Steiner, as we learn from his autobiography. 'I recognized that she had a certain right to speak about the spiritual world from her own experience. She definitely had an inner ability to approach the spiritual world with her soul. But later this was outweighed by external ambition.'[208]

Perhaps it is not quite irrelevant to say that the accent here is laid on the 'soul', that it is the soul through which Besant 'approached' the spiritual world. Could not the preclusion through 'external ambition' have occurred to a large extent because Besant's discriminatory ability was not sufficiently developed? Did not she herself also stand in urgent need of that 'mental training', for the lack of which in C.W. Leadbeater the General Secretary of the German Section had to warn Besant in 1907? And was not this General Secretary just the very best teacher she could have had to supply her with the missing ingredient of her so important soul faculties?

★

'Giordano Bruno, upon whom the new Copernican view of Nature impressed itself, could not grasp the spirit, which had been expelled from the world in its old form, except as "world soul".' With these words, Rudolf Steiner begins his characterization of Bruno in his *Mysticism and Modern Thought* (original edition 1901).[209] He continues: 'A deeper study of Bruno's writings gives one the impression that he conceived things to be ensouled, although in varying degrees. He did not, in reality, experience in himself the spirit as such, and consequently conceived the spirit after the fashion of the human soul, wherein alone he had confronted it. When he speaks of spirit he conceives of it in this way.'[210]

In such an attitude, which springs more from the soul, Bruno conceives of the uncreated, imperishable and only real archetype of everything that exists, which he calls the 'Monad' and to which, out of inner necessity, he must needs reckon the human ego, in order to guarantee it reality.[211]

'The union of "Life-Spirit" with "Spirit-Man" is that which, since early times, has been called the human *Monad*. Such monads are the basic constituent of all that exists.' Thus runs Steiner's correction (in the first edition of his *Theosophy*,[212] dedicated to Bruno, in the chapter entitled 'The Spiritland'), to the 'Monad' idea of Giordano Bruno conceived by him with too much of the soul element.

★

The great alternative graven on the biography of Annie Besant was either to acquire and cultivate knowledge of self and knowledge of the spiritual world (the experiencing of the 'Ego-Monads' of Giordano Bruno in her own Life-Spirit and Spirit-Man), under the expert guidance of the German General Secretary, or *devotion to the spirit in a single human soul*—which was the only way it would meet her in this case. We have seen on which pan of the scales it was that she eventually laid her heaviest weight. She started to search for and revere the spirit revealed in Krishnamurti's soul and this expanded in her eyes to become the 'World Soul'.

Just as one ought not to ' "misjudge" the man who had forfeited his life to the Catholic Church on account of his advanced views',[213] neither should one pass an unjust sentence, i.e. a one-sided judgement, on Annie Besant, by only taking into account the one arm of the balance.

When the 42-year-old Besant was asked in 1889 to write a review of Blavatsky's *Secret Doctrine* and thereby discovered the world of Theosophy, she had already experienced an extraordinarily intensive and full life.[214] After an early disillusioned marriage and a subsequent atheistic phase, she had successively, or simultaneously, devoted herself to causes such as freedom of opinion, women's rights, English trades unionism, Fabian socialism and birth control. When in 1889 the spark of Theosophy set alight the fire in her soul and received added fuel through her personal contact with H.P. Blavatsky, her old circle of friends, to which Bernard Shaw belonged, were horrified. In her autobiography she tells about this dramatic turning-point in her life: 'I am forced by an inner necessity to speak the truth as I see it, irrespective of whether my words please or not ... I have to preserve this fidelity towards truth unsullied, quite irrespective of how many friendships are lost thereby, or how many connections are severed. It might lead me into the unknown wilderness, I would have to follow it: it might rob me of the friendship of others, and yet I would have to follow: it might kill me, I would still trust it; and I would have no other inscription on my grave than: "She strove to follow the truth." '[215] Do not these words of Besant, spoken at the turning-point in her life, as though from the innermost kernel of her being, ultimately compensate for the darkest of her errors?

'He had witnessed the brightest gleam of her inner fire,' writes Krishnamurti's Indian biographer about his relationship to Besant, 'and had experienced along with her how it gradually became extinguished.'[216] Something of this fire had been transferred to him, even though he soon received light from other sources than those shown him by Mrs Besant.

The day Krishnamurti set out on his 'great journey through the mists towards the spiritual flame of the unseen Sun' was the anniversary of Giordano Bruno's death at the stake for his innermost beliefs in the Campo dei Fiori, Rome, in 1600.

★

Whoever seriously thinks about and ponders the facts that encircle Steiner's Bruno dedication is forced to ask: do not such phenomena, which it is not the task of this book to further elaborate, weigh heavier than the mere existence of a supposed reincarnation rumour actually circulating in anthroposophical circles?[217] In other words: why should not Rudolf Steiner, in the same sense as these rumours, though with far better reason (that is, out of concrete supersensible knowledge) have decided to write the Bruno dedication to his book *Theosophy*?

★

Yet despite such perspectives, which show at their converging point how infinitely concrete were the 'teachings' about reincarnation and karma which Rudolf Steiner started to embark upon at the beginning of the century within the circle of the theosophical movement, the one or other reader of the present volume might complain that neither Vreede nor I do justice to Rudolf Steiner's spiritual stature, but reduce it in size in an inadmissible way. It is self-evident that no one desiring to have a more concrete picture of the founder of Anthroposophy will ever be denied the freedom to regard him as the bearer of the Bodhisattva, or even the Bodhisattva-being himself, if he so wishes. Whoever would visualize it thus, however, would hardly be in a different case to one who sets out to 'solve' a mathematical equation containing two unknown factors by evaluating both unknowns, not according to their separate values, but as having one and the same value.

Whoever is not satisfied with such confusing thought complexes and would rather turn his attention to Steiner's concrete acts of knowledge and their outward consequences will find that this dreaded 'reduction' of Steiner's stature will actually present him to us as an infinitely greater riddle than before—greater than an 'unknown factor' of spiritual-historical proportions, however much ingenuity and knowledge, even enthusiastic love towards the founder of Anthroposophy, is brought to bear upon it. The 'I', as the true centre of man's being, remains invisible, even to the spiritual vision of an initiate. So, in truth, it is not surprising that the indecipherability of Rudolf Steiner's being grows greater the more one tries, from ever new sides, to approach his spiritual-scientific and practical work as being the concrete expression of his ego-being.

★

On the other hand, the Bodhisattva enigma can be put in a new light through the work of Vreede. Did not Steiner's remark to Rittelmeyer rightly point to the imminent earthly working of the already incarnated Bodhisattva? It would appear so. Yet one must not overlook the fact that during the time of the consciousness soul, and especially from the twentieth century onwards, it will depend upon man himself if and when and how certain spiritual events take place. Let us remind ourselves in this connection of Rudolf Steiner's explanations of the remarkable activity of the Angels in the human astral bodies,[218] which can only take place in the right way if individual human beings pay attention to the subtle angelic stirrings within them and are willing to let themselves be motivated by them out of their own free decision. Something similar has to be said with regard to the so-called Michael prophecy,[219] which concerns the united activity of Aristotelians and Platonists at the end of the millennium. In the age of the free conscious co-operation during the course of human evolution nothing more can be foretold as though it were to happen quite independently of the understanding attitude of man. As a result of this the age of prophesying in the old sense has come to an end. Doubtless certain things will still come about, but how, when and under what circumstances will depend more and more on man himself. Just in connection with Rudolf Steiner's *last* lecture statement about the activity of the Bodhisattva, this aspect is emphasized in an unmistakable way. It was made in August 1923 in Penmaenmawr, within the framework of the lecture cycle *The Evolution of Consciousness*, at the summer school organized by D.N. Dunlop, at which many older theosophists were present. 'Humanity may wait in vain for a successor to the old Bodhisattvas,' says Rudolf Steiner, with clear reference to the dreamy-headed theosophical expectation of the World Teacher, 'for the question as to whether one will appear or not', i.e. if he will be able actually to fulfil his mission, 'depends upon whether or not men would encounter him with understanding.'[220] Such bringing of understanding might provide the only real alternative to that of passively waiting for miracles to happen, miracles which would come about, though no one would have an urge to understand them.

★

It would be difficult to find any other subject in the history of the theosophical-anthroposophical movement of this century which has placed the adherents and representatives of the said movement before similar tests of their ability to form clear discriminatory judgements as has the Bodhisattva question. Today it does not seem to be primarily the Goethean 'concern' which, in spite of all precautions to prevent it, creeps in through the keyhole to create mischief in individual lives and in the community at large. The chief concern today is on account of 'Baron Lack of Discriminatory Ability', as Rudolf Steiner calls him—one of the three greatest enemies of the human soul. For the latter possesses, to a higher degree than the concern which is prevelant throughout the world, the technique of entering by way of the keyhole. Furthermore, this Baron seldom appears on his own, but mainly in the company of two ladies. Let us take a closer look at his companions, according to Rudolf Steiner's description:

> The first female attendant is actually very young, chubby faced, with a youthful countenance, almost childish and rather coquettish in manner—giving vent to these impulses especially, but not exclusively, in anthroposophical gatherings ... Thus this maidenly being, called *Naïveté*, is actually a very great opponent in our meetings and comes invariably without any membership card.

105

The second enemy is also feminine, considerably older than the last, with horn-rimmed spectacles on the end of her pointed nose. One might call her *Tante* [Auntie], but just as well *Tunte* [fop]. This is Lady *Illusion*. She is greatly loved, in spite of the fact that she actually creates a great deal of mischief. Those are the three great enemies about whom one could think that they creep in through the keyhole: the Ladies *Naïveté, Illusion* and the *Baron Lack of Discriminatory Ability*. We have to be very much on our guard against these three personalities.[221]

And yet Steiner does not only present the imaginary warrants of arrest for these 'personalities'; he also gives quite clear instructions about the only method of stopping them and interfering with their handiwork:

What is characterized in the final scene of the last Mystery Drama concerning certain spiritual beings—for, as you will now have seen, we are here dealing with *spiritual* beings, *spiritual* enemies—can also be applied to these enemies through the fact that their power is only retained so long as one has no consciousness of their presence. Their power ceases as soon as one is conscious of them.[222]

It could only be the result of inexact observation of these 'enemies of the soul' if one were to suppose that they merely possess a subjective human nature. Certainly man must provide the occasion, through his inner soul-spiritual attitude, for these powers to be able to creep in like this, but they are present just as objectively and independently of the human soul as are some poisonous plants which, of course, still exist even when they do not gain entry into a human body. On the other hand it would be an illusion to think that man could and should keep himself apart from all poisonous substances under *all* circumstances. As is known to an important branch of medical science, which is slowly regaining favour, in homoeopathic doses poisons are often a means of promoting health. It depends very largely on the dose that is prescribed and on the person to whom it is administered. Thus from a higher point of view evil can also be beneficial for certain beings in so far as it is able indirectly to stimulate the development of single beings or a whole community in a favourable way. It is not the evil itself, however, that man should seek to embody or receive into his soul—to do this would be to practise black magic—but the *recognition* of evil should be practised. In his *discerning* consciousness man is able to hold a mirror up to evil itself. And through the taking up of evil into the universe of knowledge, in which there can ultimately be no final isolated piece of knowledge, the actual membering of evil into the body of the universe from which it severed itself—or rather, from which it was separated for the sake of man's development—can begin to take place.

What applies to 'evil' is also true of all errors of judgement, for these are the costumes in which evil parades itself when it treads the stage of the discerning consciousness.

'Error, I will only let thee go after thou hast sat for me in front of the mirror of discernment and I have embodied the picture of thy special features into the universe of knowledge.' That would be the maxim of all those who, seeking for knowledge, do not wish to remain fixed in the seemingly irreconcilable contrast of 'true' and 'false' but who know that what is really true dissolves the discrepancy of 'true' and 'false' in a higher unity. 'What is true is the *wholeness*,'[223] says Hegel, and along with this wholeness must also be reckoned evil and error. Not an apology for evil and error is hereby intended; what underlies this Hegelian thought is penetration to the point from which a thing or thought begins to break loose from its real, respectively logical connection. For at this point, even though it might occur much later, its reintegration into the real, respectively logical world order begins.

Let us apply this thought to the erroneous comprehension of the Bodhisattva and Christ on the part of the theosophists. What was *true* about the conception of a returning Christ, apart from its confusion with the Bodhisattva? Elisabeth Vreede expresses it clearly enough: the fact that, according to Rudolf Steiner's spiritual investigation, the Christ Being would reappear in the twentieth century—not in a physical body, however, but in an etheric form. We are taught by Hegel's maxim to recognize the true in the false, and whoever understands it in this sense will not wish to let only the knowledge of truth hold sway; instead of banishing what is 'false' into the exile of complete disregard, one can become the guardian of the very gravest *errors* of judgement. There can truly be no real tolerance existing without such a 'complete' view regarding questions of understanding.

Such an integrating attitude towards evil in the guise of error,

107

rather than an exclusive one, is what Rudolf Steiner once described as an absolutely necessary endeavour for a spiritual movement. For it would really only be an Inspiration coming from '*Tante* Illusion' if one were to imagine that the sunrise of a new age could dawn without the *inevitable* simultaneous appearance of an ever-increasing shadow of objectively produced possibilities of error. 'If we were now to consider the spiritual guidance of mankind,' said Rudolf Steiner a few months prior to the planned and then cancelled Genoa Congress of 1911, 'we would have to draw the conclusion from this thought of the possibility of error—predicted with warning gesture by the occultists of all ages—that we should practise this highest form of tolerance, mentioned at the beginning of our lectures, and abandon anything which has anything to do with blind adherence to authority, for such belief in authority can be a potent seducer. It is even able to cause error. On the other hand, however, we should welcome with open and warm hearts everything which seeks to rain down upon mankind in a quite new way from the spiritual world. Hence a good theosophist will first of all be one who knows that if we wish to foster that light in our movement which is to flow into mankind's evolution, we shall have to become the guardians over all the errors which creep in with the light.'[224]

The only authority that can appoint somebody to such a guardianship is the faculty of clear judgement.

Hence it depends today far more on the cultivation of this faculty than upon good will, much learning or noble feelings. For however necessary the presence and cultivation of these faculties may be, if the former is undervalued, or even considered superfluous, they will easily come under the sway of our Baron. That is just what becomes clear to us through a comprehensive survey of the great errors within the theosophical–anthroposophical spiritual current.

How else should we grasp 'that light which is to flow into human evolution', even in its shadowless quality, if we did not illumine it ourselves with the lamp of our own free discriminatory and comprehensive understanding, like the Man with the Lamp in Goethe's Fairy Tale? And how otherwise than with the light of thought, which each must kindle for himself, can the spiritual stature of Rudolf Steiner be delineated in its true and clear outline?

# PART TWO

# INTRODUCTION TO PART TWO

Thomas Meyer

'Especially during the early years of his activity Rudolf Steiner often warned members to be cautious when they said somebody had spoken quite "anthroposophically" on the one or other occasion . . . The assumption that the person in question had spoken "anthroposophically" was often a sign that he who had said so was himself naive or lacking in discrimination.'[225] With these words, Elisabeth Vreede pointed 50 years ago to the same dangerous situation that we attempted to explain symptomatically in Chapter 11.

She has made a very elaborate attempt to clarify and circumscribe the Bodhisattva question. Every open-minded reader of Dr Vreede's lectures reproduced in this book will be able to confirm this. And yet the figure of Elisabeth Vreede, in spite of the deep insights and other qualities she possessed, is usually relegated to the background, even in anthroposophical circles, where matters of general interest are concerned. And so I shall give a short description of the life and work of this personality who, in connection with the ever-growing blurring tendency of the present day towards spiritual matters, laid such stress upon a clear and incorruptible power of discrimination. Further insight into Vreede's character and her life's work is available in German in the very able biography *Elisabeth Vreede, Ein Lebensbild*.[226]

★

When Elisabeth Vreede gave her Bodhisattva lectures in 1930 she was 51 years of age. Five years had passed since Rudolf Steiner's death and five more years were to pass before the Anthroposophical Society, newly founded by Rudolf Steiner at Christmas 1923, was rent asunder by a deep schism. As a member of the founding committee of this Society, Vreede had the task of looking after the affairs of the Astronomical-Mathematical Section, which she did with untiring diligence and a thoroughness that, according to Rudolf Steiner, extended to the very dotting of an 'i'.[227] Mathe-

111

matical thinking, deepened by Anthroposophy, took her far beyond the limits of ordinary mathematical practice and became for her the life's blood of her soul-spiritual nature. The awesome view of the nocturnal starry heavens taught her to regard the stars not as points of light to be analysed but, to use an expression of Rudolf Steiner, as 'the dwelling-place of Gods'.[228] Something of the imperturbability of the fixed-star heavens seemed to permeate Vreede's whole destiny, which outwardly was relatively calm but inwardly was repeatedly moved by great upheavals of soul.

Elisabeth Vreede was born in the Hague on 16 July 1879. The year of her birth itself seemed to want to indicate her deep connection with the spiritual Beings of the planetary spheres and their paths of spiritual influence.[229] Did not the Sun Spirit, Michael, according to the ancient occult view and the tradition newly reaffirmed by Rudolf Steiner, take over his task in 1879 as the Spirit of the Age, which is to last for the next 350 years?

The lectures given by Steiner in Düsseldorf in April 1909, *The Spiritual Hierarchies and their Reflection in the Physical World*[230]—prior to the publication of *Occult Science*—made upon her one of the deepest impressions of her life. Referring to a difficult passage in the *Bhagavad Gita*,[231] Steiner showed how four groups of elemental beings, banished from their spiritual home into more dense elements for the sake of man's development, work for his good in material objects of nature—in the rhythms of day and night, in the course of Moon and Sun. Like Ariel in Shakespeare's *Tempest,* they await with longing a fourfold response from man, which will release them from their bondage. Rudolf Steiner recommended Vreede to take the *Bhagavad Gita* as the subject for her meditation. Her contemplative view of nature, untiring industry, the humorous and benevolent basis of her temperament capable of choleric outbursts, and, above all, the clear devotional attitude of her spirituality, bearing no trace of sentimentality, are a testimony to those studying her biography of how strongly and consciously Vreede strove to unite herself with the sphere of the elemental beings.

★

Elisabeth Vreede grew up with an older brother as the second child of freethinking parents with theosophical leanings. In the free social atmosphere of the parental home (her father worked as a lawyer, her mother did charity work) visitors were entertained. Among these was Colonel Olcott, Founder-President of the Theosophical Society. The finding among her brother's books of a four-volume work by the French astronomer Flammarion gave the young Elisabeth the immediate incentive to learn French, as though it were the *only* language for learning about the stars. When she was 16 she started to study Goethe's *Faust* alongside the two years of private coaching to prepare her for taking her state examinations. Thanks to her exceptional powers of memory and great enthusiasm she soon learnt the whole of *Faust* by heart after repeated readings! After passing her *Abitur* she went on to Leyden to study mathematics, astronomy and philosophy. In the last of these subjects she felt drawn towards Hegelian philosophy, through which she acquired not only clarity of thought but also the mobility of thinking that was so characteristic of her. The study of Sanskrit was also undertaken at this time—one wonders if it enabled her to read her beloved *Bhagavad Gita* in the original?

But in spite of her enthusiasm for her studies she was never completely satisfied with what the universities had to offer her. How long would the active student life or her various sporting interests—she founded a rowing club for women—continue to compensate her for the disappointments that slowly encroached upon her in wave after wave? In the year 1900 the 21-year-old Vreede rather reluctantly followed the family tradition by joining the Theosophical Society. During the following years she gave mathematics lessons in a girls' high school alongside her studies.

In the summer of 1903, Vreede met Rudolf Steiner for the first time at a theosophical congress in London. His appearance made a deep impression on her, but not what he said. 'A countenance full of inner fire, full of the keenest attention and controlled will power'[232] is what first struck her. And 'under the force of this impression lay hidden the germ of all that was to form the later destiny'. And yet 'the whole trend of what he said was not to my liking.' For during his early years 'Rudolf Steiner spoke with tremendous vigour and with a strength of temperament which far exceeded the fiery strength of his later delivery. It was as though he wished to suffuse every sentence with the whole energy and significance of his mission to the world.'[233] That did not please her. Again, when she heard him one year later at the Congress in Amsterdam, she was not impressed, though Steiner was dealing in his lecture with 'Mathematics and Occultism', her own field of study. 'But this lecture too failed to arouse me. I was unable to make anything of it. Neither the materialistic habits of thought which surrounded me in my childhood, nor those I met with during my studies at university, nor the kind of thinking with which I had become familiar in the Theosophical Society were able to help me to discover a meaning in his words.'[234]

Her eyes were opened by Rudolf Steiner's series of articles 'Knowledge of Higher Worlds, How is it Attained?': 'The deeply inward way of leading man to spiritual knowledge spoke directly to the soul. There was no rejection or misunderstanding there.'[235] The step was taken, even though 'a long and even painful way lay ahead in order to unite scientific knowledge with a knowledge of the spirit.'[236]

Vreede travelled, whenever she could, to the lecture cycles Rudolf Steiner gave in the various European cities. Between 1910 and 1913 she continued her studies in Berlin and enjoyed the privilege for several years of living in the same house as Rudolf Steiner and Marie von Sivers. Thus there were often informal meetings and conversations with them. 'When I see by the light in his room that he has returned from his travels it gives me a feeling of security,' she writes to a friend.[237]

Vreede was present at Steiner's lectures in the Architektenhaus and at the more intimate gatherings in the rooms of the Berlin branch of the Society. In addition, she gave a preliminary course on the basics of higher mathematics. The middle of her life now having been reached, she diligently collected the spiritual treasures acquired in the varied and informal proximity of her beloved teacher and made plans for the future.

She spent the summer months of those years in Munich where she helped with preparations for the Mystery Dramas by typing the separate parts that Rudolf Steiner had written during the preceding night. In 1912 she took the part of an 'Ahrimanic dancer' in the third Mystery Play. Simultaneously the crisis that had been brewing for years within the Theosophical Society, as described in Chapter 9, now came to a head: 33 years after Michael took over his role of

114

spiritual leader, Steiner had to seek a new field of operation for the members who had retained, or re-acquired, their sense of proportion. The Anthroposophical Society was founded under his auspices. All these events were followed by Vreede at first hand with the greatest interest. She writes to her friend in Holland in September 1912: 'The general impression is that people will very soon go over to this new Society both in Germany and abroad, so that we shall soon be faced with the long-dreaded separation. For Dr Steiner it will be a much clearer position than the one at present, in which he is the General Secretary of the German Section under Mrs Besant. He will assume no official position in the Anthroposophical Society.'[238]

In 1914, Vreede moved to Dornach, where she helped with the building of the Goetheanum and formed a friendship with Edith Maryon, the sculptress and pupil of Rudolf Steiner, whose death occurred all too early.

Vreede spent the last years of the war once more in Berlin, tending the prisoners of war. In 1920, she moved to Arlesheim and took part in the first School of Spiritual Science course at the Goetheanum, which had just performed its opening ceremony. Internal difficulties and divergent opinions within the Anthroposophical Society presented Rudolf Steiner in 1923 with the alternative of either 'withdrawing from the Society',[239] or taking the affairs, in which up till then he had only served as teacher, into his own hands. After a deep inner struggle he decided to found the Society afresh under his own chairmanship. During the course of the Christmas Foundation Meeting 1923/4 he appointed a Committee comprised of Marie Steiner, Albert Steffen, Ita Wegman, Günther Wachsmuth and Elisabeth Vreede. Vreede's star of destiny now stood at its zenith; she was able to ray forth the results of her characteristic thoroughness and prolific activity in grand Jovian style. She gave lectures, held private audiences and, through the Goetheanum archives, established and looked after by her, she had guardianship over all the typewritten lectures of Rudolf Steiner, which she herself had collected and arranged. But only a few years of shared domicile in the house of the 'Esoteric' Committee were to be allotted her. The death of Rudolf Steiner brought about a hiatus in the affairs of the Society. Hidden animosities, or at least differences of opinion, that Rudolf Steiner's presence had formerly smoothed over, suddenly rose to the surface. In the Committee's car on the way back from the cremation ceremony, on 3 April 1925, a violent argument flared up between Marie Steiner and Ita Wegman in Vreede's presence over the unresolved question of the urn's future resting place. Marie Steiner resolved to withdraw from the Society and concentrate solely on her work within the Section for Music and the Rhetorical Arts with which she had been entrusted; she suggested that Eugen Kolisko and Maria Röschl should take her place on the Committee. The other members of the Committee, including the two she had intended to nominate, rejected this 'solution' and begged Marie Steiner to continue in her former post. For the moment the threatened calamity had been averted.

Between 1927 and 1930, Vreede published the Astronomical Letters for the members of her Section, which are still available today in the collected edition of *Anthroposophy and Astronomy*.[240] Yet the difficulties that had struck like lightening on the death of Rudolf Steiner increased further and reached their climax in 1930, the same year that Vreede held her Bodhisattva lectures.

★

The complex affairs of those years can, of course, only be dealt with in a very fragmentary and incomplete way in a work such as this in which we must limit ourselves essentially to what seems to us to be of symptomatic importance with regard to Vreede's biography and path of destiny. And even by limiting ourselves to what concerns Vreede alone, the full picture of the relevant happenings will only be thoroughly understood when her own reports of the events of the Society after Rudolf Steiner's death, which are still kept under lock and key, are made available to the reading public.

To pass over the aspect of Vreede's connection with the happenings in the Society, even in such a short sketch as this, is impermissible, if only for the very characteristic trait that was touched upon by the mathematician Ernst Bindel in his commemorative address at her funeral. The following is the gist of what he said: 'Where others remained silent she would voice her opinions irrespective of how they might be received. All cautious consideration of the effect of her words and action was distasteful to her. If she were faced with a choice between judiciousness and veracity she would unhesitatingly

116

decide in favour of the latter.'[241] Vreede held no brief for glossing over awkward facts when these were of special anthroposophical interest in her eyes.

★

After various attacks against her fellow Committee member Wegman, Vreede was herself attacked during an Extraordinary General Meeting, which took place in the last days of December 1930, and this was on account of just those two Bodhisattva lectures held in the summer of the same year in Stuttgart. Adolf Arenson had repeated his lecture in Dornach during the regular General Meeting in the spring of the same year, and Albert Steffen had given it his approval and pronounced it as 'particularly significant'.[242] Certain members regarded the verdict of Steffen, who had been appointed Chairman of the Society in December 1925, as an *a priori* authorization of Arenson's exposition. For this reason Arenson's lecture was much more widely known among members of the Society than were Vreede's, about which more rumours than actual first-hand reports seem to have circulated. Vreede asserted that a lecture should not be condemned 'on account of *hearsay',* and declared that she would be willing to repeat her lecture if that were wanted.[243]

During the further course of the meeting, Vreede's Stuttgart lectures were discussed and criticised in a most unworthy manner. Among other things it was asserted that 'whether one liked it or not her views were directly *opposed* to the spirit of Dr Steiner'.[244] Someone even went so far as to say, on the basis of the abridged and distorted versions and interpretations of her Stuttgart lectures, that she should be 'accused of heresy', as she was supposed to have 'denied that Dr Steiner had announced the coming of the Etheric Christ'![245]

And thus it came about that through Elisabeth Vreede's efforts to free Rudolf Steiner's name from untenable beliefs she found herself in the remarkable situation of being accused by many of his pupils of working against the spirit of his teachings. After the lapse of more than 50 years it seems not too difficult to say whether it was Dr Vreede or her detractors who were more greatly inspired by 'the spirit of Dr Steiner'.

Neither then nor later did the Stuttgart lectures Vreede offered to repeat in Dornach ever come to be given. Instead, a majority of those present voted in favour of the 'northern proposition'. This was a proposal that the fivefold order of the Committee invested by Steiner should be reduced to a threesome, and that Ita Wegman and Elisabeth Vreede should be excluded from membership of the Committee. Even though this proposition was rescinded later by the Chairman Steffen, in Vreede's eyes the very fact that it could ever have been mooted was a very ominous symptom of the general state of the Society. Vreede herself, now as before, was convinced that after Rudolf Steiner's death 'the only way for the Society to go forward was to bear in mind the necessity of holding fast to the configuration of the Committee as it had been inaugurated with deep insight by Rudolf Steiner and accepted by the members'.[246] In connection with the events portrayed here, one of the photographs in this book acquires a quite symbolic significance. It was taken in the summer of 1930 during the Youth Camp at Stakenberg, near Ommen in Holland, and shows Vreede and Wegman in a basket chair for two. Close as was the connection here of these two Dutch ladies, just as close will be their karmic connection in the years to come.

'The being of Anthroposophy,' writes Vreede to a friend in January 1934, 'has always been regarded by me as a newly created spiritual being, a being which at the same time is the first hierarchical being created by man, very young and still under-developed, as is the case with a small child—a being which, through our combined effort, as a community seeking knowledge and with the co-operation of its creator from the spiritual world, is destined to develop further. And that is just the reason why I find it so painful, when such attacks as these are made against some of the active members to exclude them from contributing to the forming of the being "Anthroposophia".'[247]

In 1935 these attacks reached a temporary climax when, at the Spring General Meeting, the motion was put forward that, along with the exclusion of various prominent and leading members of the Society and some National Societies, Elisabeth Vreede and Ita Wegman should be taken off the Dornach Committee of five. At this critical point Ludwig Count Polzer-Hoditz, anticipating the threat to the Society, gave a courageous speech in which he defended Wegman against the charges set against her. But his speech died away without an echo.

According to an eyewitness account, on the morning of that day, Elisabeth Vreede called on the spiritual world with wringing hands and beseeching gesture to help her in her need, not for her own personal destiny but because for her it went without saying that if the exclusion of members were carried out, then, as inevitably as the planets and the Sun move in their heavenly courses, far-reaching negative consequences would affect the whole destiny of the age. *That* was her main concern at this critical moment in history.

An overwhelming majority of the members voted in favour of the motion. Also the 'shared seat' of the two Dutch ladies was overturned and Vreede and Wegman found themselves excluded from the Committee founded by Rudolf Steiner.

'In spiritual-scientific matters, one unites through differentiating and individualizing, not through centralizing.'[248] Rudolf Steiner had pointed this out 12 years previously and, in view of similar splitting-up tendencies in the *old* Society, he had prepared for the extension of the individualizing process therein. But the Dornach majority decision of 1935 still wanted to pursue its aims by means of the centralizing method. Thirty-three years after Rudolf Steiner had started work in Berlin within the framework of the Theosophical Society, the Secret Police, centred in that same city, ordered the dissolution throughout the Reich of the Anthroposophical Society—which was already beginning to disintegrate from within. In a Berlin manifesto of 15 November 1935, the reason for the closure was, among other things, attributed to the fact that 'the Anthroposophical Society was disposed towards internationalism, and that Waldorf education was individualistic and directed towards the single human being'. Through that, 'there existed the danger that the further activity of this Society might damage the interests of the National Socialistic State'. How great, in a *positive sense*, could have been the 'danger' to the State if the Anthroposophical Society had remained inwardly at unity in face of all the dangers threatening it from without, in spite of all opposing circumstances and necessary individualization! Perhaps it might not then have been so easily blown into a historical limbo for several years by a decree from the Gestapo.

119

In December 1935, there appeared the last of a new series of six 'Astronomical Letters', which Vreede had prefaced exactly one year earlier with an important astronomical Christmas message. The work on the 'Calendar', which she had first edited in 1929 on behalf of the Section, still continued as before—with the difference that from 1936 until her death it had to be printed privately.

Before the outbreak of war it had been possible for Elisabeth Vreede to participate at least twice in the Summer Schools arranged by the English friends. In 1936, following on the Summer School in Wales, she travelled with a small party to Ireland—the land of the Hibernian Mysteries, where so much had to remain shrouded in silence. The group visited the famous cult chamber of New Grange and Vreede sought the centre of the Hibernian Mysteries, which she conjectured to be connected with the neighbouring tumuli of Knowth and Dowth. Do these ancient names perhaps provide a hint of the mysterious statues, 'Science' and 'Art', handed on to us through the ages? 'In savouring what are possible pictures of ancient times, a breath of heathen mystery rites hovered over our converse, stimulated by the *genius loci*,' writes one of the participants later. Yet, at the same time, through her insurmountable sense of humour, Vreede knew how to create the necessary counterbalance.[250] Everyone felt thoroughly at home with her, for she 'accepted the other person, putting them on a level with herself and never letting them feel that they were in any way of less importance'.[251]

She visited Mallorca, on the track of Ramon Lully, the important contemporary of Thomas Aquinas. In 1936, she observed the Sun eclipse in Turkey together with Lili Kolisko. In 1938, she visited Germany for the last time to assist with the emigration of Jewish people.

The war cut Vreede off from the last of her friends in Holland, Germany and Great Britain. Her life started to take a saturnine course. Her unshakable fidelity to her own inner calling and to the being Anthroposophia became more inward. She went for solitary walks through the treasure-house of her memories, which included numberless lectures given by Dr Steiner to which she could refer at will as if they had only just been given. However, it was not a mere remembrance of facts and words at such times but an occasion for hard soul and spirit exertion, for, as Rudolf Steiner had once said, she had been 'one of the very few who *understand* my lectures.'[252] How many of those who had died may have accompanied her on her path when she set to work afresh in the archive of her inmost heart, unperturbed by the destiny of the age or by the ordained destinies of the Anthroposophical Society?

In March 1943, her last remaining travelling companion, Ita Wegman, suddenly died. Vreede held the private funeral oration at the crematorium. 'Now the centre of gravity of our spiritual movement lies in the spiritual world,'[253] she stated. A few days later she became seriously ill for the first time in her life. Her last conversations were centred on her beloved *Bhagavad Gita* and the experiences of geometric figures, which she visualized as she lay in contemplation on her bed. The septicaemia spread rapidly. When a slight improvement came about she went to Ascona, the last work-place of Ita Wegman. There she died on 31 August 1943.

When Elisabeth Vreede saw Rudolf Steiner entering the lecture hall at the London Theosophical Congress of 1903, she instinctively nudged her companion and called out, 'See who is entering *there*!'[254] She might well have experienced the approach of Rudolf Steiner, in a flash of recognition, as the incarnation of the very goal of her existence. Many years later, her spiritual teacher reminded her of the colour of the dress she wore on that occasion.

Rudolf Steiner once indicated that Elisabeth Vreede had incarnated too early, on account of Anthroposophy. He added an important rider: 'This individuality does not wish to be recognized.'[255] From him who was able to see *that*, she had no need to conceal her true identity. She brought it to the light of day through the work she did for Anthroposophy and for its creator.

# THE BODHISATTVA QUESTION IN THE HISTORY OF THE ANTHROPOSOPHICAL SOCIETY:

## TWO LECTURES BY ELISABETH VREEDE HELD IN STUTTGART ON 9 AND 11 JULY 1930

Prefatory Remarks by Elisabeth Vreede to the Lectures[256]

*The text of the first of these two lectures has been put together on the basis of an extensive, although perhaps not quite exact, shorthand report. For the second lecture, a shorthand report was unfortunately not available. I worked out the text with the aid of my own very extensive notes that lay before me during the course of the lecture; and with the aid of an extremely inadequate summary of the lecture that had been brought to my attention, I checked myself as to the sequence of what was said and as to the content actually brought forward. I have included whatever I most probably left out of my notes, but this is put in square brackets.*

*Through this kind of reworking, it follows naturally that in the text of the second lecture, the literary style predominates, while in the first I have held as exactly as possible to the spoken word.*

# LECTURE 1 (9 July 1930)

When I was last able to speak before you here,[257] we did not finish with the theme undertaken, as you will remember, and I was permitted to suggest a continuation of my lecture at some time in the future. Now it has happened that, before we could consider such a continuation, I find myself in the position of speaking to you again.

I would like now to try to form this lecture in such a way that it can somewhat fill the role of a continuation of what we were speaking about before; so that you may again distinguish the style and manner in which our teacher, Rudolf Steiner, worked in our Society and how he coped with particular problems such as that of the Bodhisattva—about which we will now speak.

When we approach the question of the Bodhisattva, with which at the moment many of the friends in our Society are preoccupied, we must know that our friend, Herr Arenson, held a lecture on this subject that will be known to many,[258] especially so for the reason that it has fortunately been printed. There he gathered together the passages in Rudolf Steiner's lectures where this theme was spoken of, so that one could easily survey all the material that belongs to it.

It goes without saying that in view of the seriousness which marks Herr Arenson's lecture, we wish to show an equal seriousness in dealing with this theme ourselves.

It is certainly correct, I believe, when Herr Arenson says that there is widely spread among members a comprehension about the being of the Bodhisattva that is vague. And perhaps this is simply due to the fact that we are dealing here with a concept from oriental culture, a concept that is still remote to a western style of thinking and that was brought to our attention through Rudolf Steiner only during the period of which I would like to speak to you.

Rudolf Steiner treated this subject only in relation to oriental spiritual life as it flowed through the Theosophical Society, with which we were, of course, previously united. And so it seems right and necessary to me to place this theme into the history or pre-history of the Anthroposophical Society, and to try to find an approach to the Bodhisattva question from that side.

123

Now if you review our whole literature, the lecture cycles and other single lectures which are mostly available in transcripts of a sort, you will find that in the earlier years of his activity Rudolf Steiner took some trouble to transform the oriental Indian element living in Theosophy into a western element.[259] He wanted to teach nothing but western occultism. The situation he came upon, as he began to work in the Theosophical Society, was that of Indian Theosophy along with people who were attached to it. The whole first years were an effort to transform the expressions to which the members were accustomed, but which they basically little understood, into corresponding western concepts—in order gradually to lead these people towards a western approach to spiritual research.

You will find, then, in the years 1904 and 1905, several instances where the being of the Bodhisattva is mentioned. Therein Rudolf Steiner gave definitions from various aspects, as it was his custom to throw light on things from different points of view. So it is that he speaks of the Bodhisattvas in the so-called 'Cycle of 31 Lectures' (Berlin) in the year 1905,[260] wherein he traversed the whole range of Indian occultism and interpreted anew—in a sense, translated—nearly all the expressions that were commonly used, and explained them for the members. Later on, he did not have to return again to most of these things, because he had by then evolved concepts that are comprehensible in the context of western spiritual life.

We then find the Bodhisattva idea appearing especially strongly in the years 1909, 1910, 1911, and fading out again through 1912 and 1913.[261] From then on, stillness again reigned with regard to the Bodhisattva question. He had brought it in connection with a particular occurrence about which we will have to speak and which will, on the whole, be familiar to you. Those of us who experienced those times—I mean those in which the Alcyone or Krishnamurti affair was taking place in the Theosophical Society—have preserved extraordinarily strong impressions from them. It was a time of the most powerful experiences that one could go through. Some of this will already be familiar to you inasmuch as you have heard my last lecture.

If you would now attempt to understand the difficult indications of Rudolf Steiner about the Bodhisattvas, it can be of help to you to hear a personal version by one who participated in the extraordinarily powerful, intense experiences of the Bodhisattva question in those years. Herr Arenson mentions a whole series of lectures in which the Bodhisattva question is treated. You will find all these lectures in the years 1909 to 1912, called forth by what was then agitating the Theosophical Society, to which we were, in a sense, chained. I would like to tell you something of what was pervading hearts and souls at that time, for I believe that the description of these more soul-related experiences is just what may help towards an understanding of the problem arising now.

Yet before I come to that, I would like to speak in more detail about the teaching of the Bodhisattvas as we find it clearly depicted by Rudolf Steiner, and which you have also heard about in Herr Arenson's lecture. I wish to touch first on this sphere so as not to speak too abstractly about what we shall then have to say, and because it is good to immerse ourselves again in what Rudolf Steiner has taught us.

In particular, I would like to refer to an important lecture, which later on I shall treat as part of the history of the Anthroposophical movement, but which here I shall review in its basic content in order to further clarify for you what Rudolf Steiner means by the term 'Bodhisattva'. I am speaking of the lecture on 'The Sphere of the Bodhisattvas' in the cycle *The Christ Impulse and the Development of Ego-Consciousness*.[262] If we take what Rudolf Steiner says there, we find the Bodhisattva-beings are of a kind who are always in the spiritual world, and who, as you know, surround the Christ; they belong in their twelvefoldness to Christ, enjoy His presence, and absorb His teachings. They teach only in order to proclaim the Being of Christ on Earth, for they descend one after another to Earth. They are the great Teachers of mankind.

We must distinguish them from those beings whom Rudolf Steiner called the 'Primeval Teachers of Mankind',[263] of whom he said that from a certain time onward they had retired from the Earth and now have their dwelling on the Moon. We must distinguish them from those teachers of mankind who, in the beginnings of evolution, came down from other planets and taught early human-ity arts and sciences. What man possessed of skills and capacities, of science and art, was taught him by beings standing between the human and the angelic level, who had remained behind during the Moon evolution and therefore did not fully belong to the Angel hierarchy.[264] Rudolf Steiner called them *Luciferic beings*, from whom, however, mankind received much good—its whole culture, you might say, right down into later Greek times. The great heroes of ancient times bore a Luciferic spirit at the base of their souls.[265] That is a different stream from the one with which we now have to concern ourselves.

One cannot speak of the Bodhisattvas in the same way (although they too descend to Earth) as of those Luciferic beings. When one considers them in their twelvefoldness, one can see in them an image of the zodiac, and also an image reflected in that which Christ had around Him on Earth as His 12 apostles. Rudolf Steiner brought the name 'Buddha' into relation with the name 'Mercury',[266] the god of wisdom, as it is basically the same word. So the Bodhisattvas are actually called 'Wisdom Beings'. One can see in them a kind of Mercury being who is not, however, of a Luciferic nature, and who recognized Christ early on and followed Him—in contrast to the beings above [who indeed also stem partly from Mercury] who were, fundamentally, rebel spirits retarded in development.

Of the Bodhisattvas Rudolf Steiner says, in accord with the oriental teaching, that they descend to Earth one after the other, incorporate for a while as Bodhisattva [for the time being I shall make use of the expression], and finally rise to the rank of Buddha. A Bodhisattva who has become Buddha returns no more to Earth; then comes the next Bodhisattva. And what the Bodhisattvas had as their task up to the Mystery of Golgotha was that of preparing human understanding for the Mystery of Golgotha. And after the appearance of Christ on Earth, they helped human beings to acquire understanding of the Christ Being and His deed. Six, we can reckon, descended before the Mystery of Golgotha, and six will follow.

Now Rudolf Steiner says in this lecture[267] that in earlier times the Bodhisattvas never were fully incorporated. Rather, one would then have seen a person, and behind him—as though stretching out beyond him—a mighty spiritual figure. The figure did not enter fully into corporeality, and it sufficed for the mission of the Bodhisattva that a human being was permeated in such a manner and could take up what could be given through the Bodhisattva-being. This went on into the fourth post-Atlantean cultural epoch.

Then mankind had come so far that a Bodhisattva who had not fully incorporated would no longer have been able to make himself understood. Earthly things would no longer have been comprehensible for a being remaining so much in the background as not to have entered fully into a human being. Rudolf Steiner, in explanation, speaks about the human conscience, which came into existence in the sixth and seventh pre-Christian centuries. We know that, previously, when people had done something evil they experienced the Furies, the Erinnyes, acting from without, who pointed out to them the wickedness of their doings, whereas afterwards the voice of conscience, developing rather quickly, began to speak within human beings themselves. Such a thing would not have been comprehensible to a being not incorporated in the earthly world.

We must bear in mind that the Bodhisattvas are not in the same sense teachers as those we have described above, who actually taught people all sorts of skills (counting, reckoning, writing, etc.). Instead, their teachings are more closely related to morality. Indeed, they bring a reflection of what they have experienced of the Christ Being. You will find this in the life-story of the last Bodhisattva—who became Gautama Buddha—where he himself describes how his previous incarnations had become apparent to him. These descriptions seem quite fantastic to a contemporary human conception of things. He describes, for instance, how he had been a hare and came to a hermit who had nothing to eat and was hungry. Then, out of compassion, the hare jumped into the fire and let himself be roasted so that the hermit might have food. Thus, a deed of sacrifice, done out of compassion, is what the Buddha describes there.[268] And Rudolf Steiner spoke of the fact that from the present Bodhisattva there will go forth the teaching of virtuousness. That virtue will be teachable—so that the teaching will enter into human moral evolution. It is for this reason that the future Buddha will be called the 'Buddha of Good Will' (*Buddha der guten Gesinnung*),[269] the Maitreya Buddha, the Bringer of Goodness in Love, in Friendship.

Now, in the lecture of which we are speaking, Rudolf Steiner describes how in the incarnation when Gautama became Buddha, about 600 BC (the time when the fourth post-Atlantean cultural epoch had begun also for India), the necessity then arose for the

Bodhisattva-being to completely penetrate, to enter fully into a human body—in order to come to know what human fate on Earth is. And when you look at the life of Buddha from this point of view, you will see how step by step a being is led towards life as a human, wherein there is suffering, sickness, death, and how this one life sufficed, Rudolf Steiner says, for attaining the knowledge of what life on Earth means for a human soul. Then came the Enlightenment beneath the Bodhi tree, through which the Bodhisattva rose to Buddhahood. You can also take this same description out of a lecture that was held right here in Stuttgart and you will see how Rudolf Steiner describes this event of becoming Buddha quite anthroposophically. How western is the description in comparison with the usual oriental one! He allots chief importance to the fact that a being has become *human*, and as a human being gives forth those teachings which previously had been only inspired. I am referring to the lecture on the Gospels (Stuttgart, 14 November 1909)[270] where Rudolf Steiner speaks about the previous Bodhisattva becoming Buddha:

Earlier on he had allowed himself, so to speak, to be led from above; he had received impulses from the spiritual world and then passed them on. In this incarnation, however, 600 years before our era, he was raised to the rank of Buddha in his twenty-ninth year, i.e. in this incarnation he experienced the entry of his whole individuality into the physical body. While earlier as Bodhisattva he had to remain outside with a part of his being in order to be able to make a bridge, the step forward to Buddha-rank was now that he was incarnated wholly in the body. Thereby he was able not only to receive the teaching of compassion and love through inspiration, but he could look within and receive this teaching as the voice of his own heart. This was the enlightenment of the Buddha in the twenty-ninth year of his life under the Bodhi tree. There it was that the teaching of compassion and love flowered in him, independent of connections with the spirit world, as something belonging to the human soul; so that he could think through to the teaching of compassion and love, of which he spoke in the Eightfold Path. And the sermon following this is the great teaching of compassion and love, issuing for the first time from a human breast!

You see, the emphasis is laid on the fact that it was spoken for the first time out of a *human breast*. In the oriental view, the main importance is placed on the fact that the Buddha no longer has any need to incorporate, that he enters into Nirvana where all desires and all incarnations are extinguished—the entry into so-called 'Nothingness'.

For this conception, prevalent also in the West, it was a great surprise when Rudolf Steiner told us of the further tasks that the Buddha also carried out later. One did not get the impression that what happened to Buddha when he had entered Nirvana was a blissful cushion of rest, as it is presented in oriental teaching. One great task after the other was bestowed upon him. We know that the latest task given to him, actually by a human being, by Christian Rosenkreutz, was such that it took him right up to the sphere of Mars, and to a deed that can again be described as a deed of sacrifice.[271] This conception is a historical one, suited to western research, one which does not stop at the point where the Buddha being vanishes, so to speak, into the spirit world, but instead is capable of relating what later happens to him. On the other hand, it is the style of eastern spirituality to leave precisely these things more vague, and not to take an interest in what happened to the Buddha after he had reached Nirvana but rather to stress the rhythmical return of the repeated Earth-lives of the Bodhisattvas.

With the foregoing as a basis, I would now like to state the following. In his lecture on 'The Sphere of the Bodhisattvas', Rudolf Steiner expresses it this way: that 'if the wise World Guides had continued to pursue the policy of letting the Bodhisattva not wholly incarnate, it would not have worked, because the contact with the world of human beings would no longer have been sufficient'. So the next Bodhisattva had then to relate himself in a quite different manner with the human world.

It is certainly difficult to describe the ways in which the great World Teachers are connected to the human being, for nowhere are such profound secrets hidden as here, where we are dealing with the incorporations of the great Teachers of mankind. Even if one is able to communicate one or two single details, one is still always confronted with tremendous enigmas. Take, for example, the significant passage in Cycle 19, *From Jesus to Christ*,[272] where Rudolf Steiner speaks about Jeshu ben Pandira, and how he then suddenly mentions Moses and the Prophets. This in itself suffices to show that great secrets lie hidden here.

At the point where decisions are made in the spiritual world for the incorporation of a being, the systems that we make cease to function. The Orient loves such systems, loves to contemplate the regular coming-and-going of Bodhisattvas, and pays little attention to the individual differences that have to exist in different periods of time. But with regard to our period, starting in the fourth post-Atlantean age, Rudolf Steiner says that the Bodhisattva does indeed unite with a human being. And yet, at the same time, the individuality of that being still, in a way, *remains* present. It is not like it was in the case of Christ Jesus, when the ego of Jesus departed from his sheaths at the Jordan Baptism, but it is so that the ego of the human personality remains present when the Bodhisattva enters into him.[273] We therefore have to look to an individuality who is the bearer of the Bodhisattva-being. And if one was present at the time when Rudolf Steiner spoke about the Bodhisattva and about Jeshu ben Pandira,[274] one could not resist the impression that it was a human individuality, going through all the incorporations, who was being referred to—who stands in connection with the Bodhisattva. Certainly one can often feel enigmas arising when one reads individual passages about this question. Just because of this I would like to mention what I myself had as a personal impression: that what was meant is the ever-and-again returning individuality of Jeshu ben Pandira who, at a special moment of his life, is united over and over again in destiny with the being of the Bodhisattva.

★

After this introduction, I would now like to consider the time when Rudolf Steiner spoke so frequently and with such power about the Bodhisattvas. There is for me no doubt that this was called forth by what, at that time, took place in the Theosophical Society. The end of it is indeed even today not in sight, the curtain having still not fallen on this drama.[275]

It was during the years 1909–10 that the leader of the Theosophical Movement, Annie Besant, repeatedly wrote: 'One can feel how human hearts are becoming especially open to the spirit. People are expecting a Teacher of mankind, the Bodhisattva.' And a little later one could hear: 'People are awaiting Christ—why even in India one finds that human souls are living in expectation of a

130

Christ who will reincarnate.' And then it soon became more concrete, and one could read: 'He *will* come, he *is* here, the Christ, who is the Bodhisattva; for these two are one and the same Being!' The one—so it was said—is only the oriental, the other the occidental name. And then the Hindu boy, Krishnamurti, was pointed towards as being, supposedly, this incorporation. About this Annie Besant once remarked that 'in the West he is called Christ, in the East he is called the Bodhisattva'. And she added: 'I prefer to call him Bodhisattva.'[276] Rudolf Steiner took this very seriously; he spoke with great severity about the fact that in occult matters a subjective preference must never be allowed to prevail. When certain names are used, no subjective preference may be determinative. These names—Christ, Bodhisattva, Buddha—have quite definite meanings and may not be mixed up.

Indeed, Annie Besant also said [and this error was not new, but had persisted throughout the whole history of the Theosophical Society] that the Christ, who at the same time was said to be the Bodhisattva, was also he who was incorporated in Jeshu ben Pandira[277]—truly a complete Pied Piper's bag of misrepresentation. So now Rudolf Steiner was confronted with the fact that things were stated which, from the perspective of true occultism, were grave errors. Rudolf Steiner continuously emphasized that *teachings* can be many and various in a movement based on the spirit; in this case, however, it was a question of *beings* whose names were mentioned and who were brought into relation with incorporated human beings. Here one being must not be confused with another, just as little—to use a quite trivial comparison—as Herr Müller can simultaneously be Herr Meyer. He attempted to set this straight so that clarity might prevail in these things.

Today it may strike us as terribly muddled, from the very outset, to assert that Christ and the Bodhisattva are the same being. During that period, however, the assertion was capable of producing the greatest confusion. This whole mix-up was based on a fundamental error that had already been committed by Blavatsky.[278] Blavatsky was a personality with strong occult antipathies. Rudolf Steiner has told us that it is possible to have such subjective antipathies when one is an occultist. She had such an antipathy, for example, against the Yahveh-being as Moon god, as well as against everything connected with the Moon. She also had it against Christ and

Christianity in general, as it was embodied more or less imperfectly in its representatives.[279] And if you could get hold of the first publications of the Theosophical Society, such as the first years' issues of the paper *The Theosophist*,[280] you would find there a vile abuse of Christ Jesus that could make you feel quite sick.

Such things as this, present at the starting point of a spiritual society, can create very strong karma. That is then something that such a society is not able to work through. So it belongs to the bad karma of the Theosophical Society from the outset to have had no relationship with the Christ—indeed, to have had even an antipathy. Later on, the German branch of the Theosophical Society— long before Rudolf Steiner—tried in a rather feeble way to let Christian impulses flow in. This was not viewed favourably from 'above'. But the fact that in the Society itself people came to a point of absurdity with regard to Christ, has, no doubt, something to do with the bad karma of that Society. They confused Jesus of Nazareth with Jeshu ben Pandira. They said: 'The Jesus of whom the Gospels speak lived a hundred years before our era.' I remember how once someone said to me: 'If Blavatsky can look back into the Akasha Chronicle and can see Jeshu ben Pandira in the year 105 BC, then she surely could have also seen Jesus in the year nought!' This person thought that vision moves through time like clockwork. But it is not so. Spiritually one cannot see, or cannot see correctly, that towards which one has an antipathy.

And the effect of this error continued further. It affected Annie Besant when she attempted personally to bring something of Christianity into the Theosophical Society, after previously having passed through a long period of atheism. She then wrote a book entitled *Esoteric Christianity*, which was published in 1897.[281] It was highly praised by Rudolf Steiner because he was glad that in the Society people were trying to come to a recognition of the Christ.[282] Into this book Annie Besant put what she knew of Christianity from the years of her youth, but she also again wove in the mistaken confusion of Jesus of Nazareth with Jeshu ben Pandira, saying apparently of Jesus Christ that he was born in 105 BC[283] and was 'led to his death'[284] without speaking of a crucifixion. For it is supposed historically that Jeshu ben Pandira was not actually crucified. And therefore, as a result of confusing the two, the crucifixion of Christ Jesus is not accepted by Annie Besant. Thus

132

did the old error enter again and actually make the book ineffectual.

When Rudolf Steiner himself brought his teaching about the Christ—here in parts of Germany and also abroad where he was invited for lectures—there was at first acceptance. But then, before long, an atmosphere of opposition developed in the Theosophical Society. Quite soon thereafter came the moment when something was staged, in that the young Indian boy was brought forward who was supposed to be accepted as the reincarnated Christ, yet at the same time was purported to be the Bodhisattva who would become the next Buddha, the 'Great World Teacher',[285] with the conse-quence that extraordinary confusion prevailed. When Annie Besant noticed that people in the West were repelled by her speaking of Christ reappearing in the flesh, she immediately let this depiction drop. Later she even denied in a court of law[286] ever having spoken of Christ in connection with Krishnamurti, but the mix-up with regard to the Bodhisattva and Christ occurred nonetheless.[287]

Rudolf Steiner had to eliminate that. He had to clarify what had been thrown into confusion because of certain tendencies. He went about doing this in a wonderfully positive way—in such a way that at the same time he left human freedom untouched. He did not say: 'Krishnamurti is not the Christ,' or, 'He is not the Bodhisattva.' Indeed, you will not find anywhere in his lectures mention of the name of this Hindu boy. Rather, he repeated to us over and over, beginning in the year 1909: 'My dear friends, the Christ comes only once into the world in a physical form. He is the centre-point of Earth evolution. Just as a pair of scales can have only one balancing point, so in Earth evolution the event of Golgotha can take place only once.'

You will remember from the lectures how often this was repeated![288] He also repeatedly stated (this too you will find throughout the cycles and lectures in precisely the years 1909–12): Yes, western occultism absolutely recognizes eastern occultism, and we are in agreement with oriental occultism that the Bodhisattva goes on incorporating until he rises to Buddhahood and then has no need to incorporate further. Just as every eastern occultist knows that, so does the western occultist know that the Christ can only once be present in physical incorporation. And they have just as little right to tell us that Christ will appear again in the flesh as we would have to tell the oriental that the Buddha would go

133

on to further incarnations after he had risen from Bodhisattva to the rank of Buddha.[289]

One may ask: was it necessary, then, to repeat such a thing so often? Yes, for although Rudolf Steiner did have a movement of his own within the Theosophical Society, this false teaching definitely had a great influence on many members. The German Section was, after all, still a branch of the Theosophical Society. Many people, particularly those from countries outside Germany, had been pupils of Annie Besant before they found their way to Rudolf Steiner; and all of them actually looked up to her, filled with reverence. It was a time of the most difficult trials of the soul for the members of that period, and many soul-struggles were endured precisely because of the way Rudolf Steiner brought forward these teachings, leaving it to the freedom of each individual to draw his own conclusions. Truly difficult inner struggles occurred. Heart's blood flowed with regard to the question: is Annie Besant right in presenting Krishnamurti as the World Teacher, or as Bodhisattva, or as the Christ—or is Rudolf Steiner right?[290]

Our present time has perhaps less comprehension for such soul-struggles. It is perhaps necessary to put oneself back into a pre-war state of mind in order to understand what people's souls went through when they had to admit: if Annie Besant was not right about this, then everything else that she taught in this regard must be wrong! On the other hand, when one sees how people today suffer soul-agonies because one boxer receives a knockout punch—which they would rather see happen to his antagonist—then perhaps it does seem strange that it had such a disturbing effect on people when Rudolf Steiner had to say something other than what Annie Besant said. I could read you passages where Rudolf Steiner called upon the members to have the *courage* to discern where there is truth and where untruth. [That was at a time, of course, when the separation from the Theosophical Society had already taken place.] It was actually here in this hall that Rudolf Steiner let loose with a severe sermon to those who still could not make the decision in their souls to acknowledge to themselves that the truth was not being told on the other side, even though at that time (May 1913) a situation making this insight possible had for some time existed.[291]

I wish now, in order to follow the matter historically, to let the

134

years pass by your inner eyes during which Rudolf Steiner did not take part with his group in what the others who were in the Star of the East movement were doing.[292] You will, of course, find briefly indicated in the Düsseldorf cycle on *The Spiritual Hierarchies*[293] how Rudolf Steiner, step by step, placed the truth regarding Christianity and Buddhism before the members. Then, in June 1909, came the Theosophical Congress in Budapest. At this Congress Rudolf Steiner held a public lecture: *From Buddha to Christ*.[294] Annie Besant also spoke about Buddha. So those two personalities stood there side by side as the embodiment of two different streams, although they stood, so to speak, on the *same* podium. It was at this congress that the event took place about which Rudolf Steiner later spoke: Annie Besant made him the offer that if he would recognize Krishnamurti as the reincarnated Christ, she would recognize him, Rudolf Steiner, as the reincarnated John the Evangelist.[295] Unbelievable as that seems to us today, there was a time in the Theosophical Society when incarnations were distributed rather like orders of knighthood. This was all grafted onto the basic error that had arisen, that of considering the Bodhisattva to be identical with the Christ Being, and Krishnamurti—then still a child—as being the future 'World Teacher'. Advancing step by step, Rudolf Steiner took up the fight against this, but, as we have said, in full positivity and in the fullest measure respecting freedom.

In August 1909 there was the cycle in Munich with the remarkable title *The East in the Light of the West*.[296] Oriental spiritual life was especially illuminated therein, culminating in the question: what actually is a Bodhisattva? It is precisely in reading through this cycle that you will receive the most important insights about the Bodhisattva-beings. Then in the following September, in the cycle on *St Luke's Gospel* [GA 114], the two Jesus boys were spoken of for the first time. Following that, in October, the General Meeting of the German Section took place in Berlin.[297] Rudolf Steiner made use of this opportunity to speak about 'The Sphere of the Bodhisattvas'[298] in the lecture that presented so magnificently the Being of Christ and the teaching of the Bodhisattvas. Here, after the *difference* between the Christ and a Bodhisattva had first been clearly elaborated, the *relation* between one and the other being was explained.

It was thus made clear at this point, for anyone who wanted to hear it, that Christ will not again be incorporated in a physical body; so that whoever says He *will* must be in error. This was, so to speak, the negative side of Rudolf Steiner's task. But the positive side was quite especially represented. One could formulate that as follows, although of course it was not expressed in exactly this way: when Annie Besant says that an expectation is alive in human beings that the Christ will return, then this is correct if we do not think of it *physically*.

The moment thus approached when Rudolf Steiner told us for the first time that Christ would return *etherically*, when he quite specifically stated that Christ would indeed come, that He might be awaited, though not, however, in physical but rather in etheric form.

It was in the beginning of the year 1910 that Rudolf Steiner stated this fact quite powerfully, and, for the members, unexpectedly. It was, so I've been told, the first time—in a lecture in Stockholm in January 1910.[299] [Unfortunately there exists no transcript of this lecture, as far as I know.] And from then on you can follow the sequence: January, February, March 1910, everywhere Rudolf Steiner speaks of the fact that Christ will reappear in the etheric,[300] and everywhere—at the same time—he brought the teaching about the future Maitreya Buddha. Like a wave of enlightenment this flowed from him, leading to the situation that at last there was sufficient insight among the members in Germany for them not to join in with the nonsense perpetrated by the other side.

It was again in Scandinavia—it is remarkable how often and how penetratingly Rudolf Steiner spoke in Scandinavia about these things—in Christiania, that he held the cycle of lectures *The Mission of the Individual Folk Souls in Relation to Teutonic Mythology*[301] in the spring of 1910. You can read there how powerfully Rudolf Steiner spoke about the appearance of the Etheric Christ. He even mentioned it in a public lecture,[302] everywhere allowing the truth to flow in, confronting the falsity that had been spread about.

Then, in August 1910, there was the performance of the first Mystery Drama, *The Portal of Initiation*,[303] in which the seeress, Theodora, beholds the future Christ in etheric light. Thus by means of art it is shown how a naive seeress beholds and reveals to people what will soon be beheld by many. At the same time, this Mystery Drama—which falls within the period of impending struggle with

136

the Theosophical Society—is precisely the point where the connection is made, as you know, with Goethe's 'Fairy Tale', thereby relating to what stands as a mighty spiritual background behind this 'Fairy Tale' and behind the anthroposophical movement. We need only to remind ourselves of what Rudolf Steiner told us about the supersensible cult[304] that was working at the time when Goethe was writing it. Precisely at that moment, in August 1910, Rudolf Steiner sets his own path quite clearly up against the other, from the theosophical side.

Thus we find in this period an extraordinarily heightened activity with regard to setting forth the truth and rejecting untruth. And one can have the feeling that here, through Rudolf Steiner's efforts, not only was clarity brought into the situation for the people, the members, but also that it must have worked directly into the spiritual world—in that the way has been kept clear for the Bodhisattva-being in the face of the unbelievable mixture of error and truth that had been spread about. It must have had an enormous significance for the Bodhisattva-being when, before his appearance on the physical plane, such confusions were created as had been brought about by the Star of the East. For from those quarters a complete order had been founded for the purpose, as they said, of preparing the way for the World Teacher.[305]

Rudolf Steiner once expressed himself on this theme as follows: 'Indeed one cannot really found an association in order to further the coming of a being into the world. One can found associations for spiritual ideals, but not to further the appearance of him who is to bring those ideals to realization.' He gave as an example the fact that many Germans, in the first half of the nineteenth century, yearned for a united Germany. They founded associations to further the coming into existence of a German kingdom. 'But I have never heard,' said Rudolf Steiner, 'of an order being founded for the purpose of helping Bismarck into the world.[306] It is simply nonsense to found an association in which people are expected to wait for him who is supposed to come.' And he repeatedly let the fact emerge that when one works at Theosophy or Anthroposophy in the right way one then creates the very condition whereby the answer will come out of the spiritual world.

One has just to imagine what it means when people are supposed to remain in inactive expectation for years, almost decades, waiting for an imminent World Teacher. And in that same period of time Rudolf Steiner placed the whole powerful spiritual treasure of Anthroposophy before us and was continuously expanding it! I say this so that you can feel how, at this point, a *deed* of clarification and purity of discernment was carried out through Rudolf Steiner, which undoubtedly must also have had certain consequences for him.

Then came the time, in September 1910, when Rudolf Steiner held the cycle in Berne on St Matthew's Gospel,[307] which for all who heard it will live on indissolubly in the memory. There he spoke for the first time about Jeshu ben Pandira, who was the teacher of the writer of St Matthew's Gospel, and who had worked within the Essene order—where the physical descent of the coming Jesus was known and taught. At that time Rudolf Steiner brought Jeshu ben Pandira into connection with the Bodhisattva-being. The manner in which he spoke in Berne was such that one can only agree with what Herr Arenson has said: that it was an Inspiration, a real permeation by the Bodhisattva-being. It was an unforgettable impression for everyone there who heard Rudolf Steiner when he spoke the words in which he identified himself with the coming Bodhisattva. One could feel that through all that had gone before our Teacher had come into such a direct relationship with the Bodhisattva-being himself that it was for him tantamount to an Inspiration, a permeation. I would like to read you the passage, which at that time one could feel as being spoken out of a permeation with the Bodhisattva himself:[308]

And if Essene teaching is to be renewed in our days, if we are resolved to shape our lives in accordance with the living spirit of a new Bodhisattva, not with the spirit of a tradition concerning a Bodhisattva of the past, then we must make ourselves receptive to the Inspiration of the Bodhisattva who will subsequently become the Maitreya Buddha. And this Bodhisattva will inspire us by drawing attention to the near approach of the time when in a new raiment, in an *etheric* body, Christ will bring life and blessing to those who unfold the new faculties through a new Essene wisdom. We shall speak entirely in the sense of the inspiring Bodhisattva who is to become the Maitreya Buddha and then we shall not speak of how the Christ is to become perceptible on the physical plane—in the manner of some religious denominations. We are not afraid to speak in a different sense, because we recognize it to be the truth. We have no bias in favour of any oriental religious teaching, but we live only for the truth. With the knowledge gained from the inspiration of the Bodhisattva himself, we declare what form the future manifestation of Christ will take.

Thus it is stated here that through the Inspiration of the Bodhisattva, knowledge of the etheric return of Christ is given. A few days before this we had already had the impression during a lecture: something like an Inspiration is happening here! And then in this lecture it came in a very strong, powerful manner, so that we had the impression: now this is a direct connection; here the words are coming out of direct Inspiration.

*

Dear friends, I will never deny this impression. I have carried it for years in my soul. But I have also carried other impressions in my soul—that on other occasions, too, our Teacher allowed himself to be inspired by other beings when the karmic opportunity, so to speak, presented itself; the impression of what he conveyed to us when his spiritual investigations brought him into contact with beings of the spiritual world, so that an Inspiration could even take place directly while he was speaking to members in smaller circles. (There, in Berne, it was in the presence of all members who had come to the cycle of lectures.) This other impression had to do with something taking place within the esotericism of that time. One can express the phenomenon as follows. We experienced that Rudolf Steiner could *demonstrate* Inspiration *directly* (it is difficult to find the right expression). To describe it I will make use of a quotation from St Paul: 'I am a man, and nothing human is foreign to me.' Today it is the custom to use this phrase mostly in relation to what is 'human, all too human'. Let us use it here in the highest sense!

We know from our spiritual science, especially from the cycle *The East in the Light of the West*,[309] that there existed a whole stream of humanity, the so-called southern stream of initiation, in which men allowed themselves to be inspired, and beings took possession of them. The persons thus initiated did not need to be of particularly high standing but could be instruments for the spiritual world. This historical stream flowed through the more southerly countries, e.g.

139

Egypt and India. There existed also the other path of the northerly stream—to which, for instance, Zarathustra belonged—by which a man so strengthened himself in his own being that he himself could proclaim the spiritual world. And we know it is the task of Anthroposophy *to unite these two paths so that they come together*. It is in this sense that I would like to use the expression that nothing human was foreign to our Teacher—that he united everything in himself that could, on the whole, be experienced in human evolution. This was so, in spite of the fact that one could perceive him as being an individual who was an independent researcher of the spirit, who *researched* in such a way as in earlier times could only be *revealed* from out of the spiritual world.

I was told by members when I entered Rudolf Steiner's spiritual training that there were lessons (the so-called 'esoteric lessons') in which, by means of certain formally spoken words, he announced, in effect, that he would speak out of Inspiration. That is something that I experienced only once; it was at the lecture cycle in Düsseldorf, *The Spiritual Hierarchies*.[310] This cycle had made an overwhelming impression. Only if we are able to imagine that all those things spoken of in those lectures were at the time not yet part of the treasures of what we've been taught—all the powerful spiritual insights about the Sun system, the formation of planets in relation to the Hierarchies, etc. (the book *Occult Science*[311] had indeed not yet been published)—only then can we understand what a tremendous flowing forth of spirit this cycle signified. Then we can also imagine that the holding of such a lecture cycle, the impressing of such exalted supersensible experiences into human concepts and human words, must also have consequences for him who presents mankind with such spirit treasure, and that this soul is, moreover, capable of being quite specifically inspired—capable of entering into relationship with beings in quite another way than is usual. And so, during the cycle at that time in Düsseldorf, we had a session in a smaller circle, an 'esoteric lesson',[312] just as they were often held in those days. There Rudolf Steiner began with the words: 'My dear sisters and brothers, this esoteric lesson is of a nature that it does not stand within the responsibility of him who speaks here.' And then he described how Zarathustra was initiated by Ahura-Mazdao, how Zarathustra stood before the great Sun-being. He was himself Zarathustra in this moment. It was extremely impressive to experi-

140

ence how our great Teacher, who had conveyed to us the outcome of his research, now showed us directly how an ancient leader and Teacher of mankind could, through Inspiration, reveal himself; the way for him had been prepared, so to speak, through all that had formed the basis of teaching in that cycle.

In Berne at that time it was much the same experience, only different in that it was called forth on another level. It must be regarded as something unique. In the following years Rudolf Steiner spoke ever and again of Jeshu ben Pandira and the Essenes, but probably never with the same intensity of focus as had occurred in these particular lectures in Berne. It was a tremendous experience for everyone present.

When something like this happened, Rudolf Steiner afterwards always showed the other side, bringing about the balance, in that he again held forth fully in his own being. I would like to consider as such an occasion the first lecture that he held during the following winter (1910–11) in Berlin, which is included in the cycle 'Excursus on the Gospel of St Mark'.[313] Between the Berne cycle and this Berlin lecture, hardly any other lectures were held. It is true I know the Berlin lecture only from reading it (I came to Berlin just in time for the second lecture). I believe that if I had heard it I would be able to speak of my impression with still greater certainty. In the first Berlin lecture after the summer and autumn courses, Rudolf Steiner would often set forth a sort of 'Leading Thought' theme for the further winter lectures. So it was this time too, although the lecture consisted of a review of the previous year. In it he spoke again, as so often elsewhere, about the fact that we must always approach things from various sides if we wish to gain real knowledge. For hundreds of years, he said, we in the West have not had a conception of the Bodhisattva; indeed, it has only been in the last 150 years that we've come to cultivate research of the Orient. And he described this as something that can help us toward developing a feeling of humility in our striving after knowledge. I would like to read to you a few passages out of this first lecture:

When we permeate ourselves with this feeling, we will gladly and willingly gather from all directions the ideas and feelings that will enable us to regard the great facts of existence from the most varied aspects. More and more, the need will develop in our age to regard things from

141

many sides. Therefore, let us today cease from closing ourselves off towards other points of view or opinions, towards another path than our own (or of our culture) leading to the highest things.[314]

I cannot help but have the impression from these words and from the whole lecture that here another path is being indicated, a path usual in the Orient, to which we do not want to close the door, although our own path is a different one. For me there rings throughout this lecture the fact that Rudolf Steiner was really the first *anthroposophist*, and he pursued his investigations as a *human being*; he was not a theosophist, in the sense that up to that time everything had been revealed, actually, from out of the spiritual world. We know that the old forms of cognition had continued working on for a long time, on into the eighteenth century, in people like St Martin,[315] and also Annie Besant—who entitled her principal work *The Ancient Wisdom*.[316]

In the Theosophical Society there was so little comprehension for the independent research of Rudolf Steiner that someone even asked him[317]—as he once told us—who the medium was who had researched these wonderful things for him out of the 'Akasha Chronicle'. For in the Theosophical Society, when Blavatsky was no longer there and the 'Master' revelations had ceased, they later brought down, through especially prepared mediums, pronouncements about Atlantis, the Moon evolution, etc. They were accustomed to such things there.

Rudolf Steiner was the first person of the modern age to research these things by means of his own clairvoyance, who brought with him the capacities that enabled him to have such a vision, and who thereby made it possible for us to go that way—so that we ourselves, even if only in small measure, could become researchers of the spirit *(Geistesforscher)*, able to investigate spiritual matters independently. This seems to me to be the continuation of what Rudolf Steiner lived as a prototype for us in his life: the 'man who is looking into the heights' (as he translated for us the word *anthropos*)—the person seeking wisdom in the spiritual heights. He often said that Anthroposophy is something which one can develop only in the physical world, and which we must carry up from here into the spiritual world. We really have to bear spiritual knowledge through the portals of death, for one cannot acquire it in the spiritual world itself. He also spoke of the fact that a person who is able to do spiritual research in *this* world can be a teacher not only for people but also for spiritual beings. The spiritual beings are also dependent on hearing from human beings what spiritual science is. It can be produced only here on Earth.[318] Thus he pointed to the significance of the human being for the spiritual world. You will find this too in the Mystery Drama, where Benedictus speaks of the fact that on a certain level of his striving he was made worthy of 'serving in spiritual spheres as advisor'.[319]

To regard Rudolf Steiner in this manner, as the first researcher of the spirit who showed how every person can himself become a researcher of the spirit, seems to me to be a consideration of what makes up his greatness and can contribute also to our own dignity.

# LECTURE 2 (11 July 1930)

In the previous lecture we discussed the activity of Rudolf Steiner up until October 1910, in so far as it had to do with the Bodhisattva question. This effort at clarification was carried through the winter of 1910/11. Then in June 1911 the lectures on 'The Spiritual Guidance of Mankind' were given. At this time the lectures were for members only. But only two months later Rudolf Steiner let them appear as the well-known booklet by that title.[320] There he speaks of the two Jesus children, about the Bodhisattva, and also about the Etheric Christ. He published this in book form despite the enormous work the Mystery Dramas demanded of him in preparation, writing, rehearsal and performance (*The Soul's Probation*[321] was then being performed for the first time). And then there was the cycle of lectures held subsequently in Munich.[322] In spite of all this work Rudolf Steiner found it necessary to revise the transcript of the three Copenhagen lectures to make them ready for printing. The booklet appeared in August 1911, right at the time of the Munich cycle. Here, for the first time, was something appearing publicly that told of the two Jesus boys and the future coming of Christ. Rudolf Steiner says himself in the preface to this edition that he has reasons for publishing this work 'precisely at this moment'. If we, in turn, ask ourselves why this had to happen, we come upon the Theosophical Congress, which was to be held in Genoa in September of that year, 1911. It was intended that Rudolf Steiner would again attend this Congress. Annie Besant also had agreed to come, and it was known that she would bring 'Alcyone', i.e. Krishnamurti, with her.

The representatives of two spiritual streams would thus have confronted each other there in quite a different manner than two years before in Budapest. A clash was expected from all sides. It was in order that there would be a clear public expression of his teaching—a basis, so to speak, for a possible serious discussion— that Rudolf Steiner had put *The Spiritual Guidance of Mankind* into print so soon. The Congress, however, was cancelled at the last minute—Annie Besant had wired that she could not come. The General Secretary of the Italian Section, who was in charge, took this to be a cancellation of the whole Congress. There followed all sorts of confusion, about which we do not need to speak here,[323] but the altercation was avoided. Rudolf Steiner then held lectures in various places (Milan, Lugano, etc.) in which he went on speaking about the Bodhisattva question.[324] In Herr Arenson's presentation you will find some quotations from these lectures in particular. Rudolf Steiner spoke especially eloquently and extensively on this theme, as well as about the Etheric Christ, in the lecture that will be familiar to many of you. It was held in Basle on 1 October 1911, and usually bears the title 'On Self-Knowledge'.[325] Immediately afterwards there was the Karlsruhe cycle, *From Jesus to Christ*,[326] of which we will speak later.

I want also to mention the Leipzig lecture of 4 November 1911,[327] because Herr Arenson attributes special significance to a passage from it. Now the transcript that exists of this lecture is quite deficient, as anyone who reads it can see. But even if you take literally the transcript from which Herr Arenson quotes, you find that Rudolf Steiner said, 'It is the task of *Theosophy* to teach about the Etheric Christ.' And: 'Theosophy is here in order to prepare this.'[328] In another, fuller version of this lecture that has come into my hands since then, the sentence bears more or less the same meaning, but has a slightly different wording: 'Specifically for our time it is necessary that Christ be proclaimed. Therefore, Theosophy also has the task of proclaiming the Christ in etheric form.'[329]

I do not wish at this point to enter into the occasionally rather difficult question as to how far one should now go to always write 'Anthroposophy' wherever Rudolf Steiner said 'Theosophy'. Certainly it is justifiable or even necessary to do so in most cases. But particularly in this situation, and from the whole context of the lecture [which regretfully I did not hear myself], my sense for the passage would be: 'It is the task of Theosophy to teach about the *Etheric* Christ'—with the stress on 'etheric', i.e. not to teach about the Christ as reincarnating in the physical realm. Then the word 'Theosophy' would indeed refer also to the stream flowing though Annie Besant and her colleagues, for it is they who specifically teach about the Christ as appearing in the physical realm—and not about the Etheric Christ! This shows just how carefully we have to proceed in this direction, and for this reason I would like to tell you of my own impressions and experiences from this period.

In December 1911, the General Meeting of the German Section of the Theosophical Society[330] took place. It was on this occasion that the members discussed for the first time whether they should found their own Society, for they no longer wished to be wrongly identified with the Theosophical Society. At that time, too, an association[331] was provisionally formed which has subsequently developed into the Anthroposophical Society. Thereupon, Rudolf Steiner immediately warned us of the consequences such a step would bring in its train. I do not wish to speak about much that happened then; but I would point to the fact that—for the first time—the members made it evident to Rudolf Steiner that they, in a sense, officially agreed with him. They declared their will to support *him* and not the false doctrines of Annie Besant. It was as if this were the fruit of all of Rudolf Steiner's wonderful work of the previous two and a half years, which I have tried to recount to you in chronological order. For him this was proof that he would be able to carry his movement further, proof that sufficient insight and understanding existed.

And it did actually seem, after that confirmation of his work, as if it were no longer necessary for Rudolf Steiner to repeat so strongly what he had almost continually repeated for two years. You will find already in the lectures of 1912 that he speaks less often about the Bodhisattva question, and then only on those occasions when the Society affairs are directly concerned with it. Again, Scandinavia forms an exception. There, in Christiania (Oslo), Rudolf Steiner again raised the question strongly in the cycle *Man in the Light of Philosophy, Theosophy and Occultism*.[332] It was there, too, that he spoke for the first time about the fact that Buddha was directed by Christian Rosenkreutz towards Mars in order to fulfil his peace mission there.[333] And in the cycle in Basle, *The Gospel of St Mark*,[334] in September 1912, Rudolf Steiner again speaks quite clearly about the nonsense originating in Adyar that had been put into the world. [In the Preface to the printed cycle which, however, was not published until 1918, Rudolf Steiner even mentions Mrs Besant by name.] From then on the subject is hardly spoken about again. During the Munich cycle in August, the still loosely constructed 'Association' was renamed the 'Anthroposophical Society' by Rudolf Steiner.[335] The name came as a surprise to us. We really only knew the word from the 1909 lecture cycle[336] that is now printed in *Die Drei*. But in any case, the continued existence of Rudolf Steiner's work was now guaranteed.

You know that the severance from the Theosophical Society occurred in the year 1913 at the General Meeting in Berlin in February. You probably know too that the direct reason why we resigned [we would have been excluded otherwise] was that at the Grand General Meeting, always held by the Theosophical Society around Christmastide in India, and in front of an audience of several thousand members, Annie Besant had described Rudolf Steiner as having been educated by the Jesuits, saying also that 'because he is incapable of freeing himself from this fatal influence, he cannot allow room for freedom in his Section'.[337] The news of this reached us shortly before the German General Meeting,[338] and Rudolf Steiner stated with great emphasis that he would not have anything more to do with a personality capable of speaking such an untruth on such an occasion. With this the severance was completed.

I have to mention this matter here in this manner, because it is connected with statements of Rudolf Steiner's to which Herr Arenson particularly refers, and which I myself have to attribute to something quite different. I am referring to the General Meeting where Rudolf Steiner told us about his life-story,[339] and spoke of himself all the time in the third person: 'Rudolf Steiner did this or said that', etc. And Herr Arenson finds proof in this that it is the Bodhisattva individuality who, through Rudolf Steiner, is in some measure telling the story of Rudolf Steiner's youth.

We have to consider, now, that *never* before had Rudolf Steiner spoken to members about his own life, except perhaps to a very few who had heard a few details from him over the course of years. He had regarded it as a basic rule of the occultism that he represented—Rosicrucianism—that the personality of the teacher, as such, be allowed to recede into the background. He also behaved in such a way that a question in that direction never even arose. Only once, in a foreword to a work of Eduard Schuré (*Divine Evolution*),[340] there appeared a sort of life description. This indeed had its origin in indications by Rudolf Steiner, but seemed in a way to remain in the air, giving one the impression that Rudolf Steiner basically did not approve of it.[341] There was actually no possibility available for members [even if they were acquainted with the Schuré description] of judging whether what Annie Besant stated at the General

Meeting was true or not. The evidence was lacking for an objective judgement. Indeed I remember that I myself, before this General Meeting, was so incapable of seeing this matter as being completely fabricated that—before Rudolf Steiner had spoken—I had formed the somewhat naive thought: Well, perhaps at sometime or other the Jesuits, because they noticed that here was an especially talented child, had paid for his education, and Annie Besant had blown that up into a 'Jesuit education'. Of course this was naive thinking, for if that had happened the Jesuits would not have allowed Rudolf Steiner to just go his way, so to speak, but would certainly have held on to him for themselves! I only mention this in order to show how lacking in a basis for judgement we then were. You must remember that his autobiography, *The Course of My Life*,[342] was not yet written.

[I remember, too, how once during a question period such as Rudolf Steiner was used to holding after his lectures in the *Architectenhaus*, he suddenly said: 'As the son of a junior railway official, I could often experience this or that . . .'[343] For me, that was a moment when Rudolf Steiner seemed suddenly to be standing on Earth in the midst of common human situations.]

Rudolf Steiner, out of his tremendous objectivity and sense of propriety, could not feel otherwise than that he could indeed break off relations with Annie Besant in response to the Jesuit accusation, but that first he was obliged to tell *us* about his life. Thereby he was forced to break with the principle of keeping his personal circumstances in the background. What he resented was being forced by outer lies into action which he would not otherwise have willed to take at this time. This rings through his question at the General Meeting as to whether the members wished to listen to his life-story. He *asks* this because he believes it to be something that does not belong at a General Meeting—namely, the story of his youth, which he would have to tell in order to disprove slanderous statements. You can find this situation described in these words in the *Newsletter* of that time:[344]

> Because of this, and since truly objective matters are mixed up here with what is personal, I now have to approach you with a question. I cannot convey everything to you right now that could show you how this reproach is constructed out of nothing, how untrue and foolish it is.

I ask you, are you willing during the coming days to listen to a short sketch, a short extract from the course of my life? There is no other way that I can give you proof of how foolish and untrue such an accusation as Mrs Besant's is. Neither, however, do I want to force it on you, and so I am asking you to tell me whether you agree to hear an abbreviated synopsis of my memoirs at some suitable moment during the coming days.

[The meeting accepts the suggestion.]

Mrs Besant knows very well that all such accusations leave behind them a residue. And now ... I pause, for no words suffice to characterize what has happened. That I should be forced to the point of having to describe the course of my life is unheard of!

My ears can still hear the energy and the indignation with which Rudolf Steiner hurled these last words into the meeting. The meeting, it is recorded, 'accepted the suggestion'. And when Rudolf Steiner, after two days, was ready to tell his life-story, he began with a sort of protest, his first words being:

It is my honest conviction that what I now have to describe is more than one should ask a group such as this to listen to. You can definitely rest assured that, feeling this as I do, I resort to this description only for the reasons that came up in the last few days. These reasons require—to a certain measure it is a duty—that for the sake of our endeavours, suspicions and distortions should be put in the right light—that is, be rejected.[345]

Then, only after having said these few words in preface—

My dear theosophical friends, please regard the manner in which I shall couch my description not as affected, but as something which in many ways seems to me the most natural form.

Rudolf Steiner begins to speak of himself in the third person. His manner of speaking could be interpreted as the final protest against the enforced deed, as a last rejection of having to allow the personality of the occult teacher to come into the foreground. Then he was able to raise himself above the situation with the help of what is, after all, the freeing element in spiritual life. And that is

149

humour. Indeed, he told his life-story in such a way that we often had a good laugh. There was, for example, the delightful incident with the stationmaster who had a toothache. Someone telegraphed the dentist to come and help. Being always a very busy man, he wired that the stationmaster should wait on the platform, and the train would stop for a moment on its way through. The dentist pulled out his tooth and the train moved on immediately. The stationmaster stood there, quite stunned, inspected his tooth and said [unfortunately I cannot repeat it to you in Austrian dialect as Rudolf Steiner told it]: 'Well, actually he pulled out a perfectly healthy tooth, but now the other one doesn't hurt anymore either!'

It was in this manner that Rudolf Steiner told his life-story, notwithstanding that it was in the third person! This, too, belongs to an examination of the Bodhisattva question in the light of anthroposophical history.

We now come to the important point in the inner transformation that takes place in the Bodhisattva-being between the thirtieth and thirty-third year of his life. You will all know the passage in which Rudolf Steiner speaks of the fact that he who is the bearer of the Bodhisattva-being is, in his youth, of such a nature that no one around him can know what will be working in him in the future. He is a child with no more or less talent than another until, at the above-mentioned age, the Bodhisattva takes possession of him, and thereby a complete transformation of his life takes place.[346] This oft-repeated statement of Rudolf Steiner's is brought into connection here with what provoked it historically.

Annie Besant, we know, had appeared on the scene with a boy whom she maintained was the Bodhisattva. The highest reverence was paid to this boy. He wrote a little book at the age of 14 or 15—*At the Feet of the Master*,[347] which for someone who reads it without prejudice does not seem to contain anything very important—and yet it was actually taken very seriously as proceeding from the future World Teacher. In the Karlsruhe cycle, however, Rudolf Steiner said, when speaking of the transformation of the soul of the Bodhisattva:

This transformation occurs particularly between the thirtieth and thirty-third years. It can never be known beforehand that this body will be taken possession of by the Bodhisattva. The change never shows itself

150

in youth. The distinctive feature is precisely that the later years are so unlike the youthful ones.[348]

Compare this with the passage from the Milan lecture (21 September 1911) that was also quoted by Herr Arenson:

And one would best recognize that somehow the right thing was not being done if it were said of a young person—when he was not yet 30 years old—that the Bodhisattva was manifesting in him. This would be a sign of error.[349]

As you can see, the nonsense that was being spread about over there was being clearly indicated. This nonsense went so far that Krishnamurti, as a half-grown boy, was taken by Leadbeater to Sicily and there, as he tells, was 'initiated'.[350] It is purported that he had lain for three-and-a-half days in an initiation sleep resembling death—in Sicily of all places! Dear friends, read the cycle, *Mysteries of the East and of Christianity*,[351] held at precisely that same General Meeting in Berlin (February 1913), and you will find Sicily indicated as that place on Earth where the anti-Grail impulses dwell. It is stated further that in the spiritual aura of Sicily, to this day, the evil consequences of the works of the Grail-antagonist, Klingsor—the black magician—can be perceived. This was the light thrown by the spiritual investigator, which was dressed, one might say, in the chaste garb of a communication of knowledge, about what was supposed to have taken place there as a quasi-initiation of an immature young person. It is exactly in this manner that all communications of Rudolf Steiner in that period 'fit' into the happenings in the Theosophical Society.

Thereby, without mentioning any names Rudolf Steiner had actually pointed to the fact that Annie Besant and Leadbeater were basically not spiritual scientists, for otherwise they would know that in the boy, Krishnamurti, the future Bodhisattva could not yet be visible. Rudolf Steiner had left it to the free insight of the members to recognize the truth through his teachings. We need today to see these things in this light, in the aura, so to speak, in which they are situated.

Now Rudolf Steiner had also mentioned in connection with these things, during the Leipzig lecture,[352] that the Bodhisattva was already reincarnated: 'He is already incorporated, and he will be the actual proclaimer of the Etheric Christ.' [If we want to take just this message in the transcript literally, we must notice that the first fact is spoken of as in the present, the second as in the future].

Herr Arenson feels this to be a contradiction of the previous quotation, which said that one could never know before the thirty-third year had been reached that a particular body was going to be taken hold of by the Bodhisattva. By this reasoning Rudolf Steiner could not know that the Bodhisattva had already incorporated, unless one sees Rudolf Steiner himself as the Bodhisattva-bearer. I can only say that I, having heard nearly all the lectures of that period, did not experience a contradiction. For I did not doubt that Rudolf Steiner could know this, even though he had explained to us in manifold ways that Annie Besant in any case could possess no such knowledge, since otherwise she would not have brought the boy forward in that manner. Indeed, Rudolf Steiner had wanted to say previously that, from outer things [as, for instance, from the writing of a little book in childhood years which is proclaimed as significant] or from any behaviour whatsoever of a person before the thirty-third year on the physical plane, one cannot conclude that he is the Bodhisattva. However, it is precisely this that Mrs Besant had referred to, and therefore one could have no confidence in her spiritual proclamations about the World Teacher, for this basic fact of the inner transformation in the thirty-third year of age was obviously not known to her. Yet from the spiritual aspect, from a real knowledge, for instance, of the Jeshu ben Pandira indivi-duality, Rudolf Steiner could well know who was to be the Bodhisattva-bearer.

I do not wish to pursue this much further. Many have given thought to this problem, and among members it has been much discussed, but it is questionable whether there have been results of value. I do not regard it as helpful the way Herr Arenson, in this connection, pays attention to rumours which in any case could have been verified, in part, by asking questions. Herr Arenson supposes that if Rudolf Steiner, by means of his spiritual investigation, could have known the identity of the incorporated Bodhisattva, he would not have mentioned it, for if he had done so he would have broken a rule of the spiritual world. Therefore, those rumours could not be based on truth which said that Rudolf Steiner had indeed given indications about this to certain people, for the initiate does not infringe upon a law that derives from the spiritual world.[353]

It seems to me, however, that one cannot absolutely express as being a 'law' what the occultist may or may not communicate to other people. Rudolf Steiner always responded very deliberately in accordance with *what* the individual human personality was able to bring towards him in such situations; whether, for instance, there was present a deeper capacity for understanding occult things, or else perhaps a more purely natural one. To questions asked him, especially in private conversations, he gave very different answers in respect to the concreteness, the positivity of the answer, etc. One might even say that on occasion he went astonishingly far. And one cannot avoid the impression that actually Rudolf Steiner was glad when the karmic opportunity was offered to him, as it were, to say more about certain things than was possible in the general lectures.

As regards the infringement of a 'law' that Rudolf Steiner is supposed to have perpetrated concerning a communication about the Bodhisattva, I would certainly like to say that a 'law' in the spiritual world is not a thing of paragraphs and subsections, which would operate for the initiate just like an outer law whose violation would incur an outer punishment. Rather, it is a question of *knowledge* that the initiate has gained, and out of which he can judge what is helpful for human evolution and what is not [for instance, as regards the communication of spiritual facts]. How he handles this is certainly placed in the freedom of the initiate, who himself can know what karmic consequences will follow any infringement of the 'law'. Often, however, such consequences have to be taken on because the situation or world-development in general requires it. Here we can remind ourselves of a simple example which will be familiar to you all. In *Knowledge of the Higher Worlds*,[354] Rudolf Steiner tells of how all blaming and criticising has a hardening, disturbing influence on the soul of the student. That is certainly a law. But he immediately adds that of course the circumstances of life may entail—and not only for the 'ordinary person' but also for the spiritual investigator—having to find fault often. [The need to criticise can even belong to one's profession]. The initiate, in spite of all, must at times adversely criticise. The law simply expresses what the consequence will be. One must, then, simply bear this consequence. What an occultist does is indeed largely determined by a right balancing of what would be 'correct' according to spiritual law, as well as what one is often required to do in the face of the circumstances presented. In this sense I wish to mention the following.

Rudolf Steiner spoke once in Stockholm [and then later also in other places][355] about the strict law for Rosicrucians: they were not to speak about secrets pertaining to the leading personalities of Rosicrucianism until a hundred years had passed after their deaths. [One could perhaps ask whether *this* law had not been infringed upon!] Rudolf Steiner also said that one should not point to a leading personality who will come or who is already there, i.e., not awaken expectations for the future which are attached to personalities[356]—as indeed had been abundantly practised by 'the other side'—for such a thing contradicts true contemporary occultism.

As Rudolf Steiner spoke in the way described above about the coming of the Bodhisattva whose work it is to proclaim the Etheric Christ, there arose a quiet thought in my mind, because I had become accustomed to test everything—as he had demanded of us. 'Well,' I thought, 'is this not an infringement of the "law" that requires that the future must not be indicated concretely? And even is it possible to say, "The Bodhisattva—or his bearer—*is* already incarnated?"' A future expectation was indeed being spoken about at that time (1910–11) specifically in regard to the appearance of the Christ in etheric form. And then there occurred something that especially struck me, since it was like an answer to this unspoken question. [Perhaps it was called forth by the unspoken question. Such things often happened with Rudolf Steiner.] One day, in an 'esoteric lesson',[357] he was again speaking of these things. In these lessons he was accustomed to approach things very concretely at times. He said, as if in passing (but in me, for the reasons I have described, these words struck a strong note):

One could perhaps think that to us it had also occurred that a future event had been indicated. But this had to be, for the reason that false things were said by others. Therefore what was right had to be placed beside them. The mischief that 'the other side' had attempted to cause had to be disposed of through confrontation with clarified concepts.

154

In a similar way, Rudolf Steiner had to recount his life because others had spread lies about him, although for occult reasons he did so extremely unwillingly. Consider that before 1909 Rudolf Steiner had hardly ever spoken about Bodhisattvas, and after 1913 actually never did again, with one single exception. [That was in Penmaen-mawr in 1923. There it was probably called forth by the fact that a few theosophists were taking part in that public lecture cycle.][358] We can imagine that this frequent and extensive speaking about the Bodhisattva question in the years 1909–13 was evoked solely by the misrepresentations issuing from Adyar. We can also imagine that if Rudolf Steiner had been able to just take his own path, he would hardly have touched on this theme and the prophecy of the coming Bodhisattva. Therefore we can say that this speaking about the Bodhisattva was, to a certain extent, against his will, against the 'law', but it was *necessary* to prevent mischief on a larger scale. As regards the appearance of Christ in the etheric world, I believe that even if all the rest had not taken place, Rudolf Steiner would certainly have spoken to us about this. It may have been at a slightly different time or in other circumstances, but I believe he would not have withheld this knowledge from us. Also later on, in contrast to how he dealt with the Bodhisattva affair, Rudolf Steiner spoke repeatedly, if not especially frequently, about the Etheric Christ. When he mentioned the Bodhisattva in Penmaenmawr, he said that it is not that people have to wait for the Bodhisattva, but rather that the Bodhisattva has to wait for their understanding before he can speak to them in his language. This was, actually, a renewed rejection of the passive expectancy that had been fostered since 1911 in the Star of the East. One should wait *actively*, Rudolf Steiner was trying to say, and this active preparation does indeed consist in learning the language of spiritual science. Then one will also comprehend the language of the Bodhisattva. You can look this up in the cycle that has been printed with the title *Initiation Knowledge* (GA 243).

Of the appearance of the etheric Christ, Rudolf Steiner also said that although it will take place no matter what the circumstances, human beings can miss it through remaining asleep.[359] What effect the appearance will have depends very strongly on people's attitude. And having recently experienced with what enormous interest modern-day humanity follows a boxing match,[360] we can understand that, even though Rudolf Steiner was the first to speak about this appearance, mankind will need much clarification and instruction in order to comprehend it when it does begin to manifest for us. That is why it is said of the Bodhisattva that he will lead us to an understanding of the Etheric Christ. Who can now say that this mission has been entirely fulfilled (i.e. completed) by Rudolf Steiner? Precisely when one reads, for instance, the Basle lecture of 1 October 1911, *The Etherization of the Blood*, about the future working of the Etheric Christ in the life of mankind, one can feel that there is still much that can be taught about this subject in the future, in spite of the lofty prophecies through Rudolf Steiner.[361] But particularly if one has known Rudolf Steiner as a teacher, one will have no desire to talk much about these future perspectives. In Rudolf Steiner we had the first fully outward-going, public-orientated *human* teacher of the supersensible worlds, whereas in earlier epochs access to this knowledge was more a matter of Inspirations. In him one felt, in a sense, all the streams of the past flowing together. One could feel, too, how a great past, probably his own earlier incarnations, had reached a climax in this life. In whatever manner a World Teacher, a Bodhisattva, might work in the future, in that which was given to mankind by Rudolf Steiner in his Anthroposophy, his 'Wisdom of Man', we have something truly unique. Like no other person on Earth, Rudolf Steiner could say of himself: Not I, but Christ in me.

When one presents this view, dear friends, it can happen that, in a kindly manner, one is met with reservations from others. This has already occurred. It is then perhaps said: Yes, but *if* Rudolf Steiner had been the Bodhisattva, would he not have had to speak as he did when disproving Annie Besant? My friends, it is quite certain that one cannot simply push aside such objections with refutations and contrary proofs. This situation demands that we demonstrate a special tolerance. And yet it is necessary that we develop a *feeling* for what stream of human culture we encounter here, and what lives in the deeds and intentions of a certain personality, etc. In short, one has to be capable, actually, of a bit of karma investigation—not, of course, in a high-flown manner but with the means that Rudolf Steiner himself entrusted to us. I have already said that through the years one could gain the impression that, although he had connections to *all* spiritual streams, Rudolf Steiner belonged to quite another stream than that of the Bodhisattvas, which is related to oriental spiritual life. Having said this, we can now return to our historical perspective.

In the spring of 1913, the severance of the Anthroposophical Society from the Theosophical Society was completed. For Rudolf Steiner it was a matter of satisfaction (he even expressed this verbally at the time) that this transition had taken place without any further disturbance. We, as 'Anthroposophical', had simply withdrawn from the Theosophical Society. I will not now pursue the question as to whether all that Rudolf Steiner visualized as possible consequences of this liberation was actually realized. In many respects, we simply continued onwards in well-accustomed ways. But it does seem significant that Rudolf Steiner, in May 1913, i.e. shortly after the severance, held two lectures here in Stuttgart which have been entitled 'From Gabriel to Michael'.[362] At that time it was a novelty to hear of Michael, to think of Michael as a Spirit-Being especially united with our movement. Up to then he had hardly ever spoken of Michael. These lectures were delivered with great power and, above all, with tremendous exhortational earnestness. One could thus experience them as portending a new programme. Rudolf Steiner spoke there for the first time about Michael the Archangel having risen now to the rank of Time Spirit. From having been the 'Countenance of Jehovah', he has become the 'Countenance of Christ'.

There now arises the question: who is it who steps into the place of the Archangel? As you know, Rudolf Steiner taught us that there is evolution also in the realm of Hierarchies. One Being rises up, another moves in to take its place. This teaching of evolution, in reference to the spiritual worlds, is a basic pillar of Rudolf Steiner's treasure of wisdom. One finds it nowhere else in the world. In the second of the two lectures Rudolf Steiner gives the answer to the question arising at the end of the first: who has taken the place freed by the ascent of Michael from Archangelic rank to that of Time Spirit? Rudolf Steiner tells us that it is the Angel of Buddha who has risen to be an Archangel in the place of Michael. This Angel was freed, so to speak, from his office of accompanying a human being from incarnation to incarnation, for of course a Buddha does not again incorporate! When we now consider on the one hand the relationship of Michael to our movement, and on the other the fact

157

that Buddha himself received his mission on Mars through Christian Rosenkreutz,[363] then we cannot avoid the feeling that what is being shown to us here is a point of origin, as it were, of our own independent Society. (Indeed, our movement is also closely bound together with the stream of Christian Rosenkreutz.) Specifically, it is that the *previous* Bodhisattva line is connected with our own stream, and that through the being of Christian Rosenkreutz *and* of Michael, that line flows into our, i.e. Rudolf Steiner's, movement.

We have only to remember the Christmas Foundation in order to indicate how strongly Rudolf Steiner brought our movement into union with the Michael stream. Thereafter he spoke, during the unforgettable months that followed the Christmas Foundation, of the supersensible cult[364] that took place in the spiritual world around Michael and his hosts in the eighteenth and nineteenth centuries. The souls who took part in this were those who were preparing, on their descent to Earth, to live as Anthroposophists in that incarnation. He spoke of the Michael School in the supersensible world having preceded this in the fifteenth, sixteenth and seventeenth centuries.

Dear friends, I must admit I have never been able to imagine otherwise than that our Teacher himself was there taking part! Only recall what I mentioned once already, that the mighty Imaginations of the supersensible cult of the end of the eighteenth century were reflected in miniature pictures in Goethe's 'Fairy Tale',[365] and how Rudolf Steiner's Mystery Dramas themselves are again a metamorphosis of Goethe's 'Fairy Tale'. For me the moment has always been especially moving when Rudolf Steiner, in a members' lecture in Arnheim,[366] spoke of the fact that Michael admonished those souls who imbibed his impulses in the supersensible school which led to Anthroposophy to work during their incarnations on Earth as much as possible through the *spoken word*; not primarily through writings, through the printed word. Who more that Rudolf Steiner, the creator of Anthroposophy, has fulfilled this mission! He did not mean, obviously, that amongst us nothing should be written or printed, for then we could not be a really contemporary movement. But through lectures, through the countless individual conversations, he was pointing to the manner of his own working. Regarding all this, one needs to ask, where does the Bodhisattva come in? I think one really could develop a feeling for how different the Bodhisattva stream is from ours.[367]

Here I must again touch upon what has been said about the transformation that takes place in the present Bodhisattva between the thirtieth and thirty-third years of age. One would have to be able to indicate this transformation in Rudolf Steiner himself.[368] Dear friends, if one thing is certain it is this: Rudolf Steiner himself denied in the strictest manner any such impulse of transformation in his life. He very energetically repulsed such an assertion made by antagonists. He always pointed to the homogenous progression going through his whole spiritual life. Herr Arenson thinks he can find a spiritual transformation indicated in Rudolf Steiner's *The Course of My Life*, but that was by any reckoning not until the thirty-sixth year of his life—not in the thirty-third. And Rudolf Steiner describes there not how he was spiritually transformed but how for the first time he achieved an inner relationship to the *physical* world. The fact that what happens for other people much earlier in their lives takes place in him so late fits exactly into the whole tendency of his life. [When as a natural scientist one is commissioned to work out of Anthroposophy, and then has to turn repeatedly to the 'Introductions' to Goethe's natural scientific works written by the 22-year-old Rudolf Steiner in order to progress also in one's own Anthroposophical studies, then one experiences no upheaval, but rather a tremendous logical consistency in this life within the spirit.]

If it were not until a Bodhisattva had given Rudolf Steiner his mission, how could the 24-year-old have developed his life's programme in the way Rudolf Steiner did in the letter he sent to Friedrich Theodor Vischer, together with his book *A Theory of Knowledge Implicit in Goethe's World Conception*? We find the most important passage of this letter reproduced in *Das Literarische Lebenswerk Rudolf Steiners* [The Literary Life-work of Rudolf Steiner (Dornach 1926)] by C.S. Picht:

As regards Goethe's world conception, it was not the solidly based conclusions that were of decisive importance for me but rather the tendency of his manner of viewing the world. Goethe's and Schiller's scientific results are for me a centre to which beginning and end have to be sought: the beginning, through describing the basic principles upon which we have to conceive this world-view as resting; the end, through discussion of the consequences which this way of looking at things has for our own view of the world and of life.[369]

My dear friends, one who is so capable of foreshadowing his spiritual life-path can honestly say of himself that he has always possessed a unified outlook on life. In these words we can already see the creator of Anthroposophy and expounder of Goetheanism. He fulfilled to the end what he had announced in his twenty-fifth year.

I wanted to describe all this, my friends, because I think it good to reconsider how it was that Rudolf Steiner led us out of the old Theosophical and into the new Anthroposophical Society. [Perhaps in one or another person the question may yet arise: can we therefore *expect* the coming of the Bodhisattva? One can only say that certainly no one should be prevented from directing his expectancy and hope wherever he likes. Only he should not insist on making these a constituent part of the Society. Instead, for such a person, 'active waiting', which consists in learning the language of spiritual science, should continue to be the guiding principle. All else should be left to the wise Cosmic Guidance of the world, who will surely not send superflous teachers to mankind, but will send them at the right time and to the right place. We should not speculate about these things, but try to keep silent. This would most befit a truly occult bearing towards life. On this point, as you can see, the wishes of Herr Arenson coincide in a certain sense with my own.]

Perhaps an anxious question may still haunt many a soul. What then is right, and what is false? Doubt might creep in and could cause soul struggles as it did in those days when, for many souls, the question was: who is actually in the right, Rudolf Steiner or Annie Besant? Dear friends, Rudolf Steiner himself was the first who could fully understand such soul struggles. In between the two Stuttgart lectures of which I have just spoken, he said very sternly that in regard to the whole Annie Besant–Krishnamurti affair one should not give *more* weight to personal friendship than to truth. [This was when events had already made it clear where the untruth lay.] Yet Rudolf Steiner nevertheless always showed the greatest tolerance regarding all that gave cause for such doubts. If differences of opinion are now present amongst us, they can be an impulse for us to practise that true inner tolerance which must, of itself, flow out of spiritual knowledge.

In conclusion, I would like to read to you the beautiful words of comfort which Rudolf Steiner spoke once during the time when we were standing in the midst of battle. It was in Copenhagen in 1911, when he was giving the lectures which were then printed in the little book *The Spiritual Guidance of Mankind*. The three lectures that were then used as a basis for the book were preceded by his introduction, which, however, was not included in the printing, and which indeed also would not have fitted there. I would like to read to you the conclusion from this lecture. It is my own transcription—I do not have any other—and regrettably incomplete in places. But even if it were complete, it could hardly convey the immeasurable love, forgiveness and comfort that streamed from Rudolf Steiner to his listeners in this lecture. These were approximately his words:

A period of time such as ours, portending such tremendous events of soul, presents a special opportunity for us to enter profoundly into ourselves. In addition to the many duties that flow out of the Theosophical movement, we must draw into our own hearts, our own souls, so that we may clearly appreciate that only through sacrifice are we able to follow the way which can bring us certainty in regard to the Mystery of Golgotha. Significant times such as these must necessarily bring us something confirming the truth of the old saying, 'Where there is a great light, there is much shadow'—shadows that arise along with those gifts of which we have spoken here. This possibility of error necessarily exists in combination with the outpouring of great truths. Thus, more than in other times the human soul is at present open to error. It is also true that in the coming days of enlightenment, the greatest possible errors may occur. Error is easily possible for the weak human heart precisely because we shall be experiencing enormous events.

In consideration of what the occultists of all ages, with clear warning voices, have spoken about this possibility of error, we must learn to practise the tolerance of which we have spoken here. A blind subjection must, on the one hand, be avoided, for that can actually foster the possibility of error. On the other hand, it is also necessary to have an open heart for the New that wills to flow now from spiritual worlds into mankind. Whoever is a good theosophist knows that if we wish to foster the Light that is now wanting to stream into mankind, then we must recognize the errors that will flow into us along with the light.

Let us take confidence in knowing that there has never been a movement in which such open, loving hearts could be fostered as in our present-day movement. May we realize that it is better to be attacked by those who believe they have the only truth, in their own opinion, than it is to attack them ourselves . . . Between those two extremes there lies indeed a long path. Despair may descend on us with the thought: In these difficult times how can I distinguish truth from error? In our striving, let us try to live in such a way that we can be strengthened by the idea that the truth will indeed be what can provide the highest impulses for mankind: the truth shall be closer to me than I am to myself. If I have this relationship to truth, and if I should err in this incarnation, then in the next incarnation the truth itself will lead me back to what is right. It is better to err in this frame of mind than to cling to dogmas.

With this in mind, we can feel that if we should turn out to be too weak ourselves to rise up to the truth then may that which we have embraced perish, for it would not have the strength to live on, and therefore it should also not be allowed to remain in existence. If we honestly strive for truth, then truth will be the victorious impulse in the world; not through us, but through its inherent power. If what we have embraced be an error, may it pass from existence. If we feel this, if this is our guiding principle, then we can also say, 'We may trust that error will cease to exist, and truth will continue to live—no matter what our antagonists may say.' This feeling can live in every theosophical heart.

If the communications of spiritual truths can awaken such feelings in the human soul, then there will be fulfilled in these souls the mission of the new spiritual revelation which has come into mankind—and will come ever more strongly in the future—in order to lead us up into spiritual worlds.[370]

With this I would like to bring these lectures to a close.

# NOTES

*Notes referring to Rudolf Steiner's works and lectures (or explanations about them) are indicated by their number in the catalogue of his complete works in German, shortened to GA [Gesamtausgabe]. The English title is appended, when published in English (available from Rudolf Steiner Press, Bristol, or Anthroposophic Press, New York), otherwise the German title is quoted and a provisional English title added by the translator, where this is deemed necessary. Such additions, and any other explanations by the translator are enclosed in [ ].*

## Notes to the chapters by Thomas Meyer:

1. Quotation from Rudolf Steiner, Düsseldorf, 7 March 1907 (GA 97). The whole lecture is in GA 264 (not yet published in English).
2. *Rudolf Steiner Enters my Life*, London, 1929, p. 85.
3. Rudolf Steiner, *Briefe* (Band II), [*Letters*, Vol. II], Dornach 1953. Letter to Wilhelm Hübbe-Schleiden, 16 August 1902.
4. Rudolf Steiner, lecture given at Dornach, 21 September 1923, *Eine Erinnerung an die Grundsteinfeier zur Befestigung des anthroposophischen Wesens* [Recollections of the Foundation Stone Festival held to consolidate what is presented by Anthroposophy], privately printed, 1942.
5. Mary Lutyens, *Krishnamurti—The Years of Awakening*, London, 1975, p. 5.
6. Ibid. pp. 5–6.
7. Annie Wood was born in London in 1847 and married the Anglican minister Frank Besant in 1867, whom she divorced five years later, after having given birth to two of his children. In 1889, the turning-point of her life was the meeting with H.P. Blavatsky (1831–91), after whose death she became the leader of the Esoteric School. She died in Adyar in 1933.
8. Henry Steel Olcott was born in 1832. He worked as a lawyer after the American Civil War. His interest in spiritualism brought him into contact with H.P. Blavatsky, with whom he founded the Theosophical Society in 1875. He died in Adyar 17 February 1907.
9. Rudolf Steiner spoke about H.P. Blavatsky many times and in various ways. See, for example, the lectures of 11 October 1915, in *The Occult Movement in the Nineteenth Century* (GA 254), 28 March 1916, in 'Things of the Present and of the Past in the Spirit of Man',

typescript (GA 167), and 10–17 June 1923, *The Anthroposophic Movement* (GA 258). See also Jean Overton Fuller, *Blavatsky and her Teachers*, London, 1988.

10. Referred to in the lecture of 22 March 1909 (in GA 107), and that of 15 April 1909 (in GA 264).
11. Lecture of 1 October 1905, in *Foundations of Esotericism* (GA 93a).
12. Lecture of 5 May 1905, quoted from GA 264.
13. Lecture of 15 February 1909, in GA 107.
14. Ibid.
15. Ibid., and lecture of 22 March 1909 (GA 107).
16. Ibid.
17. Lecture of 31 August 1909, in *The East in the Light of the West* (GA 113).
18. See lecture of 17 September 1911, given in Lugano, *Esoteric Christianity and the Mission of Christian Rosenkreutz* (part of GA 130); and in German, remarks by H. Wiesberger in GA 264, p. 251.
19. Lecture of 22 March 1909 (in GA 107), see note 15.
20. Ibid.
21. See the 'Barr Documents' in the Introduction to *Rudolf Steiner/ Marie-von Sivers: Correspondence and Documents 1901–1925* (GA 262), p. 17ff.
22. Ibid.
23. Olcott died 17 February 1907, in Adyar. See also note 8.
24. See lecture of 15 June 1923, in *The Anthroposophic Movement* (GA 258).
25. Referred to by H. Wiesberger in her biographical sketches of Marie Steiner-von Sivers (in German).
26. 'Barr Documents', p. 18, see note 21.
27. Ibid.
28. *Cäsaren und Apostel*, Stuttgart, 1983, 6th ed., p. 350.
29. Ibid.
30. Ernst Haeckel, *Die Welträtsel*, popular edition 1903, Chapter 17, p. 131.
31. Annie Besant, *Esoteric Christianity or the Lesser Mysteries*, London, 1897.
32. See lectures of 4, 5 and 6 September 1910, in *Gospel of St Matthew* (GA 123), and also Vreede's first lecture in this book.
33. See lecture 4 of above note, 4 September 1910.
34. Annie Besant became Blavatsky's personal pupil in May of the same year.
35. *Krishnamurti—The Years of Awakening*, p. 12, see note 5.
36. Leadbeater's birthday is usually reckoned to be 17 February 1847.

His birth certificate, however, gives 16 February 1854. See Hugh
Shearman, *Charles Webster Leadbeater, A Biography*, Adyar 1980, p. 2.

37. *Krishnamurti—The Years of Awakening*, p. 16ff, see note 5.
38. Howard Murphet, *Hammer on the Mountain, The Life of Henry Steel
    Olcott (1832–1907)*, Wheaton (Illinois), 1972, p. 305.
39. Ibid. p. 305ff.
40. Ibid. p. 306ff. The Olcott biography characterizes the first of the
    aforementioned appearances of the Masters as 'astral' ones or, in
    spiritual-scientific terms, as imaginative ones experienced by several
    people simultaneously. On the second occasion, on 11 January, the
    Masters seem to have appeared in a kind of materially visible form (a
    condensed etheric body?), for which reason the elements have a part
    to play.
41. See note 24.
42. Published in GA 264.
43. Ibid.
44. Ibid.
45. Ibid.
46. Ibid.
47. Ibid.
48. *Occult Science, an Outline* (GA 13).
49. Ibid. (The italics are the author's.)
50. Ibid.
51. Ibid.
52. Ibid.
53. Ibid.
54. Ibid.
55. Ibid.
56. Ibid.
57. D.N. Dunlop, *The Path of Attainment*, London, 1916, pp. 26 and
    34.
58. D.N. Dunlop, *The Science of Immortality*, London, 1918, p. 28.
59. *Krishnamurti—The Years of Awakening*, p. 21, see note 5.
60. Ibid.
61. Ibid. pp. 22 and 23ff.
62. Ibid. p. 23.
63. Ibid. p. 24.
64. Ibid. p. 12.
65. Ibid. p. 26.
66. Ibid. p. 26.
67. Ibid. p. 26.
68. Ibid. p. 31.

69. Ibid. p. 34.
70. Ibid. p. 37.
71. Ibid. p. 39.
72. Ibid. pp. 39–40.
73. Ibid. p. 41.
74. See first of Elisabeth Vreede's lectures in this book. No copy of Steiner's lecture has been preserved. Steiner spoke of this event to members of the Esoteric Section as early as 15 April 1908 (see GA 265).
75. Christoph Lindenberg, *Rudolf Steiner, Eine Chronik*, Stuttgart 1988. p. 289.
76. Address given in Helsingfors (Helsinki) contained in GA 158.
77. Ibid. p. 41.
78. See, among other things, Rudolf Steiner's *Philosophy of Spiritual Activity* (GA 4), where the following sentence in Chapter 9 seeks to substantiate it: 'We determine the content of a concept through pure intuition on the basis of an ideal system.'
79. Rudolf Steiner, *A Theory of Knowledge Implicit in Goethe's World Conception* (GA 2), Chapter 9.
80. Ibid. Chapter 13.
81. See also Steiner's arguments in *The Stages of Higher Knowledge* (GA 12) where he does not start from thinking but from the ego.
82. Referred to in GA 264.
83. *Krishnamurti—The Years of Awakening*, p. 23ff, see note 5.
84. Rudolf Steiner spoke in Rome on 11, 12, and 13 April 1910, and in Palermo on 18 April 1910, on this theme with which he had previously dealt in a number of German cities. Published in German, GA 118.
85. Published as above (GA 118).
86. *Krishnamurti—The Years of Awakening*, p. 46, see note 5.
87. Josephine Ransom, *A Short History of the Theosophical Society*, Adyar, 1938, p. 391.
88. *Krishnamurti—The Years of Awakening*, p. 52, see note 5.
89. Lecture of 17 September 1911, in *Esoteric Christianity and the Mission of Christian Rosenkreutz* (part of GA 130). This is comparable to lecture 10 in GA 131, *From Jesus to Christ* (14 October 1911).
90. Ibid. See also note 18.
91. Ibid.
92. *Krishnamurti—The Years of Awakening*, p. 59, see note 5.
93. Ibid.
94. Ibid.
95. Ibid. p. 60.

96. *Mitteilungen für die Mitglieder der Anthroposophischen Gesellschaft (Theosophischen Gesellschaft)*, published by Mathilde Scholl, No. 1, Part 1, Cologne, 1913, p. 6. [News-sheet for the members in German.]

97. Ibid.

98. Address given at the General Meeting of the German Section of the Theosophical Society on 14 December 1911 (contained in GA 264).

99. Letter to Marie Steiner of 9 January 1905, in which he further asserts that he would otherwise 'only have written philosophical books and lectured on literary and philosophical subjects also *after* 1901'. In *Correspondence and Documents* (GA 262).

100. *Krishnamurti—The Years of Awakening*, p. 62, see note 5.

101. Rosemarie Dinnage, *Annie Besant*, London, 1986, p. 103.

102. On 9 July 1812, in the vicinity of Palermo. See Johannes Mayer, *Lord Stanhope—Der Gegenspieler Kaspar Hausers*, Stuttgart, 1988, p. 108ff. [Lord Stanhope, Opponent of Kasper Hauser].

103. See John Symons, *The Great Beast*, London 1951.

104. Lecture of 10 December 1916 in GA 273 [*Das Faust-Problem*, Vol. 2, not translated].

105. Ibid.

106. Besides Hübbe-Schleiden it was mainly Hugo Vollrath who was engaged in extending the Order in Germany.

107. *Mitteilungen* [News-sheet], p. 7, see note 96.

108. This Lodge was opened on 20 November 1912 by Hugo Vollrath with permission coming directly from Adyar (i.e. Mrs Besant).

109. *Rudolf Steiner, Eine Chronik*, p. 323, see note 75. The initiative for this decision was also not from Rudolf Steiner.

110. Ibid. p. 324.

111. The following words by Besant were published in the official *Adyar Bulletin* of 15 January 1913.

112. *Mitteilungen* [News-sheet], p. 10, see note 96.

113. Ibid. p. 9.

114. *Rudolf Steiner, Eine Chronik*, p. 330, see note 75.

115. GA 144.

116. As above, lecture on 7 February 1913.

117. See *Mitteilungen für die Mitglieder der anthroposophischen (theosophischen) Gesellschaft*, No. 1, Part 2, April 1913, p. 7.

118. Ibid. p. 2.

119. It numbered about 2,550 members in February 1913.

120. Lecture of 8 May 1912, published in GA 143, and in *Anthroposophical Quarterly*, 18, 1.

121. *Krishnamurti—The Years of Awakening*, p. 81, see note 5.

122. Ibid. p. 85.
123. Mary Lutyens, *Krishnamurti—The Years of Fulfilment*, London, 1983, p. 4.
124. *Krishnamurti—The Years of Awakening*, p. 126, see note 5.
125. Ibid.
126. We are referring to Gurdieff, the founder of 'The Institute for a Harmonious Development of Man' in Fontainbleu, near Paris, who organized his 'anti-eurhythmic' dances in Paris at the time of the Dornach Christmas Meeting. Further details, among other things, are given in P.D. Ouspensky, *In Search of the Miraculous*, London, 1947. Ouspensky was a former pupil of his.
127. *Krishnamurti—The Years of Awakening*, p. 133, see note 5.
128. Ibid. p. 157. (The italics are the author's.)
129. Ibid. p. 162. Letter of 12 August 1922.
130. Ibid. p. 162ff.
131. Ibid.
132. Ibid.
133. Ibid.
134. Ibid.
135. Ibid.
136. Ibid.
137. Ibid.
138. Lectures of 18, 19 and 20 July 1924, in *Karmic Relationships*, Vol. VI (GA 240).
139. *Krishnamurti—The Years of Awakening*, p. 217, see note 5.
140. Ibid. p. 242ff.
141. Ibid.
142. Ibid.
143. *Krishnamurti—The Years of Fulfilment*, p. 15, see note 123.
144. Ibid. p. 14.
145. *Krishnamurti—The Years of Awakening*, pp. 293–97, see note 5.
146. Ibid. p. 299.
147. Mary Lutyens, *Krishnamurti—The Open Door*, London, 1988, p. 3.
148. At the beginning of May 1933, in Adyar. See Lutyens, *Krishnamurti, The Years of Awakening*, p. 307.
149. Ibid.
150. See the lecture of 17 September 1911, *Esoteric Christianity and the Mission of Christian Rosenkreutz*, and that of 1 October 1911, *The Etherization of the Blood*, both in GA 130. (See also note 89.)
151. Quoted from the diary of W.J. Stein, in Adolf Arenson, *Ergebnisse aus dem Studium der Geisteswissenschaft* [Results of Spiritual Scientific Study], No. 2, p. 82 (published by Rudolf Steiner Study Centre,

Freiburg, 1980). Arenson himself expresses it thus: 'In answer to a question about the coming of the Bodhisattva, Rudolf Steiner is reported to have said: 'The Bodhisattva was born at the beginning of this century and looks with interest on the development of the Anthroposophical Society.' (Arenson, op. cit. p. 66). It might appear from this statement that Rudolf Steiner had infringed the rule, discussed in Chapter 9, that he himself had established. But compare what Elisabeth Vreede has to say about it in her Lecture 2 in this book.

152. Ibid. p. 82. And see Herbert Wimbauer, *Die Individualität Rudolf Steiner's—Das offenbare Geheimnis der Anthroposophie* [Rudolf Steiner's Individuality—The Open Secret of Anthroposophy], Bollschweil, 1984. In connection with the Bodhisattva question, see further H. Finsterlin, *Erde und Kosmos*, No. 1, 1982, Finsterlin's valuable contribution in *Aus der Geschichte der Adyar—Theosophie*, and an article by Robert Powell, who essentially supports Vreede's view (in No. 4, 1981). Finally we would refer to Robert Rother's *Zur Bodhisattvafrage* (no date or locality).

153. Lecture of 10 September 1910, *The Gospel of St Matthew* (GA 123). See also part of Vreede's first lecture in this book.

154. Ibid.

155. Walter Vegelahn (1880–1959) was one of the stenographers who recorded more than 500 lectures of Rudolf Steiner from 1903 on. Among these were the Berne cycle on the St Matthew Gospel, September 1910, and the immediately following Berlin cycle. *Background to the Gospel of St Mark*. Shortly before his death he made the following statement, in October 1958, to a visitor to Berlin: 'It was in Berne that Rudolf Steiner spoke about the Bodhisattva. The members were curious to know whom Dr Steiner had in mind with this statement. They put their heads together and chose the most suitable among them, Günther Wagner, to approach Dr Steiner about it. Steiner's answer was: "I am not the one." At the following meeting, Dr Steiner gave a report of all that had happened during the previous months and mentioned also the Berne lectures. While doing so he interrupted what he was saying by an aside: "I wish to add in parenthesis to all those, who are ever ready to invent incarnations from their fantasy, that in my own individuality I have no connection with Jeshu ben Pandira." ' The communication of this important fact (from a member of the Rudolf Steiner Nachlassverwaltung), was given to the author by the person who received it, to whom he is very grateful.

156. Valentin Tomberg, *Lazarus komm heraus*, four treatises (published by Martin Kriele, Basle 1985), p. 77. (English edition: *Covenant of the*

*Heart, Meditations of a Christian Hermeticist on the Mysteries of Tradition,*
trans. Robert Powell and James Morgante, Element Books Ltd.,
Longmead, Shaftesbury, Dorset, 1992, p. 70.) Tomberg has also
been discussed in *Info3*, No. 5, 1988, and in *Erde und Kosmos*, 1986,
Nos. 1–3.

157. Ibid.
158. *Goethe the Scientist*, Chapter 6, 'The Nature of Goethe's Knowledge'.
159. *Lazarus komm heraus*, see note 156.
160. Ibid.
161. Ibid. (p. 205 of English edition.)
162. Verlag Herder, Basle.
163. As above (italics are the author's).
164. Valentin Tomberg, *Die grossen Arcana des Tarot*, published by
     Martin Kriele and Robert Spaemann, with introduction by Hans
     Urs von Balthasar, Basle, 1983, Vol. 4, p. 674. A selection from
     this four-volume work appeared in 1987 in the series 'Texte zum
     Nachdenken' [Texts to Ponder] under the title *Schlüssel zum
     Geheimnis der Welt* [Key to the World Mystery] (Freiburg: Herder).
     In Robert Powell's translation, *Meditations on the Tarot* (Amity
     House, New York), the above quotation is on p. 174, lines
     23–28.
165. Ibid.
166. Ibid.
167. Joseph Cardinal Ratzinger, *Zur Lage des Glaubens—Ein Gespräch mit
     Vittorio Messori*, 2nd ed., Munich 1986, p. 8. [The State of Faith, A
     Conversation with Vittorio Messori.]
168. Ibid. p. 27.
169. Ibid.
170. *Die Exerzitien und aus dem Tagebuch des Ignacio de Loyola*, Munich,
     1978, p. 188. [Exercises and Excerpts from the Diary of Ignatius
     Loyola.]
171. *From Jesus to Christ* (GA 131).
172. See note 164.
173. *Lazarus, komm heraus*, p. 14.
174. Ibid.
175. Ibid.
176. 'Zur Gegendarstellung Prof. Spaemanns', by Pietro Archiati, *Das
     Goetheanum*, 13 December 1992.
177. Besides the two works by Tomberg, the following should be noted:
     *Rudolf Steiner 'Erkenne dich im Strome der Welt'*, in the series 'Texte
     zum Nachdenken', 1986 (see note 164); *Schlüssel zum Geheimnis der
     Welt, Meditationsübungen zum Tarot*, 1987 (see note 164); *Wörterbuch*

*der Esoterik, Zugänge zum Spirituellen Wissen*, 1989 [Dictionary of the Esoteric, Approaches to Spiritual Knowledge].

178. See lecture of 24 August 1924, in *Karmic Relationships*, Vol. VIII (GA 240).

179. See lecture of 30 May 1904, in *The History of Spiritism, Hypnotism and Somnambulism* (GA 52).

180. Karl Heyer, *Vom Genius des Mittelalters* (Basel, 1991) p. 114. [The Genius of the Middle Ages.]

181. A *glasnost* step from the direction of the Church can be observed in B. Grom, *Anthroposophie und Christentum* (Munich, 1989), even though in this case the Ignatian wish to make converts is quite obvious; in order to make of Anthroposophy a discussible subject for the Church the article concludes with the question: 'How far can Anthroposophy depart from the basic views of Rudolf Steiner?' The spiritual *superficiality* of such *glasnost* products is so evident to a thoughtful observer, that he will try in vain to immerse himself in the subject ... The latest symptom of this can be seen in the 'Dictionary' mentioned in note 177. The compiler—author, among other things, of an extensive biography of Rudolf Steiner, published by Kösel—is at pains to show, for instance, by means of his own stock phrase 'Execitia spiritualia', the supposed free approach of Ignatius, and under the catchword 'Tarot' the 'extraordinary spiritual profundity and universality of spirit' that can be drawn from *Meditations on the Tarot*: 'Here western and oriental, heathen (pre-Christian) and Christian spirituality, anthroposophical insight and personal religious experience have coalesced.' Also the authority von Balthasar says in the same article about Tomberg: 'A Christian thinker and supplicant of compelling purity spreads before us symbols of Christian Hermetics which he seeks to lead back by meditative means to the all-embracing wisdom of the Catholic (i.e. universally Christian) Mystery'.

182. Answers to questions, 2 January 1921 in GA 338: *Wie wirkt man für den Impuls der Dreigliederung des sozialen Organismus?* [How does one work for the Threefold Social Order?]. Course for public speakers. (Italics by author.)

183. *Die grossen Arcana des Tarot*, Vol. 3, p. 438; pp. 401–03 in English (see note 164).

184. Ibid.

185. Benjamin Creme, *The Reappearance of Christ and the Masters of Wisdom*, London, 1980. p. 54ff.

186. *Frankfurter Allgemeine Zeitung* of 24 April 1982.

187. *The Reappearance of Christ and the Masters of Wisdom*, see note 185.

188. *Krishnamurti—The Open Door*, p. 145, see note 147.
189. Ibid. p. 82.
190. Ibid.
191. *Krishnamurti's Journal*, published by Mary Lutyens, London, 1982, p. 26.
192. *Krishnamurti—The Open Door*, p. 92ff, see note 147.
193. *Krishnamurti's Journal*, note 221, p. 23.
194. Rom Landau, *God is my Adventure*, London, 1935 (1964), p. 206.
195. Ibid. p. 222.
196. Pupul Jayakar, *Krishnamurti, A Biography*, Harper & Row, San Francisco, 1986, p. 50. From this second great Krishnamurti biography, which especially stresses his deep connection with India, we learn some important details about Krishnamurti's first 'initiation', which took place while Mrs Besant was in Benares. It was there that she was brought into contact, through Swami Vihudhanand and his pupil Gopinath Kaviraj, with certain Tibetan occult teachings. Beyond Lake Mansarovar, where this teaching is said to have been preserved in its pure form, 'many learned sages and Bodhisattvas' are supposed to have congregated. These facts, and also the existence of the above mentioned Tibetan manuscripts, point to an essential Tibetan ingredient of the World Teacher farce. The two 'Teachers' spoke with Besant at the beginning of the Twenties 'about the imminent appearance of the Bodhisattva Maitreya and his manifestation in a human body'. The Swami 'told her that the one preordained for this manifestation was Krishnamurti' (see above, p. 43). A further key to the understanding of the Star-of-the-East attack made on Rudolf Steiner and his mission by the theosophical camp can be seen in these Tibetan-occult components.
197. Ibid. p. 92.
198. See letter of 9 January 1905 in GA 262.
199. *Briefe*, Vol. 2, Dornach, 1953, p. 309.
200. Ibid. p. 308.
201. Ibid. p. 309.
202. It is a remarkable fact that Steiner felt obliged to absent himself for a while on the day of the Foundation Meeting, in order to deliver the third of his Monday lectures to the circle of *die Kommenden* in a lecture cycle entitled 'Anthroposophy'. The fact that Steiner did not postpone or cancel this lecture on such an important occasion gives rise, in a quite unobtrusive way, to an equally important question: will the Theosophical Society remain content with Theosophy as it has been represented up till now, or will it accept the extension of its boundaries to include what Steiner has already reported, on the day

the German section was founded, under the heading 'Anthroposophy?'

203. *Esoteric Christianity*, see note 31.

204. See lecture of 14 June 1923, *Geschichte und Bedingungen der anthroposophischen Bewegung im Verhältnis zur Anthroposophischen Gesellschaft* (GA 258). [History and conditions belonging to the anthroposophical movement as compared with those of the Anthroposophical Society.]

205. *Rudolf Steiner, Eine Chronik*, p. 218, see note 75. (Italics are the author's.) The second edition of *Theosophie* appeared in 1908.

206. According to Elekehard Meffert, Bonn.

207. See Jürgen von Grone, 'Rudolf Steiner und Karl Julius Schröer', in: *Mitteilungen aus der Anthroposophischen Arbeit in Deutschland*, Vol. 15, Part 1, Easter 1961. See also 'Das Haager Gespräch' in *W.J. Stein/ Rudolf Steiner, Dokumentation eines wegweisenden Zusammenwirkens*, Dornach, 1985, p. 293ff.

208. Rudolf Steiner, *Mein Lebensgang*, p. 374. [The Course of My Life— An Autobiography.]

209. *Die Mystik in Aufgange des neuzeitlichen Geisteslebens*, chapter on 'Giordano Bruno and Angelus Silesius', p. 193 of 1901 edition.

210. Ibid.

211. Concerning Bruno's Monad theory, see among other things Rudolf Steiner's *Riddles of Philosophy*, GA 18, Chapter 5, 'The World Conception of the Modern Age of Thought Evolution'.

212. These sentences are omitted from the 2nd edition of 1908.

213. See note 209.

214. For biography of Annie Besant, see Arthur Nethercot, *The First Five Lives of Annie Besant*, London, 1961; and Nethercot, *The Last Four Lives of Annie Besant*, London, 1963; Rosemary Dinnage, *Annie Besant*, London, 1986; Anne Taylor, *Annie Besant, A Biography*, Oxford University Press, 1992. See also note 7.

215. Annie Besant, *An Autobiography*, London, 1893. Quoted by P. Jayakar in *Krishnamurti, A Biography*, p. 36.

216. Ibid. p. 92.

217. See Mary Lutyens, *Krishnamurti—The Years of Awakening*, p. 51. Lutyens says: 'On the strength of an indication by Besant in a lecture in the Sorbonne on Giordano Bruno: "As Mrs Besant herself had been Bruno in one of her past incarnations her lecture must have been convincing..."' *The Adyar Bulletin*, 15 January 1913, published the invective flung at Rudolf Steiner during the Adyar Convention of December 1912, which led to his final separation from the Theosophical Society. From a symptomatological point of

view it seems remarkably strange that just at the moment of her break with Steiner Besant was announcing the above mentioned Sorbonne lecture about Bruno on the back page of the latest December *Bulletin*. At the same moment that she received the telegram from the German Committee with its demand for her to withdraw her words, she retires, so to speak, into her own karmic past, which she glorifies in an appropriate publication at this critical stage in her life—in some ways, not such a harmless step to take. That Mrs Besant did actually regard herself as the reincarnated Giordano Bruno is confirmed by Mary Lutyens in a letter to the author which states: 'I heard her say that this was so.'

218. See lecture of 9 October 1918, *The Work of the Angels in Man's Astral Body* (part of GA 182).
219. Steiner speaks about this 'prophecy' several times during 1924 in his karma lectures, e.g. in Dornach and Arnheim (*Karmic Relationships*). It appears that he only once used the expression 'Michael prophecy' and that was in London on 27 August 1924 (GA 240). For the aspect of freedom of this 'prophecy', see the end of Lecture 2 (14 August 1924) in *Karmic Relationships*, Vol. VIII, where it is stated that the *understanding* of certain karmic realities is an indispensable precondition for such a rapid reincarnation of early anthroposophists to take place.
220. Lecture of 29 August 1923 in GA 227, *Evolution of the World and of Humanity*.
221. Lecture of 21 September 1923, at Dornach. See note 4.
222. Ibid.
223. Introduction to *Die Phänomenologie des Geistes* [Phenomenology of the Spirit].
224. Introductory words to the cycle 'Die Geistige Führung des Menschen und der Menscheit', Copenhagen, 5 June 1911, *Die Mission der neuen Geistesoffenbarung* (GA 127), p. 180. [Mission of the New Spirit Revelation.]

**Notes to Part Two**

225. Elisabeth Vreede, 'Über die Anthroposophische Arbeit', in *Anthroposophische Arbeitsberichte*, Vol. 1, Part 1, January 1938 (Prague), p. 3. See also note 4.
226. M.P. van Deventer and Elisabeth Knottenbelt, *Elisabeth Vreede, Ein Lebensbild* [Biography], Arlesheim, 1976 [not yet translated into English].

227. See lecture of 24 December 1923 [at the Foundation Meeting of the General Anthroposophical Society, 1923/24], in GA 260.

228. See lecture of 2 May 1924 (GA 241b).

229. Ibid.

230. GA 110.

231. Evening lecture, 12 April 1909, from above volume.

232. *Ein Lebensbild*, p. 16ff, see note 226.

233. Ibid.

234. Ibid.

235. Ibid.

236. Ibid.

237. Ibid. p. 42. Letter of 15 February 1910.

238. Ibid. p. 47ff. Letter of 2 September 1912.

239. Remark on 23 December 1923; see Elisabeth Vreede, *Zur Geschichte der Anthroposophischen Gesellschaft seit der Weihnachtstagung 1923*, privately printed, Dornach, 1935, p. 3.

240. Second edition, Dornach, 1980.

241. *Ein Lebensbild*, p. 29, see note 226.

242. Lili Kolisko, *Eugen Kolisko—Ein Lebensbild*, privately printed, 1961, p. 219.

243. Ibid. p. 239.

244. Ibid. p. 240.

245. Ibid.

246. Letter, see note 239, p. 4.

247. Vreede, *Ein Lebensbild*, p. 10, note 246.

248. *Rudolf Steiner und die Zivilisationsaufgaben der Anthroposophie, Ein Rückblick auf das Jahr 1923* [Rudolf Steiner and the Cultural Tasks of Anthroposophy, Review of Year 1923], published by Marie Steiner, Dornach, 1943, p. 69.

249. *Ein Lebensbild*, p. 59, see note 226.

250. Ibid. p. 61.

251. Ibid.

252. M.J. Krück v. Poturzyn, 'Elisabeth Vreede 16 July 1879–31 August 1953', in *Mitteilungen aus der anthroposophischen Arbeit in Deutschland* [German Anthroposophical News-sheet] No. 25, 1953, p. 133.

253. *Ein Lebensbild*, p. 11, see note 226.

254. Ibid. p. 16.

255. Ibid. p. 36.

256. It is not certain when Vreede wrote these notes, which were obviously intended by her to accompany the publication of her lectures. It is most likely that they were written in 1930. The source used by the publishers was a typescript version in the Goetheanum

Archive, Dornach. Apart from the title 'Dr' usually inserted by Vreede before Rudolf Steiner's name, the text is reproduced verbatim. The few additions or corrections by the editor are indicated by round brackets.

257. Lecture of 14 May 1930. No written version of this lecture has yet been found.

258. Lecture of 30 March 1930, Stuttgart. Arenson repeated this lecture at the General Meeting of the Anthroposophical Society on 28 April of the same year in Dornach. See Adolf Arenson, 'Rudolf Steiner und der Bodhisattva des 20. Jahrhunderts', in *Beiträge zum Studium der Geisteswissenschaft*, 1980, No. 2.

259. Regarding this, see the first edition of Rudolf Steiner's *Theosophy*, in which the familiar Indian terminology is replaced by its German equivalent.

260. See *Foundations of Esotericism* (GA 93a).

261. See: *The Spiritual Hierarchies and their Reflection in the Physical World* (GA 110); *The East in the Light of the West* (GA 113); *The Gospel of St Luke* (GA 114); *The Christ Impulse and the Development of the Ego-Consciousness* (1909)(GA 116); *The Gospel of St Matthew* (GA 123); *The Background to the Gospel of St Mark* (1910)(GA 124); 'Esoteric Christianity and the Mission of Christian Rosenkreutz', in GA 130; *From Jesus to Christ* (1911)(GA 131); *Man in the Light of Occultism, Theosophy and Philosophy* (1912)(GA 137); 'Occult Development and Christ in the Twentieth Century' (1913) (GA 152).

262. Lecture of 25 October 1909, in *The Christ Impulse and the Development of Ego-Consciousness* (GA 116).

263. Among others, lectures of 15 and 16 April 1909 in *The Spiritual Hierarchies and their Reflection in the Physical World* (GA 110).

264. See Rudolf Steiner, *Occult Science: An Outline* (GA 13), the chapter 'Evolution of the World and of Humanity'.

265. Among others, the lectures of 21 and 22 August 1911, in *Wonders of the World, Ordeals of the Soul, Revelations of the Spirit* (GA 129).

266. For example, the lecture of 13 March 1911, in *Background to the Gospel of St Mark* (GA 124), and also that of 13 April 1912, in *The Spiritual Beings in the Heavenly Bodies and in the Kingdom of Nature* (GA 136).

267. Vreede refers once again to the basic lecture (25 October 1909), *The Christ Impulse and the Development of Ego-consciousness* (GA 116).

268. See the lecture of 17 September 1909, in *The Gospel of St Luke* (GA 114).

269. See the lecture of 27 February 1910, 'Buddhism and Pauline Christianity', in GA 118.

270. See the lecture of 14 November 1909, in *Deeper Secrets of Human History in the Light of the Gospel of St Matthew* (GA 117).

271. See lectures: 11 June 1912, in *Man in the Light of Occultism, Theosophy and Philosophy* (GA 137); 18 December 1912, in *Esoteric Christianity and the Mission of Christian Rosenkreutz* (GA 130); and 22 December 1912, in *Between Death and Rebirth* (GA 141).

272. Lecture of 14 October 1911, in *From Jesus to Christ* (GA 131).

273. Ibid.

274. Especially lectures of 4 and 5 September 1910 in *The Gospel of St Matthew* (GA 123).

275. See Chapter 11 of this book.

276. In the July/August 1912 issue of the periodical *Theosophy in India*, the official organ of the Indian Section of the Theosophical Society, Annie Besant writes: 'I believe that within the next 30 years the highest teacher of Gods and Men, *called Jagat Guru and the Bodhisattva in the East and Christ in the West*, will appear on Earth. I believe he will take on an Indian body on this occasion.'

277. This remark could not be traced.

278. See pp. 20–21 of this book.

279. See the lecture of 18 October 1915, in *The Occult Movement in the Nineteenth Century* (GA 254), and that of 11 June 1923 in *The Anthroposophic Movement* (GA 258).

280. The monthly magazine was established October 1879 by H.P. Blavatsky. After moving to London in the spring of 1887, she inaugurated the periodical *Lucifer*.

281. The German edition appeared in 1903, published in Leipzig by Grieben (translated by Mathilde Scholl, later leader of the Giordano Bruno Branch of the Theosophical Society). The original English edition was published in London, 1897.

282. See Rudolf Steiner's essay *Einweihung und Mysterien* [Initiation and the Mysteries], published in *Lucifer-Gnosis* (GA 34).

283. *Esoteric Christianity*, see note 31.

284. See p. 20 of this book.

285. See p. 34 of this book.

286. Krishnamurti's father filed a petition against the application of the rights of guardianship imposed upon his two sons, Krishnamurti and Nitya, by Annie Besant in 1910. See also p. 52f of this book. Court proceedings were started in March 1913.

287. See note 276.

288. See the lecture of 25 October 1909, *The Christ Impulse and the Development of Ego-consciousness* (GA 116).

289. For example, the lecture of 25 October 1909 (GA 116).

290. An impressive example of such soul struggles is recorded in the address given by Ita Wegman in Arlesheim on the eighth anniversary of Rudolf Steiner's death (contained in *Erinnerungen an Ita Wegman* [Memories of Ita Wegman], 3rd ed., Arlesheim, 1987).

291. See also the lecture given by Rudolf Steiner on 20 May 1913, in Stuttgart, with the title: 'Die Verpflichtung zum Unterscheidungs-vermögen', to which Vreede refers. Published in: *Was in der Anthroposophischen Gesellschaft vorgeht*, Vol. 13, Nos 20 and 21, 1936.

292. See p. 55 of this book.

293. See the lectures of 15 and 16 April 1909, in *The Spiritual Hierarchies and their Reflection in the Physical World* (GA 110).

294. The Budapest Congress took place between 30 May and 12 June 1909. Rudolf Steiner gave his explanatory lecture on 31 May 1909 (contained in *From Buddha to Christ*, GA 109).

295. Rudolf Steiner described this grotesque proposal on 28 March 1916, seven years after it was put forward: 'I had something quite definite to say to Mrs Besant at the Budapest Congress of 1909. It was on that occasion that a compromise solution was offered me concerning the intentions with regard to the announcement of the Alcyone as the bearer of the Christ spirit. I was offered to be acknowledged as the reincarnated John the Evangelist in return for my recognition of the Alcyone.' See 'Things of the Present and of the Past in the Spirit of Man' ['Flashlights on the Deeper Impulse of History'—typescript], in GA 167.

296. *The East in the Light of the West* (GA 113).

297. The meeting opened on 24 October.

298. See note 267.

299. On 12 January, on the same day that Krishnamurti was 'initiated' in India. See pp. 41–42 of this book.

300. See GA 118. Two of these lectures are contained in *The True Nature of the Second Coming*.

301. *The Mission of the Individual Folk Souls in Relation to Teutonic Mythology* (GA 121).

302. On 13 June; no written account of this lecture has so far been discovered.

303. *Four Mystery Plays* (GA 14).

304. Rudolf Steiner referred to this supersensible 'cult' on several occa-sions during his karma lectures of 1924. See his lectures in *Karmic Relationships*, Vol. 6 (19 and 20 July), GA 240, and Vol. 4 (16 September), GA 238.

305. See pp. 48–49 of this book.

306. See lecture of 20 June 1912 in *Earthly and Cosmic Man* (GA 133).

307. *The Gospel of St Matthew* (GA 123).

308. Vreede quoted from the lecture of 10 September 1910, in GA 123 (see note 307).

309. GA 113.

310. *The Spiritual Hierarchies and their Reflection in the Physical World* (GA 110).

311. *Occult Science: An Outline* (GA 13). The work appeared in 1910.

312. The date of this Esoteric Class lesson has not yet been ascertained. See the report of the Esoteric Section lecture, Berlin, 9 July 1904, in GA 264 [Concerning the History and Contents of the First Class of the Esoteric School, 1904–14]. Not yet published in English.

313. *Background to the Gospel of St Mark* (GA 124).

314. Lecture of 17 October 1910 (in GA 124, see above).

315. St Martin (1743–1803) was a French mystic and occultist. See *Beiträge zur Rudolf Steiner Gesamtausgabe*, No. 32, Christmas 1970.

316. London 1897; the German edition appeared in 1898 (Leipzig).

317. See lecture of 11 October 1915 in GA 254, *The Occult Movement in the Nineteenth Century*.

318. The relevant lectures by Rudolf Steiner cannot be ascertained.

319. *The Portal of Initiation*. Scene 3 (in GA 14).

320. *The Spiritual Guidance of Mankind* (GA 15).

321. *Four Mystery Plays* (GA 14).

322. The lecture cycle *Wonders of the World, Ordeals of the Soul, Revelations of the Spirit* (GA 129) is here alluded to.

323. See p. 49 of this book.

324. Lectures contained in GA 130, *Esoteric Christianity and the Mission of Christian Rosenkreutz*.

325. Later published as a single lecture under the title *The Etherization of the Blood* (included in GA 130).

326. *From Jesus to Christ* (GA 131).

327. See note 324.

328. In the latest version of this lecture, in which a different copy has been used from that employed by Vreede and Arenson, the corresponding passage reads: 'For that reason Anthroposophy [verbatim "Theosophy"] has the task of proclaiming the Christ in etheric form ... in order to prepare for this, spiritual science [verbatim Theosophy] exists.'

329. Corresponds—except for the use of the word 'Theosophy' in place of 'Anthroposophy'—with the present printed version.

330. Opened in the usual way on 10 December in Berlin.

331. During 15–16 December 1911.

332. *Man in the Light of Occultism, Theosophy and Philosophy* (GA 137).

333. This occurred during the lectures of 11–12 June 1912. See also note 363.
334. *The Gospel of St Mark* (GA 139).
335. This proposal was made on 29 August 1912 during the lecture cycle *Initiation, Eternity and the Passing Moment*, GA 138 [typescript].
336. *The Wisdom of Man, of the Soul and of the Spirit* (GA 115).
337. See pp. 55f. of this book.
338. Opened on 2 February 1913.
339. Vreede is referring to Rudolf Steiner's autobiographical report, given on 3 February, in refutation of the Besant lie about his imputed Jesuitical education, made at a members' meeting. Published in *Rudolf Steiner, Briefe 1. 1881–90* and in *Beiträge zur Rudolf Steiner Gesamtausgabe*, No. 83/84, Easter 1984 [neither translated].
340. The work by Schuré, published in Paris, 1912, contains a foreword by the author dedicated to Rudolf Steiner, mainly giving his impressions of the latter but hardly touching on the course of his life. On the other hand, Schuré's foreword to his translation into French of *Christianity as Mystical Fact* gives important biographical details of Steiner. Vreede very probably had this foreword in mind but referred to the other one.
341. It is unclear what is meant here. Schuré once explained to Paolo Gentilli: 'The content of this section of his life was communicated to me by Rudolf Steiner himself in the course of many conversations... He showed what he had written to Rudolf Steiner before it was printed and the latter had no objection to it.' See *Beiträge zur Rudolf Steiner Gesamtausgabe*, No. 83/84, Easter 1984, p. 28.
342. GA 28.
343. This could not be verified, but see an almost identical remark in: Rudolf Steiner, *Geisteswissenschaft und Lebensforderung der Gegenwart*, Dornach, 1950, p. 33. [Spiritual Science and the Demands of Life Today.]
344. See *Mitteilungen für die Mitglieder der Anthroposophischen Gesellschaft (Theosophischen Gesellschaft)*, published by Mathilde Scholl, No. 1, Section 1, Cologne, 1913, p. 12. [Members' News Bulletin of the Anthroposophical (Theosophical) Society.
345. See last part of Note 339. Vreede's wording shows some slight stylistic differences compared with the one currently published.
346. See, among others, the lectures of 17 and 21 September 1911, *Esoteric Christianity and the Mission of Christian Rosenkreutz* (part of GA 130) and that of 14 October 1911, *From Jesus to Christ* (GA 131).
347. *At the Feet of the Master* was first published in December 1910. It concerns Krishnamurti's first 'initiation' and was probably largely

edited by C.W. Leadbeater. See, in this respect, p. 37 of this book.

348. See note 346.
349. See note 353.
350. Krishnamurti's first 'initiation' took place in January 1910 in Adyar. Taormina was the scene of the second 'initiation', which took place 1 May 1912. (See pp. 52–54 of this book.)
351. Lecture of 7 February 1913, *The Mysteries of the East and of Christianity* (GA 144).
352. Lecture of 4 November 1911, *Esoteric Christianity and the Mission of Christian Rosenkreutz* (part of GA 130).
353. In this connection, see the lecture of 27 September 1911 (part of GA 130). Steiner speaks of the law concerning the work of Christian Rosenkreutz, which states that 'only those things may be spoken about which took place more than a hundred years previously, for that is the length of time which must have elapsed before anything can be revealed concerning them'.
354. *Knowledge of the Higher Worlds: How is it Attained?* (GA 10).
355. Lecture of 17 April 1912, in *The Three Paths of the Soul to Christ* (GA 143). See note 353.
356. See note 306.
357. The place and time of this 'esoteric lesson' could not be determined.
358. See the lecture of 29 August 1923, in *The Evolution of Consciousness* (GA 227). See also p. 105.
359. The wording could not be verified.
360. A German, Max Schmeling, became World Boxing Champion in 1930.
361. Apart from the fact that the present Bodhisattva and future Maitreya Buddha was characterized by Rudolf Steiner as 'the true herald of the Etheric Christ' (Leipzig, 4 November 1911), we find in his notes for the lecture he delivered on 13 April 1910 the following statement: 'The Bodhisattva, who took the place of Gautama ... will be the greatest announcer of the Christ Impulse'. In the sense of this passage too, Rudolf Steiner is presented as the most exalted prophet of the Etheric Christ, not as the last and the only one to announce Him. Both lectures are published in *Esoteric Christianity and the Mission of Christian Rosenkreutz* (part of GA 130).
362. The lectures in question are those of 18 and 20 May 1913, now published in an extract in the collection 'Michaelmas' under the title 'The Michael Impulse and the Mystery of Golgotha', in GA 152.
363. See, among others, the lectures of 11 and 12 June 1912, in *Man in the Light of Occultism, Theosophy and Philosophy* (GA 137), that of 22

December 1912, in *Between death and Rebirth* (GA 141), and of 18 December 1912, *Esoteric Christianity and the Mission of Christian Rosenkreutz* (part of GA 130).

364. See note 304.

365. See, among others, the lecture of 19 July 1924, in *Karmic Relationships*, Vol. VI (GA 240) and also that of 16 September 1924, in Vol. IV (GA 238).

366. Lecture of 20 July 1924 in GA 240, as above.

367. As Vreede herself laid especial emphasis upon the epoch-making importance of Rudolf Steiner's researches into the Bodhisattvas as the Great Teachers of Humanity and especially as Teachers of Christianity, the critical reader might well ask himself if the 'Bodhisattva current' that Vreede mentions towards the end of her exposition, in connection with Rudolf Steiner's Anthroposophy, might not on the whole have been accorded too little attention.

368. See pp. 72–75 of this book.

369. Letter of 25 November 1886, now included in *Briefe 1, 1881–90* (GA 38). Same as facsimile of Vreede's quoted passage.

370. This introductory lecture is now included in *Die Mission der neuen Geistesoffenbarung* [The Mission of the New Spirit Revelation] (GA 370). It contains a number of stylistic variations from other copyists, which diverge from Vreede's version.

# INDEX

Adyar, visitations of Masters at, 23–28, 38, 42
Ahura–Mazdao, 140–41
Angel of Buddha, 157
Anthroposophical Society, formation of, 55–56, 115, 146; severance from TS, 147, 157; naming of, 146–47; Christmas Foundation Meeting, 99, 111, 115, 158; Spring General Meeting 1935, 118–19; National Societies, 118; Astronomical-Mathematical Section, 111–12; Music and Rhetorical Arts Section, 116; splitting tendencies, 119; dissolution throughout Third Reich by Gestapo decree, 119
Antichrist, 90
Aquinas, Thomas, 56–57, 86
Arenson, Adolf, relating Steiner to the Bodhisattva, 1–2, 3, 58, 72, 73–74, 75, 117, 123, 125, 138, 145, 147, 151, 152, 159
Arundale, George, 48, 53, 58
Arupe, Pedro, 81, 87
Avatar principle, 79

Balthasar, Hans Urs von, 80, 82
Besant, Annie, 19, 98–103, 130–131, 132–34, 145, 150, 152, 160; bond with Krishnamurti, 97; Giordano Bruno reincarnation rumour, 99, 100, 103; personal contact with H.P. Blavatsky, 102; takes up theme of World Teacher, 22; doubts about C.W. Leadbeater, 23, 24; as leader of Esoteric School of TS, 23, 51, 100; nomination and election as President of the TS, 24–27; first meeting with Steiner, 98; first meeting with Krishnamurti, 37; warned by Steiner

about CWL's lack of mental training, 46; 'Giordano Bruno' lecture, Sorbonne, 49; Queen's Hall lecture, 'The Coming of the World Teacher', 49; cancels visit to Genoa Congress, 49, 50, 144–45; at Annual Convention of the TS, Benares (1911), 51; at General Meeting of TS, Adyar (1912), accuses Steiner of being 'educated by Jesuits', 55–56, 147; sends Krishnamurti to Paris, 60; appoints 12 'Apostles', 66; at 1929 Ommen Camp, 69; last farewell to Krishnamurti, 71; *The Ancient Wisdom*, 98–99, 142; *An Autobiography*, 102; *Esoteric Christianity*, 21, 98
Bindel, Ernst, 116
Blavatsky, H.P., 15, 17, 18, 22, 58, 131–32; antipathy to Christianity, 131–32; personal contact with Annie Besant, 102; *Isis Unveiled*, 21, 57, 58; *Secret Doctrine*, 102
Bodhisattva (Maitreya Buddha), The, 1, 2, 3, 50, 72; confusion with Christ principle, 41, 42, 90, 107, 130–31, 133; incarnation law, 50, 150–53; relationship to Steiner, 74, 138–39; Steiner's teachings on, 21, 50, 74, 104–05, 124–25, 127, 129, 130, 136, 138–39, 141, 150–55, 158–59; Tomberg's conception of, 79–80. *See also* Krishnamurti, 'initiations'.
Bodhisattvas, 1, 2–3, 16, 21, 22, 50, 124–27, 129, 135; rise to Buddhahood, 2, 21, 50, 126; relationship to Christ, 13, 16, 125, 126, 127, 135
Bruno, Giordano, 99, 101–02, 103

183

Pallandt, Baron van, 66
Picht, C.S., *Das Literarische Lebenswerk Rudolf Steiners* (The Literary Life-work of Rudolf Steiner), 159–60
Pleroma, *see* Holy Ghost
Polzer-Hoditz, Ludwig Count, 118–19
Pope Leo XIII, encyclical 'Aeterni Patris', 86
Pope Paul II, 80, 83
Primeval Teachers of Mankind, 125
Pupul Jayakar, *Krishnamurti, A Biography*, 96, 97, 102–03

Ratzinger, Cardinal Joseph, 80, 86
reincarnation and the Catholic Church, 82–83, 84, 85, 86
Rittelmeyer, Friedrich, 72, 104; *Rudolf Steiner Enters my Life*, 10
Röschl, Maria, 116
Rosicrucianism, 147, 154
Russak, Marie, 24, 37

Scholl, Mathilde, 98
Schröer, Karl Julius, 100
Schuré, Eduard, 20, 41, 58; *Divine Evolution*, 147; *The Great Initiates*, 58
sense-free intuitive thinking, 46
Serapis, The Master, 38
Sicilian Mystery Centre, Caltabellotta, 53
Sinnett, A.P., 22, *Esoteric Buddhism*, 22, 23
Soloviev, V.S., *The Antichrist*, 90
Spaemann, Professor Robert, 83
Spirit of Truth and Knowledge, *see* Holy Ghost
spiritualism, 86
St Ignatius of Loyola, 2, 79–80, 81, 85, 87
St Martin, 142
Stakenberg Youth Camp, 118
Stanhope, Henry Lord, 53
*Star Review*, 69
Steffen, Albert, 115
Steiner, Rudolf, his mission and life

work, 1, 3, 9–10, 73–75, 85, 100, 103–04, 133–43, 144–62; on the Adyar visitations, 25–28; on the Catholic Church, 87–88; on discrimination, 11–12, 30, 105–06, 108, 111; on sources of error and illusion, 29–31, 105–06, 108, 161–62; on subjective antipathies, 131; rumour of his relationship to the Bodhisattva, 1–2, 72–75 (*see also under* Arenson); teachings on reincarnation and karma, 99, 103; first meets Annie Besant, 98; first meets Elisabeth Vreede, 113; is made Gen. Sec. at foundation meeting of German Section of TS, 99; lecture 'Monism and Theosophy', 98; invites AB to lecture in Berlin, 99; Berlin lecture cycle (1905), 124; warns AB of Leadbeater's lack of mental training, 46; lecture cycle *The Spiritual Hierarchies* (1909), 135, 140; lecture cycle *From Buddha to Christ* (1909), 135; lecture cycle *The East in the Light of the West* (1909), 135, 139; lecture cycle *The Gospel of St Luke* (1909), 135; lecture cycle *The Christ Impulse and the Development of Ego–Consciousness* (1909), 125; lecture on the Gospels (14.11.09), 128; Stockholm lecture (12.1.1910), 41, 47, 136; lectures in Europe (1910), 41, 47–48; first performance of his Mystery Drama *The Portal of Initiation* (1910), 136–37, 143; lecture cycle *The Mission of the Individual Folk Souls* (1910), 136; lecture cycle *The Gospel of St Matthew* (1910), 75, 138; lecture cycle *Background to the Gospel of St Mark* (1910/11), 141; lectures *The Spiritual Guidance of Mankind* (1911), 144, 161; first performance of his Mystery Drama *The Soul's Probation*, 144; lecture cycle *Wonders of the World, Ordeals of the Soul, Revelations of the Spirit* (1911), 144; lectures in

186

187

# A POSTSCRIPT, 21 YEARS ON: 'A MAN INFINITELY GREATER THAN ANY OF US'

## The Bodhisattva question in anthroposophical circles

The present book attempts to help elucidate the spiritual confusions that arose around the Bodhisattva question. To both the author and to Elisabeth Vreede (1879–1943), as well as to Adolf Arenson (1855–1936), the starting point was the question of the individuality of Rudolf Steiner. Furthermore, the question of Steiner's connection with the Bodhisattva of the twentieth century. Essential to the latter question is one of Rudolf Steiner's statements made 100 years ago. As temptations occurred among his disciples to identify him with the Bodhisattva, Steiner gave a clear answer to a direct question posed by Günther Wagner (1842–1930), one of the eldest members of the German Section (of which Steiner was the head at that time) of the Theosophical Society: '*That* I am not'. This oral statement was passed on by Walter Vegelahn, the shorthand typist of the Berne lecture cycle on St Matthew's Gospel, delivered by Steiner in September 1910. It was made available to me by Hella Wiesberger, who edited Rudolf Steiner's lectures for many years and who had received the statement personally from Vegelahn (for further details see note 155). Steiner did not make this significant statement during one of the lectures, but during a conversation between the two of them. That is why it is not to be found in the printed edition of the course. It must be assumed that neither Elisabeth Vreede nor Adolf Arenson knew of it. It is therefore all the more admirable that Elisabeth Vreede's investigations led, quite independently, to the same result. Yet, it is also all the more surprising that, despite the first publication of Steiner's statement in 1989, Arenson's theory of Rudolf Steiner's oneness with the Bodhisattva could be taken up anew and advocated. One instance is Heinz Eckhoff's book *Rudolf Steiners Aufgabe unter den großen Eingeweihten* ['Rudolf Steiner's Mission among the Great Initiates'] (Stuttgart 1997).

Vreede's investigations, exemplary in their own way, needed a few corrections based on the original notes placed at my disposal by Peter Selg (who has recently presented a comprehensive monograph on Vreede). Whereas Arenson's theory may, through Vreede's lectures and Rudolf Steiner's quoted statement, be regarded as once and for all refuted, the case of Valentin Tomberg (1900–1973) called for a completely new kind of approach. Decades after Steiner's death, he too was identified with the Bodhisattva. Initially Tomberg was a zealous and undoubtedly gifted pupil of spiritual science, yet during the Second World War he converted to Catholicism. Important information has appeared on this matter since the

188

first publication of our book. In the first place, we have the letter that the 70-year-old Tomberg addressed to the anthroposophist Willi Seiß on 9 March 1970. Seiß announced that he intended to visit Tomberg in Reading. In his reply Tomberg advised him against doing so. He states his utter estrangement from anthroposophy, which he regards as having quintessentially failed as a spiritual science. Referring to himself he speaks, objectively, in the third person, about his spiritual development: 'This is the spiritual metamorphosis that has befallen Valentin Tomberg from the thirties onward: he has become unable to relate to spiritual science, which he regards as untenable.' Tomberg refuses to even talk about his erstwhile relationship to anthroposophy: 'Nothing could be further from my mind at the moment, and I cannot imagine anything more fatiguing than to be forced to see the ashes of the anthroposophical past raised up again.' To trace the true nature of this radical change of spirit is not the object of this book. That the letter has been published is thanks to Sergei Prokofieff, who likewise dealt with the case of Tomberg in the nineties.[*]

A Bodhisattva as an opponent of Rudolf Steiner's spiritual science? According to Steiner, spiritual science is indispensable in paving the way for the workings of the Bodhisattva. Yet, those who acknowledge the Bodhisattva-hood of Tomberg have drawn their knowledge of the Bodhisattva almost exclusively from Steiner's supersensible research. Thus they come into conflict with their own source, a contradiction of a rather grotesque kind. Tomberg's adherents had for many years set the tone for the journal *Novalis*, edited by Michael Frensch, which is no longer in publication today; however, such adherents still exist today. They do not always express their views openly and directly and, as a rule, they orientate themselves towards the eurythmist and astrosophist Robert Powell, who in his book on the Maya calendar made a renewed, implicit declaration of belief in Tomberg's Bodhisattva-hood.[†]

After the publication of the first German edition of this book, the influential German lawyer Martin Kriele wrote a critical review. Kriele edited the Catholic-inspired volumes by Tomberg after the latter's death, published by the Catholic Herder Verlag. Having left the Anthroposophical Society, Kriele considers the Roman Catholic Church to be *the* spiritual authority. In his book *Anthroposophie und Kirche: Erfahrungen*

---

[*] Sergei O. Prokofieff, *Die Beziehung des späten Tomberg zu Rudolf Steiner und zur Anthroposophie*, Dornach 2003, p. 10ff. (English edition: *Valentin Tomberg and Anthroposophy, A Problematic Relationship*, Sussex 2005). See also Sergei O. Prokofieff, *The Case of Valentin Tomberg*, London 1997.
[†] See Robert Powell, *Christ and the Maya Calendar, 2012 and the Coming of the Antichrist*, New York 2009.

*eines Grenzgängers* ['Anthroposophy and the Church, Experiences of Walking a Borderline'], he states with reference to the Bodhisattva: 'What Rudolf Steiner outlined about the future appearance of the Bodhisattwa [...] is quite naturally fitting to Tomberg' (p. 185). He misrepresents *The Boddhisatva Question* and its authors in the following way:

Firstly, he claims, Elisabeth Vreede, who was positive about Tomberg's early writings and provided a preface to the English edition of Tomberg's *Essays on the Old Testament*, had insinuated in this preface that she believed Tomberg to be 'the one'. There is simply no trace of a such a suggestion in Vreede's preface! Secondly, Kriele suggests that Meyer thinks the reappearance of the Bodhisattva would only take place 'in etheric form', which explains why (for Meyer) neither Steiner nor Tomberg could be the Bodhisattva—a statement nowhere to be found in this book.

Within the circle of former followers of Tomberg, some continued to search for new candidates for the Bodhisattva of the twentieth century. Uwe Todt, who had previously written for *Novalis*, published (in the publishing house of the same name) a monograph on a Danish seer, Martinus, born in 1890, and put him in Tomberg's place. But Martinus proves to be even less compatible with Steiner's spiritual science, as he categorically rejects Steiner's cognition of the cosmic Christ-being who incarnated into the sheaths of Jesus of Nazareth during the baptism in the Jordan. Todt also circulates an alleged statement of Steiner, according to which twenty-first century anthroposophy needs to be replaced by something completely new.* Anton Kimpfler's essay, published in *Der Europäer* in Nov. 2010, gives a good overview of some further variants of speculations concerning the Bodhisattva issue.

### 1910—elucidation and the source of spiritual confusion

All spiritual-scientific insight, but also the speculations and the partly very obvious confusions related to the Bodhisattva question, culminated as early as 1910. On 12 January that very year, Rudolf Steiner decided that all the confusions that had been smouldering for years about the identity of Christ and about the Bodhisattva of the twentieth century would need to be untied like a Gordian knot. He spoke to members in Stockholm for the first time of the appearance of the etheric Christ, while at the same time, in India, Annie Besant, President of the Theosophical Society, called the 14-year-old Krishnamurti a 'vehicle' for the new Maitreya-Bodhisattva, that she identified with the 'reincarnated' Christ.

---

* Uwe Todt, *Martinus—Leben und Werk Bd. 1* ['Martinus, His Life and His Work Vol. 1'], Schaffhausen 2007, p. 88ff.

As is known, during the months following this memorable day Rudolf Steiner bore the truth of the etheric Christ event like a torch, from the north through Europe, down to the south of Palermo. And in September 1910, Rudolf Steiner finally felt compelled to put an end to the speculations over his alleged connection with the Bodhisattva with the above cited statement.

Less known, or at least less noticed, was the contribution he had made to the elucidation of the confusion over the Christ and the Bodhisattva question in his first mystery drama *The Portal of Initiation*, in the lengthy opening scene. This drama was premièred in Munich in August 1910. We must be aware of the fact that both this first and the second drama, *The Soul's Probation*, which premièred in the following year, had been written for a theosophical audience. This accounts for the fact that the higher truth of the etheric return of Christ is not announced by the spiritual leader Benedictus, but by a seeress, Theodora. The theosophists generally knew of no other method of spiritual research than the one which was pursued through mediums. Rudolf Steiner shows that it is perfectly possible for higher spiritual truths to be revealed through a medium, even though the spiritual science founded by him rejects the mediumistic approach. He then discloses the dangers and restrictions attending mediumism in the third scene of the third drama, *The Guardian of the Threshold*, where it becomes obvious that the same seeress, Theodora, temporarily fails to escape Lucifer's clutches, in spite of her noteworthy clairvoyance.

Christ, who has appeared in the etheric realm, speaks through Theodora, and is followed by a 'human individual', a teacher of Christ's new appearance. This being speaking through Theodora is the Bodhisattva of the twentieth century. Furthermore, it becomes evident that Benedictus also knows of the new etheric event, although he is not identical with the latter being. Similarly, Rudolf Steiner also knew of the exalted teaching tasks of the Bodhisattva, without being identical with him (see Appendix p. 198 ff.).

### Spiritual developments

Anyone seeking to illustrate erroneous historical insights and spiritual fallacies runs the risk of rendering an all too rigid and inflexible picture of those who commit such errors, ignoring the potential spiritual development of such figures. While, 'in the midst of the spiritual struggle', it is perhaps unavoidable that an injustice is done to the bearers of spiritual errors—in as much as the prospects of a rectification of such errors by the very same individualities is ignored—today, 100 years later, such a rectification is not only possible but also necessary. For otherwise one would come into conflict with a most profound aspect of the Christ-impulse—the extraordinary impulse towards the finest possible cultivation of the innermost, sublime kernel slumbering in every human soul.

We shall give instances of three bearers of Christological errors, who have also helped sow the seeds of various Bodhisattva-errors, and thereby attempt to trace such a development in their later life, as revealed either in Steiner's statements or the statements of the respective individualities—or even from impartial observations of our own. We have in mind H.P. Blavatsky (1831–1891), Annie Besant (1847–1933), and Krishnamurti (1895–1986).

## Blavatsky and her post-mortem development

H.P. Blavatsky, whose pioneering impact on a new spiritualization of culture and science was acknowledged by Steiner, was all her life blinded to the truth about the Christ-individuality. She had reached an understanding of Yahweh, but at the same time became a fierce objector to the Yahweh-impulse, which is in fact part of the Christ-impulse. She even confused the historical Christ with the leader of the Essenes, Jeshu ben Pandira, who was likewise crucified, about 100 years before Jesus Christ. Steiner often criticizes the unsystematic and illogical nature of her presentations, yet at the same time he emphasizes the exceptionally significant and profound element in her writings, for instance the difficult 'Stanzas of Dzyan' of *The Secret Doctrine*. Steiner's *Occult Science* was, even in the title, a correction to and an extension of Blavatsky's *Secret Doctrine*; in lieu of 'doctrine', which always bears the imprint of something dogmatic and, as it were, something like a shot fired from the pistol of the 'absolute', Steiner uses the term 'science'. In some passages in his lectures Steiner pointed out the fact that his correcting of certain spiritual errors perpetrated by Blavatsky came about with the spiritual consent of her individuality.* This already indicates that her post-mortem development was of a kind that permitted of her realizing erstwhile errors, and of becoming spiritually receptive to truths that had previously remained inaccessible to her perception. But there is more to it than that. During her post-mortem evolution she had even developed the urge where possible to draw the attention of people, who concerned themselves seriously with her writings, to Steiner's work. We find the best instance known to us in the life of Eleanor C. Merry (1873–1956), the spiritual friend of D.N. Dunlop (1868–1935), who organized, together with the latter, Rudolf Steiner's great lecture cycles in Penmaenmawr and Torquay. Like many of

---

* See, among other things, the lecture of 27 September 1911 on Christian Rosenkreutz, in GA 130 (*Esoteric Christianity and the Mission of Christian Rosenkreutz*, Sussex 2000).

Steiner's pupils, Merry had for many years previously also been a serious student of Blavatsky's writings. While studying *The Secret Doctrine*, she had a peculiar experience, feeling guided by an invisible hand. Whenever she had difficulties in comprehending the text, and whenever there arose a question, the hand guided her to another passage, sometimes further away, where her question was then answered. When E.C. Merry related this experience to Rudolf Steiner, he confirmed that behind the invisible hand was Blavatsky's spiritual guidance, and he added the following weighty words: 'She has led you to me'.* This means, if taken seriously, no more and no less than that the Blavatsky-individuality, during her post-mortem development, perceived Rudolf Steiner as one, or even as *the* one, who would truly further pursue her own mission, and that she therefore wished to lead seeking souls to him. It is also said that, since that point in time, the former founder of the Theosophical Society literally belongs to and furthers the anthroposophical movement.

### Annie Besant's death in the Christ-year 1933

Annie Besant adopted Blavatsky's fundamental Christological error and perpetuated it. Therein lies the reason for her evident confounding of the Christ-individuality with the individuality of the Bodhisattva, formerly Jeshu ben Pandira. Furthermore, she was increasingly searching, above all under the influence of C.W. Leadbeater (1847–1934), for the reincarnated Bodhisattva, whom she thought to have found in the young Krishnamurti, on 12 January 1910. Since Steiner could not accept this, his expulsion from the Theosophical Society, at the close of 1912, became inevitable.

Yet Annie Besant acknowledged, during the first years of the twentieth century, Steiner's great abilities, even his superiority regarding spiritual science. He acknowledged her spiritual courage and knew of her significant karmic background, and he expressed it openly, with a dedication ('to the spirit of Giordano Bruno') in the first edition of *Theosophy*. Could it be that this first phase, of the interaction between Besant and Steiner, did not bear fruit after Besant's death due to the fact that it was superseded by the second phase, i.e. that of increasing opposition? Could it be that an after-death review of this first phase may have sown the seeds of a spiritual reorientation in a new earthly life in the future? These questions have not been brought up as theoretical concerns, but in view of the peculiar moment of Besant's transition to the spiritual realm: she passed away in the autumn of 1933. Steiner's first announcement of the fundamental Chris-

---

* Quoted from: T.H. Meyer, *D.N. Dunlop—ein Zeit- und Lebensbild*, Basel, 2nd edition 1996, p. 190ff. (English edition: *D.N. Dunlop, A Man of Our Time*, London 1992.)

tological truth of the twentieth century—the appearance of Christ in the etheric realm since 1933—was, as regards the time when it was communicated (on 12 January 1910), related to the culmination of Besant's error.

If we survey Besant's spiritual evolution, we realize that the period of time from the beginning of 1910 up to the end of 1912 (when Steiner was expelled from the Theosophical Society), marks the low point of this development. And these three years are each flanked by a period of 21 years: in 1889 Besant is asked to write a review of Blavatsky's *Secret Doctrine* (that is how she comes upon the author and her writings); 21 years after 1912, Besant dies in India. Annie Besant had requested to have the following inscription on her gravestone: 'She tried to follow Truth'.

It is in many respects noteworthy, therefore, that Besant passed away at the Christologically crucial moment, which Steiner had referred to in Stockholm. And what particularly motivated us to consider the likelihood of a—perhaps somewhat protracted—post-mortem correction of her fundamental Christological error is, apart from the positive relationship to Steiner during the time previous to 1909, the fact that her fundamental error concerning the physical incarnation of Christ, and centring upon the figure of Krishnamurti, was shattered a few years before her death, when Krishnamurti dissolved the 'Star of the East', which had been set up especially for protracting this very error.

### Krishnamurti, Daskalos and a post-mortem intervention by Rudolf Steiner

Now we have come to the third instance, to Krishnamurti himself. Regarding this subject, we have a statement from Rudolf Steiner, although one which he did not make during his lifetime, but many years after his death. The recipient and conveyor of this statement appears to us to be sufficiently credible for us to receive it impartially. The Swiss anthroposophist and key member of the Paracelsus-branch in Basel, Günther Zwahlen, conducted a conversation with the Cypriot healer Daskalos (1912–1995) in August 1990. The latter stated that he had been regularly and for a long period in supersensible contact with Steiner. Daskalos asked Zwahlen whether he would be interested in hearing 'how he had encountered Rudolf Steiner and his teachings in this life'. According to Zwahlen, Daskalos continued as follows: 'After I had answered in the affirmative, he asked whether I knew what theosophy was. Yes, I did know. Then, whether I knew why Rudolf Steiner had withdrawn from the Theosophical Society. Yes, that was because of Krishnamurti, whom the theosophists had passed off as the reincarnation of Christ. Did I know who Leadbeater was? Yes, I knew. Daskalos went on: Leadbeater, who was clairvoyant, had perceived that a master had incarnated in Cyprus. Daskalos pointed at himself and said: "That was me". A delegation of the Theosophical Society had come to Cyprus and had summoned him to join the Theosophical Society and the work therein. He related that while he was reflecting upon this, Rudolf Steiner suddenly stood beside him and said: "Don't do this, or else you'll soon end up like Krishnamurti". Thereupon he declined the invitation. (Daskalos, so I learned later, was at that time 26 years old.)'* Thus did Zwahlen report this conversation. Providing the chronological details are correct, this spiritual communication between Steiner and Daskalos unfolded in 1938. That would be five years after Besant's, and four years after Leadbeater's, deaths and four times seven years after the momentous year 1910. Consequently, this suggests that, during his post-mortem development, Steiner followed, in his spiritual body, the evolution of Krishnamurti. Steiner did not directly concern himself with Krishnamurti during his lifetime; Krishnamurti was an innocent victim of theosophical machinations. We may even raise the question as to whether it was not Steiner's individuality behind the motivating impulse that inspired Krishnamurti towards his tremendously courageous act of liberation in 1929. In this case, it would be all the more natural for Steiner's individuality to seek, out of his spirit, to prevent the theosophical machinations of old from finding a new victim in the person of Daskalos.

### Krishnamurti's statements on Besant, Steiner—and Christ

The only statements, known to me, that Krishnamurti made regarding Steiner and Besant suggest neither rancour against the latter, nor any rejection of the former. These statements can be found in an interview with Krishnamurti, published for the first time in 1936, which extended over several days, and was conducted by the English author Rom Landau. When Landau made enquiries about Krishnamurti's relationship to Rudolf Steiner, Krishnamurti replied: 'I have never studied Steiner, and I wish you would tell me more about him. All I know about Steiner comes from Dr Besant's occasional remarks. I think she had a great admiration for Steiner's unusual gifts, and was sorry that their relationship had to be broken, but I never studied him properly.'†

And when, on another occasion, Landau came to speak of the difficulty that most men have in ascending the path to Krishnamurti's solitary heights, the following scene transpired: 'Krishnamurti came quite near me—as he had often done before—looked deep into my eyes and said in

---

See *Das Goetheanum*, Nr. 34, 3 December 1995.

† Rom Landau, *God Is My Adventure. A Book on Modern Mystics, Masters and Teachers*, New York 1936, p. 344.

his melodious voice: "You are right. They live in the plains and I live, as you call it, on the mountain top; but I hope that ever more and more human beings will be able to endure the clear air of the mountain top." Then he added: "*A man infinitely greater than any of us had to go His own way that led to Golgotha*, no matter whether His disciples could follow Him or not".'* This is an astonishing acknowledgement of the uniqueness of Jesus Christ and of the singularity of the deed on Golgotha.

If one ponders on such statements, one sooner or later comes to realize that in Krishnamurti's life, which was marked by serious physical and emotional suffering, even after he had freed himself from the Theosophical Society, something *did* happen which could be described as a kind of miracle of change. And to this miracle he contributed in that he, who had been indoctrinated for two decades over who he was, ventured forth into becoming no less than *himself*, in the deeper sense, and acting accordingly.

As the author of these lines had the occasion, at the beginning of the 1980s, to attend one of the yearly summer-talks held by Krishnamurti in a large tent at Saanen near Gstaad, he gained the impression that this was a man in whom all passions had merged into a single great passion: into that of attaining to truth on his own and of inspiring others into doing the same. Each of the firm and yet sprightly steps of the already very aged man, each of his gestures, each of his words, spoke of this truth. Krishnamurti attached no importance to having supporters or a following. He lived in the hope that he would be understood. It would be a trespass against the spirit of development if we now ignored such images from the later years of this man's life.

## C.W. Leadbeater as the centre of a karmic group of people

As far as the actual kingpin of the erroneous theosophical evolution of 1910 is concerned, his inner developments seem to be rather obscure. Charles Webster Leadbeater died as a bishop of the Liberal Catholic Church of Australia, whereas previously he had been a member of the Anglican Church—not much of a deviation in the broad scheme of things. And yet, the death dates of those who were closely connected with him in their theosophical work, point to a karmic group in which developments of the kind referred to were becoming manifest. Krishnamurti died on 17 February (1986); the co-founder of the Theosophical Society, Henry Steel Olcott, had died on the very same day (1906); 17 February was also the death date of Giordano Bruno, who had been burned at the stake in 1600 for his courage to speak out the truth; and it was also the day on which Charles Webster Leadbeater was *born* (1847). Concrete spiritual research

---

* Op. cit., p. 369.

alone can shed light upon the details of the development of the Leadbeater-soul since its passing in 1934. But that, at least in his initial development, the evolutionary course of old had been preserved, may be divined in connection with the visit from the theosophical delegation to Daskalos in 1938. In fact, this visit had been prompted by a statement once made by Leadbeater on the birth of a master in Cyprus. What would seem more reasonable than to suppose that it was at least partly inspired by the post-mortem impact of Leadbeater's soul? And, Steiner's spiritual 'intervention' points to the possibility that a pseudo-spiritual Daskalos-tussle, analogous to the Krishnamurti-tussle ignited by Leadbeater, could well have unfolded.

## Conclusion

A truly spiritual-scientific view of history should not restrict itself to ascertaining what has happened in the past, or to identifying the players with those deeds for time immemorial. As much as it needs to focus on the facts and events clearly and unambiguously, equally such history needs to draw our attention to those occasionally subtle facts or occurrences that indicate future developmental tendencies in the spirit of these very players. These tendencies do not necessarily have to be of a positive kind. Goethe said that the best we could access from history was the enthusiasm it enkindled, and this holds true for the seeds sown for future development. We may find these seeds in the past and in the present. And is not an error which has been consciously overcome, more deeply and firmly rooted in truth than a thoughtlessly assumed truth?

The dramatic facts and events depicted in the present volume are at times subjected to thorough examination, especially with regard to the kingpins involved in the theosophical tragedy that occurred from the year 1910 onward. But certain representatives of the universal impulse of the Catholic Church, an impulse that has become obsolete in world history, or certain supporters—a group which still exists today—of illusionary blendings of ecclesiastical and truly scientific spirituality, are also portrayed in a clarity that verges on the satirical. However, he who reads this book in the developmental spirit which inspired its birth 21 years ago, and which we have endeavoured to present in particular detail in this afterword, will neither take objection to the clear-cut depiction of some of the details, nor will pass 'definitive' judgements on certain personalities portrayed here, which would go against the developmental principle referred to. May the present expanded edition of *The Bodhisattva Question* be received in this very spirit!

## APPENDIX: THE BODHISATTVA QUESTION IN THE LIGHT OF THE MYSTERY DRAMA *THE PORTAL OF INITIATION**

In 1997 the 'Bodhisattva question' acquired, through Heinz Eckhoff, renewed topicality in anthroposophical circles. Eckhoff advocated Arenson's old theory, and also the latter's line of reasoning: Rudolf Steiner identified the Bodhisattva as, among other things, one that had the mission to proclaim the etheric Christ. Who was it that actually announced the etheric Christ? Rudolf Steiner. Hence, he claimed, Steiner himself must be the Bodhisattva.

From Arenson to Herbert Wimbauer and up to Heinz Eckhoff, reference has repeatedly been made to statements by Steiner such as the following (from a lecture on 4 November 1911, GA 123) [Italics by TM]: 'The successor to Gautama Buddha, to the Bodhisattva, was the individuality that at that time, 100 years before Christ, had been incarnated as Jeshu ben Pandira, as a foreteller of Christ in the physical body; he [the successor to Gautama-Buddha as a Bodhisattva] is already incarnated, and he *will be the actual proclaimer of Christ in etheric guise*, just as he then foretold the Christ as the physical Christ.'

In a review of Eckhoff's book published in the Michaelmas 1998 issue of *Mitteilungen der anthroposophischen Arbeit in Deutschland*, Herbert Pfeifer comments on this cited passage as follows: 'Given these explanations, it is beyond doubt that the Bodhisattva of our century is the one who foretells of the etheric Christ. If we now set out in search of the individual who actually proclaimed the etheric Christ, we find no less a person than Rudolf Steiner himself. That can be inferred from many passages in his writings; he mentioned the appearance of the etheric Christ in more than 30 lectures.' This may seem logical. Yet already the attribute of the 'actual' proclaimer (not 'one who foretells', as Pfeifer says) in the above wording of Steiner's statement, denotes the possibility that this 'actual' proclaimer does not necessarily have to be the *only* proclaimer. A closer look at Rudolf Steiner's first mystery drama shows that, at least in this instance, there is indeed a second proclaimer.

In the first scene of *The Portal of Initiation* the naïve seeress Theodora appears on the stage. Two beings speak through her: in the first place, the etheric Christ (though not explicitly mentioned by this term). Theodora describes him thus:

----
* First published in *Der Europäer*, vol. 3, nr. 2–3, December/January 1998/99.

[. . .] before my spirit / Stands an image within a shining light, /And from it words sound forth [. . .] / They ring out thus, / 'You have lived in faith, / You were comforted by hope, / Now be comforted by vision, / Now be enlivened by me. / I lived in the souls / Who sought me within themselves / Through the words of my messengers, / Through the power of their devotion. / You have looked on the senses' light / And had to believe in the Creator's realm of spirit; / Yet now is won for you / A drop of the noble gift of seership. / O may you feel it in your soul.'

Secondly, through Theodora there speaks a certain human individuality who has the task of portending the Christ beheld by Theodora:

An individual struggles free / From that shining light. / It speaks to me, / 'You are to proclaim to all / Who want to heed you / That you have looked upon / What people are yet to experience. / Christ once lived upon the earth, / And the consequence of that life /Is that in soul form he hovers over / The development of human beings. / He has united himself with the earth's spirit part. / People could not yet look upon him then, / On how he showed himself in that form of existence [. . .] / Yet the future draws near / When the people of the earth / Are to be endowed with the new seeing. / What the senses once looked upon / During Christ's time upon the earth, / Shall be looked upon by souls / When soon the time has been fulfilled.'

The sceptical professor Capesius, who witnesses Theodora's utterance of the revelation, assumes that she is merely relating in her own way, something that the spiritual teacher Benedictus has already portended several times:

We have been informed / The man we've been told / Is the soul of this circle / Has also often reported / About this future gift, / Of which she spoke as if dreaming. / Is it possible / The content of her speech derives from him, / And only the style comes from her?

That is also how Heinz Eckhoff has interpreted these passages (loc. cit., p. 88). Yet Maria firmly denies it. She responds to Capesius' words:

If the matter were like that, / It wouldn't be important for us. / However, the facts have been carefully checked. / Our friend was completely unacquainted / With our guide's addresses / Before she entered our circle, / And from among us as well, / No one had heard of her previously.

On the level of drama, it would be rather tasteless if Theodora were to attend one of Benedictus' lectures, and then shortly afterwards perceive him again from spiritual sight saying the very same thing, that others had already had the occasion to hear via their physical ears. There is no need for the proclaimer of the etheric event, who has just appeared before her physically, to be presented afterwards to her spiritual vision! What appears to her spiritual sight (the 'individual') is the 'actual' high proclaimer-individuality, that has never before appeared to her in physical shape.

Thus, in this drama, we find two objectively different proclaimers of the future faculty of seeing the etheric Christ: Benedictus and the 'individual' that 'struggles free from that shining light'. One could even say: there is 'one who foretells' appearing on the physical plane and an 'actual' proclaimer that initially acts only on the occult plane. Thus, the much-debated relationship of Rudolf Steiner to the Bodhisattva of the twentieth century may also be considered in the light of this passage from the first mystery drama. And this very much corresponds with Eckhoff's understanding of it. Yet he fails to see the strongly emphasized distinction between Benedictus and the 'individual' in Theodora's perception, and therefore can only see the passage as being in support of his and Arenson's theory. However, he who approaches this passage objectively will interpret the above-cited passage from Rudolf Steiner's lecture in a different way to that of Arenson, Wimbauer, Eckhoff and many others. Elisabeth Vreede held the view that Rudolf Steiner was, as far as the seeing of the etheric Christ was concerned, the one who foretold of this seeing, inspired by the actual *proclaimer* of the etheric Christ. The above-quoted passage from *The Portal of Initiation* is dramatic evidence in support of this view—one that has, surprisingly enough, hitherto gone unnoticed.